# Swiss Constitutional Law

# Swiss Constitutional Law

Thomas Fleiner
Prof. Dr.iur., Dr.h.c., LL.M. (Yale)

Alexander Misic
lic. iur., LL.M. (Cornell)

Nicole Töpperwien
Dr.iur., LL.M. (Cardozo)

This book was originally published as a monograph in the International Encyclopaedia of Laws/Constitutional Law

2005

KLUWER LAW
INTERNATIONAL

Stæmpfli Publishers Ltd. Berne

*Published by:*
Kluwer Law International
P.O. Box 85889
2508 CN The Hague, The Netherlands
sales@kluwerlaw.com
http://www.kluwerlaw.com

*Sold and Distributed in North, Central and South America by:*
Aspen Publishers, Inc.
7201 McKinney Circle,
Frederick, MD 21704, USA

*Sold and Distributed in all other countries by:*
Extenza-Turpin Distribution Services
Stratton Business Park
Pegasus Drive
Biggleswade
Bedfordshire SG18 8TQ
United Kingdom
E-mail: sales@kluwerlaw.com

**A C.I.P. Catalogue record for this book is available from the Library of Congress**

*Printed on acid-free paper*

*Cover design:* The Bears Communications, Amsterdam

ISBN Kluwer Law International 90 411 24047
ISBN Staempfli Publishers 3 7272 91133



Printed and bound by Antony Rowe Ltd, Eastbourne

# The Authors

Thomas FLEINER,
Prof. Dr.iur., Dr.h.c., LL.M. (Yale)

Thomas Fleiner is professor for constitutional and administrative law and director of the Institute for Federalism at the University of Fribourg, Switzerland. He was president of the Legal Department and Dean of the Faculty, visiting professor at the Hebrew University of Jerusalem, the University of Rouen, the University of Belgrade, the University of Trier, the University of Louvain, the European College of Bruges and Cardozo Law School, New York. He was President of the International Association of Constitutional Law. He publishes in the field of federalism, human rights and general theory of the state in several languages. Prof. Fleiner is an internationally recognized advisor and is involved in legislative drafting.

Alexander MISIC,
lic. iur., LL.M. (Cornell)

Alexander Misic studied law at the University of Fribourg (Switzerland), Louvain Law School (Belgium) and Cornell Law School (USA). He worked as a research fellow at the Chair for Constitutional and Administrative Law in Fribourg, published in the field of federalism and human rights and co-edited a book on the new Swiss Constitution. He is currently preparing his doctoral thesis in evidence law and working in a Zurich law firm with focus on constitutional litigation.

**The Authors**

Nicole TÖPPERWIEN,
Dr.iur., LL.M. (Cardozo)

Nicole Töpperwien studied law at the University of Fribourg (Switzerland), she received a masters degree of Benjamin N. Cardozo School of Law (New York, USA) and a doctorate degree (Dr.iur.) of the University of Fribourg. After working as a senior research fellow at the Institute of Federalism (Switzerland) she is currently acting as a legal adviser to the Government of the Republic of Macedonia. She published in the fields of the general theory of the state, federalism and decentralisation, with the focus on multicultural societies.

# Table of Contents

**Table of Contents**

**Table of Contents**

# List of Abbreviations

| | |
|---|---|
| AG | Aargau (Swiss Canton) |
| AJP/PJA | *Aktuelle Juristische Praxis* (law review) |
| AI | Appenzell Inner Rhodes (Swiss half Canton) |
| AR | Appenzell Outer Rhodes (Swiss half Canton) |
| BE | Berne (Swiss Canton) |
| BGE 126 I 1 | Decision of the Federal Court, Book 126, Volume I (Constitutional Law), page 1 (for an explanation of the citing system *see* Part I, Chapter VII, § 2) |
| BL | Basle-Land (Swiss half Canton) |
| BS | Basle-City (Swiss half Canton) |
| BV | Bundesverfassung |
| CHF | Swiss Franc(s) |
| Constitution | Federal Constitution of the Swiss Confederation of 18 April 1999 (SR 101) |
| e.g. | for example |
| ECHR | European Convention on Human Rights of 4 November 1950 (SR 0.101) |
| ed. | Editor/edition |
| eds. | editors |
| EMRK | German version for ECHR |
| esp. | especially |
| *et al.* | and others |
| *et seq.* | and the following pages |
| FOCJ | Functional Overlapping Competing Jurisdictions |
| FR | Fribourg (Swiss Canton) |
| GE | Geneva (Swiss Canton) |
| GL | Glarus (Swiss Canton) |
| GR | Grisons (Swiss Canton) |
| i.e. | for example |
| JU | Jura (Swiss Canton) |
| LU | Lucerne (Swiss Canton) |
| NE | Neuchâtel (Swiss Canton) |
| NGO | Non-Governmental Organization |
| NW | Nidwalden (Swiss half Canton) |
| NZZ | *Neue Zürcher Zeitung* (newspaper) |
| *opt. cit.* | cited above |
| OW | Obwalden (Swiss half Canton) |

**List of Abbreviations**

| | |
|---|---|
| recht | *Zeitschrift für juristische Ausbildung und Praxis* (law review) |
| SG | St. Gallen (Swiss Canton) |
| SH | Schaffhausen (Swiss Canton) |
| SJZ | *Schweizerische Juristen-Zeitung* (law review) |
| SO | Solothurn (Swiss Canton) |
| SR | Systematic Register of Federal Statutes (http://www.admin.ch/ch/d/sr/sr.html) |
| SZ | Schwyz (Swiss Canton) |
| TG | Thurgau (Swiss Canton) |
| TI | Ticino (Swiss Canton) |
| UN | United Nations |
| UNO | United Nations Organization |
| UR | Uri (Swiss Canton) |
| VAT | Value Added Tax |
| VD | Vaud (Swiss Canton) |
| VPB | Verwaltungspraxis der Bundesbehörden (http://www.vpb.admin.ch) |
| VS | Valais (Swiss Canton) |
| Vol. | Volume(s) |
| ZG | Zug (Swiss Canton) |
| ZH | Zurich (Swiss Canton) |
| ZSR | *Zeitschrift für Schweizerisches Recht* (law review) |

# Preface

Although the founding fathers of the American Constitution guiding principle was 'let us be guided by experience, as reason might mislead us', anyone who has the intention of understanding Swiss constitutional law will have to take into consideration the vastly different situations Switzerland has encountered during its history.

Since the 16th century, the Diet, which was the first common institution, not only brought but also held together the historical, religious, cultural and linguistic diversity in the country. Therefore, Swiss federalism, as the constitutionally guaranteed balance between self and shared rule can only be understood as a means of consolidating and maintaining diversity. This balance is not only a constitutional instrument to separate powers, it aims to accommodate and even to promote diversity thus guaranteeing that it will never be intergraded into a melting pot, such as with American and German federalism. The aim of the Constitution is not only to limit governmental power in order to promote more freedom but also to provide instruments for conflict management among different cultural and religious communities. Communal peace is a public value, for which individual liberties, such as freedom of religion and linguistically diversity may be limited.

By simply reading the different constitutional provisions, which regulate direct democracy, the spirit behind said provisions guiding the Swiss concept of freedom and democracy cannot be understood without in-depth investigation. The Swiss, in fact, have a four-dimensional view of freedom: freedom from the state (inalienable rights), freedom within the state (democracy), freedom to the state (group rights of local authorities) and freedom by the state (social rights).

Democracy, as such, is for example not seen as a means of producing an efficient majority of 51 per cent, but it is an additional freedom for the community members through the shared rule principle with state power structured from the bottom up, with all different levels of municipal, cantonal and federal government. This constitutes the very basis to understanding consensus-driven democracy. Unlike many other democracies, the compromise which enables an inclusion of more than 51 per cent into a majority decision is, in our political culture, understood as a strength and not as a weakness. As Swiss democracy does not exclude the 49 per cent minority from power, it is inclusive, not exclusive.

Direct democracy forms the state at all levels into a specific political model not easily comparable to other governmental systems. Almost every political decision is influenced by democracy in the end. Therefore, the political elite must always bear in mind that almost any decision can be revoked by a popular referendum, thus making the prevention of referendum the main aim of Swiss politics. The influence of political parties is strongly diminished compared to other democracies based on the Westminster model. Thus, the executive on all different levels, although composed of different party members, is never a coalition cabinet based on a coalition program of the majority coalition. Like Parliament, the executive has to find the consensus that would most likely be successful in a referendum.

We have tried to limit ourselves to presenting a brief and rather positivistic overview of Swiss constitutional law without lengthy explanations and we have relied only on the most accepted theories and doctrines. Therefore, we recommend to interested readers that they seek the aim behind the different constitutional provisions asking why these provisions might be different in comparison to other constitutions. As the reader becomes familiar with notions such as freedom and democracy, they should be aware that these might be labelled for a different content which can only be understood by analysing the reality and history of Switzerland.

At this point, we would like to thank the editors for their patience. We also would like to thank Ms. Lisa Lieberherr, language teacher at KBZ in St. Gallen, and Ms. Adrienne Lieberherr for their invaluable support in correcting the language as well as for contributing many suggestions concerning style and content, which helped keep the text clear and easy to understand.

We would cordially like to thank Dr. iur. Pierre A. Karrer, LL.M. (Yale), FCI Arb., for the authorization to use and update his English translation of the constitutional text. We are grateful to Ms. lic. iur. Natalia Misic, LL.M. (NYU), Attorney-at-law, who corrected the text and suggested precious changes, and Mr. Naim Memeti, legal adviser, who provided us with the index, for their important contribution.

The Swiss Constitution is in a constant flux. It is our intention to keep up with the constitutional changes and the case law of the Federal Court by regular updates. Please do not hesitate to contact us if you have further suggestions, comments or questions (asm36@cornell.edu).

The Authors
August 1, 2004
Fribourg/Zollikon/Gstaad

# General Introduction

## Chapter 1. Outline of Swiss Constitutional History

### § 1. Introduction

*1.* Switzerland is a country of about seven million inhabitants. Its neighbouring territories are Austria, France, Germany, Italy, and the Principality of Liechtenstein. Although situated in Central Europe, it is not a member of the European Union. Switzerland has four official languages (German, French, Italian, and Romansh) as well as a population that mainly consists of Protestant and Catholic religious denominations. Over the last centuries, long before the creation of the Swiss Confederation in 1848, the Cantons and the approximately 3,000 municipalities, have developed their own political identity and traditions, which is reflected even nowadays in the cultural diversity, in the diversity of political decision-making procedures, and in the diversity of cantonal and communal organizational structures. The borders between the linguistic, religious and cantonal groups are not overlapping but rather intersecting.

*2.* From a comparative constitutional law perspective, Switzerland is insofar an interesting and unique example as it did not follow the same path as many other European countries: Switzerland did never try to homogenize its population nor did it split the territory according to linguistic, religious or cultural lines. Primarily through federalism and democracy, Switzerland managed to create and preserve institutions that respected the given diversity while also unifying the Swiss population. This Swiss model of peaceful co-existence in a multiethnic society will be elaborated in Part II and III of this monograph on Swiss constitutional law. The Swiss model and the question of its applicability on other multiethnic societies (esp. in the process of nation-building after conflict) have drawn the attention of political actors and scholars from all over the world. Therefore, it is justified to outline the historical background before and after the creation of the Swiss Confederation in 1874.[1]

1. For a further account on *general* Swiss history, *see* Im Hof Ulrich *et al.*, *Geschichte der Schweiz und der Schweizer*, Helbing & Lichtenhahn, Basle/Frankfurt a.M. 1986; for a 19th century account of constitutional history, *see* Bluntschli Johann Caspar, *Geschichte des schweizerischen Bundesrechts von den ersten Bünden bis zur Gegenwart*, Vol. 1, Topos Verlag AG, Vaduz 1977 reprint of 1875; for the main historical constitutional documents *see* Bluntschli Johann Caspar, *Geschichte des schweizerischen Bundesrechts von den ersten Bünden bis auf die Gegenwart*, Vol. 2, Topos Verlag AG, Vaduz 1977, reprint of 1875; Kölz Alfred, *Neuere schweizerische Verfassungsgeschichte – Ihre Grundlinien vom Ende der Alten Eidgenossenschaft bis 1848*,

Stämpfli Verlag, Zurich 1992; Kölz Alfred, *Neuere schweizerische Verfassungsgeschichte – Ihre Grundlinien in Bund und Kantonen seit 1848*, Stämpfli Verlag, Zurich 2004; for concise outlines of Swiss constitutional history, *see* Steinberg, 8–72; Auer/Malinverni/Hottelier, Vol. I, 1293 *et seq.*; Häfelin & Haller, 12–24; Kölz Alfred, 'Geschichtliche Grundlagen', in: Thürer *et al.*, 111–127 (with further references to the works of Aubert, Curti, His and Rappard); Schneider Hans-Peter, 'Der eidgenössische "Bündnisstaat"', in: *Festschrift Fleiner*, 201 *et seq.*; Tschannen, § 2.

## § 2. Foundation of the Confederation

*3.* The official starting point of Swiss history is 1291, when three Cantons (at this time called *Orte*) signed a treaty and created a defence union combined with a system of arbitration for conflicts among the Cantons. The union's aim was to prevent the predominance of neighbouring powers and guarantee a balance of power within. Other Cantons joined in by concluding further treaties, thereby developing a treaty-based confederation. The purpose of the alliance was to facilitate as much cooperation as necessary to defend the independence of Switzerland, while safeguarding the sovereignty of the Cantons. Therefore, in order to preserve diversity the Cantons accepted unification to a certain extent.

*4.* Up to the end of the 18th century the different entities that formed Switzerland were not equal, making their status dependent on the treaty which linked them to the union. Status was negotiable, for example when Fribourg and Solothurn requested entrance into the union, they had to accept fewer rights than most other entities in order to avoid a predominance of cities over rural Cantons (*Stanser Verkommnis* of 1481) whereas other areas were subjected territories, such as the Vaud which was under control of the Canton of Berne.

*5.* The only common institution was the *Diet*, an assembly of representatives from the Cantons.

*6.* Because of the continuance of cantonal sovereignty, the Cantons developed different political regimes. Most Cantons had oligarchic systems, which were centralized to differing degrees. For many decisions, the mountainous Cantons relied on the so-called *Landsgemeinde*, an assembly of the citizens who ruled through direct democracy.

*7.* During the Reformation period, Switzerland became a patchwork of different religious (Catholic and Protestant) communities resulting in a division which soon developed into an issue of political debate.

*8.* The Thirty Years' War (1618–1648) increased this division and threatened the unity of the country. Neutrality became a question of survival, as Switzerland decided to set up a common foreign policy that excluded any involvement in the conflict, which was dividing Europe. Towards the end of the war, the Swiss even managed to organize a common Protestant and Catholic defence against intrusion from the outside (*Wiler Defensionale*).

*9.* The independence of Switzerland was legally recognized after the Thirty Years' War in the Westphalian Peace of 1648.

## §3. Modernization

*10.* At the end of the 18th century, modernization in neighbouring countries, industrialization and the professionalization of armies, along with the ideas of the French Revolution, triggered demands for a stronger centralization and modernization of Switzerland. In 1798, Napoleon invaded Switzerland and created a centralized state in accordance with the French prototype. The Cantons were then transformed into equal although purely administrative units. But Switzerland soon proved to be ungovernable as a centralized state. During the Mediation Act, Napoleon re-introduced the Cantons as main and equal power holders.

*11.* After Napoleon's defeat, Switzerland opted again for a loose Confederation, but the equal status of the Cantons remained. In the Vienna Congress (1815), the borders and the neutrality of Switzerland were internationally recognized. While the formerly subjected territories and mainly Protestant Cantons adopted a progressive democracy, the old influential families regained power and introduced conservative structures in the predominately Catholic Cantons. As a result, the tensions between progressive and conservative Cantons rather were of socio-economic nature than religious conflicts.

*12.* In order to limit the pressure for centralization and democratization of the Protestant Cantons, the conservative Catholic Cantons formed a secret union (*Sonderbund*) which violated the treaty of the Confederation. When it was revealed and the Catholics refused to dissolve it, the Protestant Cantons did it by force. The year of 1847 entered in Swiss history as the year of civil war (*Sonderbund* War).[1]

1. For an account of the Sonderbund War, *see* Remak Joachim, *Bruderzwist nicht Brudermord, Der Schweizer Sonderbundkrieg von 1847*, Orell Füssli, Zurich 1997.

## § 4. Switzerland as a Federal State

### I. The Federal Constitution of 1848

*13.* In 1848, the People and the Peoples of the Cantons of Switzerland adopted a federal constitution which was a compromise between victors and defeated of the civil war. Not only did it introduce partial centralization and fundamental rights and liberties, it also guaranteed, through the institutional setup and the limitation of competencies of the central government, respect for cantonal diversity.

*14.* With its new constitution, Switzerland took an important step towards modernity. It became a federal state based on constitutionally guaranteed self and shared rule. Over the years, the institutions and political processes were pragmatically enhanced.

*15.* From the 1860s onward, a democratization of the Cantons took place and many of the direct democratic instruments within the Cantons were introduced between 1860 and 1874.

## II. The Federal Constitution of 1874

*16.* In 1874, a new Federal Constitution was adopted which did not change the state organization decisively. Main novelties included the establishment of a unified army, the introduction of a facultative referendum, and the permanent institution of the Federal Court. Furthermore, the Federal Constitution of 1874 introduced further fundamental rights and liberties, such as the right to free primary school education, the economic freedom clause, the right to marriage, and the freedom of religion. In later years, there were approximately 150 partial revisions of the Federal Constitution, such as the creation of the new Canton of Jura in 1979, the introduction of equal rights for men and women in 1971, the further strengthening of direct democracy (initiative for the partial revision of the Constitution in 1891), the introduction of a national social security system, and a gradual centralization of powers.

## III. The Federal Constitution of 1999

*17.* Finally, in 1999, a second total revision of the Constitution took place after a reform project in the 1970s was defeated. On 1 January 2000, this new Constitution became effective. Its total revision was not an ambitious project, but rather a limited revision of the text without introducing substantial novelties.

*18.* In spite of numerous constitutional revisions, the overall constitutional design first adopted in 1848 remains the same today. Although the Swiss Constitution is one of the most frequently revised constitutions, Switzerland has one of the most stable political systems in the world.

*19.* The Federal Constitution continues to be the basis for peaceful co-existence of the Cantons, and of the different cultural, linguistic and religious groups.[1]

1. For constitutional reform in Switzerland from a sociological perspective, *see* Kreis Georg, 'Totalrevisionen als soziale Bewegungen – Zu den fünf Verfassungsphasen der neueren Schweizergeschichte', in: Sitter-Liver, 169–197, on the reform of 1999 and its interpretation, *see* Häfelin & Haller, 68–69; Rhinow René, 'Zur Aktualisierung der Bundesverfassung, oder: Nachführung ist mehr als Nachführung', in: Sitter-Liver, 563–572; Tschannen, § 2 N 26.

# Chapter 2. The Foundations of the Swiss Political System

## § 1. The Democratic Principle

*20.* Switzerland, being one of the oldest democracies in the world, has managed to slowly transform and democratize formerly oligarchic forms of government and to pragmatically develop a diverse set of flexible and locally anchored democratic institutions. Surrounded by monarchies and aristocratic countries for several ages, the belief in the specificity of Swiss democracy forms an essential part of the Swiss identity.[1]

1. Auer Andreas, 'Problèmes fondamentaux de la démocratie Suisse', in: ZSR 1984 II 1 *et seq.*; Grisel Etienne, *Initiative et référendum populaires – Traité de la démocratie semi-directe en droit suisse*, 2nd ed., Stämpfli Verlag, Berne 1997; Hangartner Yvo & Kley Andreas, *Die demokratischen Rechte in Bund und Kantonen der Schweizerischen Eidgenossenschaft*, Schulthess, Zurich 2000; Mastronardi Philippe, 'Der Zweck der Eidgenossenschaft als Demokratie', in: ZSR 1998 II 317 *et seq.*; Müller Jörg Paul, *Demokratische Gerechtigkeit*, Munich 1993; Rhinow René, 'Grundprobleme der schweizerischen Demokratie', in: ZSR 1984 II 111 *et seq.*; Rhinow, Verfassungsrecht, 34 *et seq.*; Tschannen, § 6 II.

*21.* The democratic principle, although absolutely fundamental, is not mentioned in the Constitution. However, it is indirectly embodied in it through diverse provisions.

*22.* Evidence of the primacy of the democratic principle is set out in Article 148(1) of the Constitution according to which Federal Parliament is the highest authority of the Confederation *subject to the rights of the People* and the Cantons. The People not only elect their representatives in Parliament (*infra* Part II, Chapter 2, § 2), they also decide on substantive matters through the means of the initiative, the constitutional referendum, the statutory referendum and the treaty referendum (*infra* Part II, Chapter 2, § 3 and § 4).

*23.* Additionally, the Constitution sets minimum requirements for the democratic organization of the Cantons. According to Article 51 of the Constitution, every Canton shall adopt a democratic constitution, which must be approved by the People and must be subject to revision, if required by a majority of the cantonal People. Furthermore, the cantonal constitutions must be approved by the Confederation to assure their conformity with federal laws (Article 51(2) of the Constitution, *infra* Part III, Chapter 2, § 1, II., B.).

*24.* This primacy of the democratic principle over the *Rechtsstaat* principle (*infra* D.) can also be deduced from Article 190 of the Constitution, according to which the Federal Court may not declare federal statutes as unconstitutional (*infra*, Part IV, Chapter 2, § 4, I.) because the democratic legitimacy of Parliament is deemed higher than the legitimacy of the Court.[1]

1. *See* Linder, Schweizerische Demokratie (with further references); Linder, Swiss Democracy; Auer/Malinverni/Hottelier, Vol. I, 183 *et seq.*; Häfelin & Haller, 53–54; Rhinow, Verfassungsrecht, 34 *et seq.*; Rhinow, 231–234; Tanquerel Thierry, 'Les fondements démocratiques de la Constitution', in: Thürer *et al.*, § 18.

## § 2. The Federal Principle

*25.* Switzerland is a federal state, although unlike other federal constitutions, e.g., the German Basic Law or the Belgian Constitution, the Swiss Constitution does not explicitly denominate Switzerland as such. Rather, federalism is taken for granted. The Swiss state is based on a double legitimacy, stemming from the federal principle and Article 1 of the Constitution, which proclaims that the Swiss People *and* the Cantons form the Swiss Confederation.

*26.* Switzerland is composed of three governmental levels (federal, cantonal and municipal), each of which has its own powers. The three-level polity is mirrored in the concept of a threefold citizenship (federal, cantonal and municipal citizenship). The Constitution transfers certain powers to the federal level, while residuary powers lie with the Cantons (Articles 3 and 42 of the Constitution). The federal level can only act in the area of expressly enumerated powers, the Cantons confer autonomy to the municipalities. The Federal Constitution protects the autonomy of the municipalities only within the limits fixed by the cantonal constitutions (Article 50(1) of the Constitution; *see also infra* Part III, Chapter 3, § 1, II.).

*27.* Swiss federalism is based on the constitutionally guaranteed balance between shared rule and self-rule. The Constitution provides for the distribution of powers and determines therefore the areas of self-rule. Formerly, the self-rule principle was the predominant one in the concept of Swiss federalism.

*28.* In addition, the Constitution provides for shared rule, for instance, through the representation of the Cantons in a second chamber of Parliament (*infra* Part II, Chapter 3) and through the participatory rights of the Cantons at the Federal level (e.g., revision of the Constitution, participation in the preliminary law-making procedure; *infra* Part I, Chapter 3, § 2; Part III, Chapter 1, § 2, II.). Due to the political interdependence of the Confederation and the Cantons, there has hardly remained any area in which the Cantons are completely and absolutely autonomous. In the Constitution of 1999, the element of cooperation, embodied *inter alia* in the shared rule principle, has gained importance as a recompensation for the diminished cantonal autonomy.[1]

1. *See* Auer/Malinverni/Hottelier, Vol. I, 293 *et seq.*; Fleiner & Basta Fleiner, 533 *et seq.*; Häfelin & Haller, 54, 263 *et seq.*; Fleiner & Misic, 'Föderalismus als Ordnungsprinzip der Verfassung', in: Thürer *et al.*, § 27 (with further references); Hangartner Yvo, *Die Kompetenzverteilung zwischen Bund und Kantonen*, Berne 1974; Gerotto Sergio,

*La partecipazione di Regioni e Cantoni alle funzioni dello Stato centrale–Gli ordinamenti italiano e svizzero a confronto*, Basle 2003; Hänni Peter, *Schweizerischer Föderalimus und europäische Integration*, Schulthess, Zurich 2000; Kägi-Diener Regula, 'Zweck und Aufgaben der Eidgenossenschaft aus bundesstaatlicher Sicht', in: ZSR 1998 II 49 *et seq.*; Knapp Blaise, 'Le fédéralisme', in: ZSR 1984 II 275 *et seq.*; Koller Heinrich, 'Der Preis des Föderalismus aus juristischer Sicht', in: *Festschrift Fleiner*, 109 *et seq.*; Linder, *Schweizerische Demokratie*, 135 *et seq.*; Saladin Peter, 'Bund und Kantone – Autonomie und Zusammenwirken im schweizerischen Bundesstaat', in: ZSR 1984 II 431 *et seq.*; St. Galler Kommentar, Schweizer Rainer J., Vorbemerkungen ad Article 42–135, 553–556 (with further references); Rhinow, Verfassungs-recht, 34 *et seq.* and §§ 5–10; Tschannen, § 6 V.; Zimmerli Ulrich, 'Neue Bundesverfassung und föderalistische Strukturen', in: Gauch Peter & Thürer Daniel (eds.), *Die neue Bundesverfassung*, Schulthess, Zurich 2002, 79 *et seq.*

## § 3. The Neutrality Principle

### I. Principle

*29.* After a long tradition of warfare and mercenary service rendered to other countries, Switzerland adopted a policy of neutrality in order to avoid fragmentation and conflicting loyalties of its multicultural population. This necessity arose for the first time in the Thirty Years' War, which threatened the political unity of Catholic and Protestant Cantons.

*30.* On 20 November 1815, Switzerland's perpetual neutrality was internationally recognized and guaranteed in the Charta of Paris. The Swiss neutrality was reconfirmed several times, for example in the Treaty of Versailles on 28 June 1919, in the aftermath of World War I and in the London Declaration of 13 February 1920.

*31.* Again, the Constitution does not expressly mention the neutrality principle, which – together with democracy and federalism – seems to be taken for granted. Neutrality is only mentioned in Article 173(1)(a) of the Constitution. According to this Article, Federal Parliament shall take measures to safeguard the neutrality of Switzerland.[1]

1. *See* Goetschel Laurent/Bernath Magdalena/Schwarz Daniel, *Schweizerische Aussenpolitik: Grundlagen und Möglichkeiten*, Zurich 2002, 42–45; Rhinow, Verfassungsrecht, 550 *et seq.*

### II. Concept of Active Neutrality

*32.* The notion of neutrality developed over the course of time, and today Switzerland abides by a concept of active neutrality through which perpetual, armed neutrality shall be preserved. However, at the same time, Switzerland pledges to conduct an active foreign policy based on solidarity and participation.

*33.* The concept of a perpetual armed neutrality dictates that Switzerland will not initiate a war or take part in any military aggression. Additionally, Switzerland shall remain neutral in all wars, independent of the parties involved, the place and the time, and will not support any of the parties in the conflict. Through an adequately equipped army, Switzerland ensures its defence and aims to prevent a vacuum of power on its territory.

*34.* The concept of an active foreign policy is designed to prevent isolation as well as to promote cooperation and solidarity in order to enhance security within the Swiss territory, while also fulfilling Switzerland's responsibility towards the world. These goals are enumerated in the Constitution. For example, Article 2(4) of the Constitution states that Switzerland shall promote an equitable and peaceful international order. Article 54(3) of the Constitution adds that its foreign policy shall be directed at enhancing respect for human rights, democracy and the peaceful coexistence of nations.[1] The Federal Council has stated that the participation of members of the Swiss Army in international peace-keeping operations are compatible with the neutrality principle insofar as the operation corresponds (1) with the principles of Switzerland's foreign affairs and security policy and is (2) based upon a mandate by the UN or the OSCE. Furthermore, the participation of members of the Swiss Army in international peace-keeping operations is (3) optional and (4) does not include military involvement in combat situations in order to appease a party of the conflict by force. *See* the new Articles 66 and 66(a) of the Federal Military Act (SR 510.10), as effective since 1 September 2001, and 1 January 2004.

1. *See* Auer/Malinverni/Hottelier, Vol. I, 313; Epiney Astrid & Kälin Walter, *Völkerrecht*, Stämpfli, Berne 2003, 289–307; Hottelier Michel, 'L'adhésion de la Suisse à l'Organisation des Nations-Unies: aspects constitutionnels' in: *Revue française de droit constitutionnel* 2002, 485 *et seq.*

## III. Neutrality and the Adhesion to the United Nations

*35.* In 3 March 2002, the Swiss People and the Cantons voted in favour of joining the United Nations (54.6 per cent of the population, twelve of the twenty-three Cantons). On 18 July 2002, Switzerland was accepted as the 190th member of the United Nations.

*36.* According to a Federal Council statement, Swiss neutrality is compatible with the UN Charter and thus will not be affected by the adhesion to the UN. Of course, Switzerland has already participated in coercive measures adopted by the UN since 1990 and has given about CHF500,000,000 to the disposal of the UN per year. The UN membership does not demand Switzerland's active participation in armed conflicts.

## § 4. The *Rechtsstaat* Principle

## I. Principle

*37.* The *Rechtsstaat* principle is expressly mentioned in the Constitution of 1999. The meaning of *Rechtsstaat* as 'rule by law' instead of 'rule of law' differs from the rule of law concept in the Anglo-American understanding. According to Article 5 of the Constitution, state activity shall be based upon and limited by the Law. Conceptually, the *Rechtsstaat* principle is essentially characterized by the principle of separation of powers, the legality principle limiting agency action, as well as constitutional and administrative review.

*38.* As the *Rechtsstaat* principle is not completely implemented in the field of constitutional and administrative review, reforms are envisioned (*see infra* C.) The Federal Court usually distinguishes between the formal and substantive *Rechtsstaat* principle. The content and function of the formal *Rechtsstaat* principle is set out in Article 5 of the Constitution (principle of legality, respect of international law), in Articles 29–32 (procedural due process, right to substantive review by an impartial court), and the principle of separation of powers. The substantive *Rechtsstaat* principle is based upon the idea that all state activity must be in the public interest and proportionate to the goals pursued (Article 5(3) of the Constitution) and respect fundamental liberties.[1]

1. *See* Auer/Malinverni/Hottelier, Vol. II, 469 *et seq.*; Häfelin & Haller, 52–53; Kohler Georg, 'Philosophische Grundlagen der liberalen Rechtsstaatsidee', in: Thürer *et al.*, § 15; Moor Pierre, 'Principes de l'activité étatique et responsabilité de l'Etat', in: Thürer *et al.*, § 16; Schmid & Uhlmann, 'Idee und Ausgestaltung des Rechtsstaates', in: Thürer *et al.*, § 13 (with further references); St. Galler Kommentar, Hangartner Yvo ad Article 5, 51–59 (with further references); Rhinow, 36–38; Rhinow, Verfassungsrecht, 419 *et seq.*; Tschannen, § 6 III.

## II. Historic Development

*39.* Until the early 1980s, due to the ideology of the superiority of the (direct) democracy principle, the Swiss *Rechtsstaat* was underdeveloped, particularly in the field of administrative law where citizens did not always have the right to an impartial court. Since Switzerland's accession to the European Convention on Human Rights in 1974 the situation has changed considerably. In comparison to the size of their population, the Swiss are among the most frequent registrants of human rights complaints in Europe, second only to the Austrians. This is due mainly to the underdeveloped system of remedies against unconstitutional federal statutes and administrative action (or omission). Since the adoption of the European Convention, the Federal Court has made extensive efforts to create harmony in its interpretation of fundamental rights guaranteed in the Convention and the Constitution of 1874. These decisions had a very concrete impact on the new Swiss Federal Constitution of 1999. Taking the lack of *Rechtstaatlichkeit* into account, the authors of the new Federal Constitution decided to structure it according to the following two principles. First, they introduced the above-mentioned Article 5 in the *general part* of the Constitution. Second, they included an extensive Bill of Rights with a set of justiciable procedural guarantees in the second part of the Constitution. The constitutional review of federal laws, however, is still not granted (Article 190 of the Constitution).

## III. Reform

*40.* The People and the Cantons agreed on a constitutional reform of the Judiciary on 12 March 2000. Because the reform requires considerable modification of statutory law, the enforcement date has not yet been set. The reform contains the following innovations:

(1) In legal disputes, every person shall have the fundamental right to a decision by a *judicial* authority (Article 29(a) of the Constitution);
(2) the delegation of power to unify civil and criminal procedure law – formerly a traditional domain of the Cantons – at the federal level (Articles 122–123 of the Constitution);
(3) the extension of the Federal Court jurisdiction over federal elections and voting (Article 189(1)(f) of the Constitution);
(4) the reduction of the heavy case load of the Federal Court through the creation of a Federal Criminal Court in Bellinzona (Ticino) and a Federal Administrative Court in St. Gallen (Article 191(a) of the Constitution), as well as the creation of additional cantonal judicial authorities (a new issue will be that Cantons can establish joint judicial authorities) (Article 191(b) of the Constitution); and
(5) express guarantee of the independence of the judge (Article 191(c) of the Constitution).[1]

1. *See* St. Galler Kommentar, Kiss & Koller ad Article 191 (Justizreform), 1941–1968; Häfelin & Haller, 24; Rhinow, Verfassungsrecht, 475 *et seq.*

*41.* The introduction of an exhaustive constitutional review of federal laws constitutes the still missing element for the fulfilment of the *Rechtsstaat* principle (*see* Part IV, Chapter 2, § 4, I.). It is unlikely that a reform will be set on the political agenda in the near future.

# Chapter 3. State Territory

## § 1. Overall Territory

*42.* Switzerland covers an area of 41,285 square km, approximately two hundred times smaller than the territory of the United States of America.[1]

1. For statistics, *see* Swiss Federal Statistical Office at http://www.statistik.admin.ch.

## § 2. Cantons

*43.* The Swiss territory, as enumerated in Article 1 of the Constitution, is divided into twenty-three Cantons: Zurich, Berne, Lucerne, Uri, Schwyz, Unterwalden, Glarus, Zug, Fribourg, Solothurn, Basle, Schaffhausen, Appenzell, St. Gallen, Grisons, Aargau, Thurgau, Ticino, Vaud, Valais, Neuchâtel, Geneva, and Jura.[1] The Canton of Jura was created in 1978 as a result of a secession from the Canton of Berne (*infra* Part III; Chapter 2, II.).

1. The Constitution of 1999 no longer lists the Cantons Unterwalden, Basle and Appenzell, but enumerates the half Cantons Nidwalden and Obwalden, Basle-City and Basle-Land, Appenzell Inner Rhodes and Appenzell Outer Rhodes.

*44.* Three of the twenty-three Cantons are divided into *half Cantons*. In the Middle Ages, the Canton of Unterwalden decided to separate into two half Cantons, Obwalden and Nidwalden. For mainly territorial reasons, the geographical location made the cooperation between the two parts of the canton difficult. The division of the Canton of Appenzell into Appenzell Inner Rhodes and Appenzell Outer Rhodes was a result of the counter-reformation. The Canton was split into a Catholic and a Protestant part in 1597.

*45.* In 1832–1833, the Canton of Basle divided into Basle-City and Basle-Land due to a dispute between the city of Basle and the countryside, which essentially felt dominated by the city. When a referendum on the separation of the two parts failed, the canton expelled all municipalities that had not voted to remain with the canton of Basle. These municipalities then formed the half canton of Basle-Land, which was later joined by other municipalities. The Diet (the governing institution in Switzerland at that time), however, denied both Cantons the right of a full vote. Like the half Cantons of Appenzell Inner Rhodes and Outer Rhodes, and Nidwalden and Obwalden, they had to share a common vote in the Diet. Today, the half

Cantons each have only one seat in the Senate, while the other Cantons dispose over two seats each (*infra* Part II, Chapter 3, § 1, II. and III.). With minor exceptions, the half Cantons' status is very similar to that of ordinary Cantons. Due to this similarity of status, one can often find the statement that there are 26 Cantons or 26 cantonal regimes, even though there are officially only 20 ordinary Cantons and six half Cantons. Whether there are 23 or 26 federal subdivisions depends on the way of counting.

*46.* The mountainous Canton of Grisons is the largest territory with 7,105 square km, whereas the Canton of Basle-City is the smallest with 37 square km.[1]

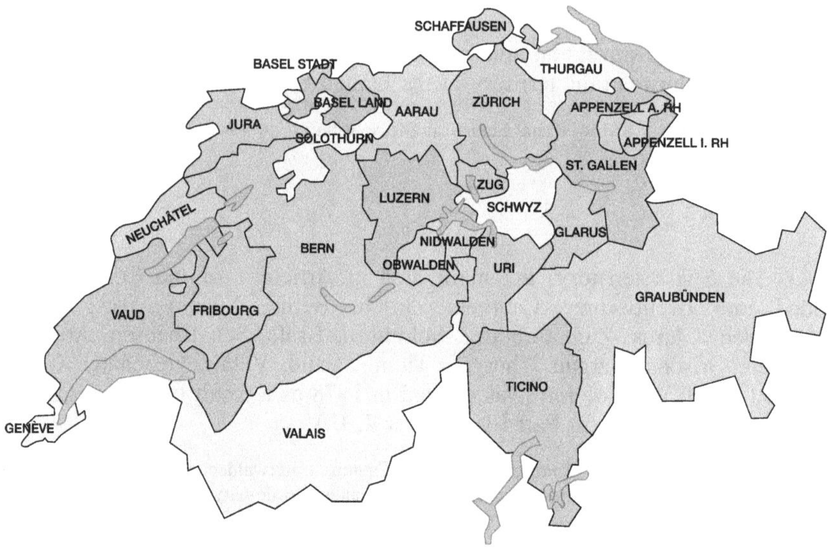


*Figure 1. Cantons*

| Canton | Territory in square km[2] |
|---|---|
| Grisons | 7,105 |
| Berne | 5,961 |
| Valais | 5,225 |
| Vaud | 3,212 |
| Ticino | 2,812 |

| | |
|---|---|
| St. Gallen | 2,026 |
| Zurich | 1,729 |
| Fribourg (Freiburg) | 1,671 |
| Luzern | 1,493 |
| Aargau | 1,404 |
| Uri | 1,077 |
| Thurgau | 991 |
| Schwyz | 909 |
| Jura | 837 |
| Neuchâtel | 803 |
| Solothurn | 791 |
| Glarus | 685 |
| Basle-Land | 517 |
| Obwalden | 491 |
| Schaffhausen | 299 |
| Geneva | 282 |
| Nidwalden | 276 |
| Appenzell Outer Rhodes | 243 |
| Zug | 239 |
| Appenzell Inner Rhodes | 173 |
| Basle-City | 37 |

1. For statistics, *see* Swiss Federal Statistical Office at http://www.statistik.admin.ch.
2. For statistics, *see* Swiss Federal Statistical Office at http://www.statistik.admin.ch.

## § 3. Municipalities

*47.* The Cantons decide on the organization of their territory, which is then divided into municipalities, and confers autonomy upon them.[1] Overall, Switzerland has approximately three thousand political municipalities, although their numbers are continually decreasing, largely due to mergers. On the average, each Swiss municipality has 2,100 inhabitants. However, 45 per cent of the Swiss municipalities have less than five hundred inhabitants, and more than two hundred municipalities have less than one hundred inhabitants. The City of Zurich, which also forms a municipality, has about 400,000 inhabitants.

1. The Canton of Appenzell Inner Rhodes calls its lowest level of government *Bezirk*, instead of *Gemeinde*, the term that is usually used for municipality.

*48.* In 1998, the Canton of Fribourg consisted of a total of 246 municipalities. Of these, 192 have less than one thousand inhabitants. In 1998, the average number of inhabitants per municipality throughout Switzerland was 940. Therefore, the average community in the Canton of Fribourg is clearly smaller than the average Swiss one. However, Fribourg created an incentive system for mergers, under which Fribourg authorities expected the average number of inhabitants to increase to 1,200 by the year 2003. So far, the policy of merging municipalities has been more successful in the French, Italian and Romansh speaking areas than in the German-speaking ones.

## § 4. Districts

*49.* Seventeen Cantons additionally divide their territory into districts. While the municipalities have a relatively large degree of autonomy, these districts are in most cases purely administrative units. The head of the district can be compared with a *préfet* in the French system. Only the Cantons of Schwyz and Grisons confer to their districts (Bezirke resp. Kreise) autonomy and an independent public law status, thereby introducing an additional level in the federal system.[1]

1. *See* Constitution of the Canton of Schwyz of 1898, § 3, §§ 22–23, § 25, §§ 70–85; Constitution of the Canton of Grisons of 1892, Article 38 *et seq.*

## § 5. Regions

*50.* For strategic planning purposes, the Federal government divided Switzerland into regions. So far, these regions remain artificial entities and their importance in the Swiss state structure is minimal.

## § 6. Capital

*51.* The capital of Switzerland is Berne and the City of Berne is part of the territory of the Canton of Berne. The City of Berne has 122,469 inhabitants (2001).[1]

Unlike to the capitals of the United States or Mexico, the federal institutions of the Swiss Confederation do not form a distinct federal district.

1. For statistics, *see* Swiss Federal Statistical Office at http://www.statistik.admin.ch.

# Chapter 4. Population (Demographic Data)

## § 1. Overall Population

*52.* Switzerland has 7,262,210 (December 2001) permanent inhabitants. Of these, 3,712,121 are female and 3,549,089 are male. The number of people permanently living in Switzerland is increasing by an average of 0.6 per cent per year, largely due to immigration.[1]

1. For statistics, *see* Swiss Federal Statistical Office at http://www.statistik.admin.ch.

## § 2. Cantonal Populations

*53.* The Canton of Zurich has the largest number of inhabitants (1,252,800 according to the provisional results (2002) of the 2000 census), whereas the half Canton of Appenzell Inner Rhodes has the lowest population total with 14,700 inhabitants.[1]

| **Canton** | **Population (2000)**[2] |
|---|---|
| Zurich | 1,252,800 |
| Berne | 956,800 |
| Vaud | 639,200 |
| Aargau | 549,600 |
| St. Gallen | 453,200 |
| Geneva | 406,700 |
| Lucerne | 351,500 |
| Ticino | 301,600 |

| | |
|---|---|
| Valais | 270,800 |
| Basle-Land | 259,700 |
| Solothurn | 244,900 |
| Fribourg (Freiburg) | 240,700 |
| Thurgau | 229,550 |
| Basle-City | 189,000 |
| Grisons | 187,800 |
| Neuchâtel | 168,000 |
| Schwyz | 129,300 |
| Zug | 100,250 |
| Schaffhausen | 74,200 |
| Jura | 68,150 |
| Appenzell Outer Rhodes | 53,650 |
| Glarus | 38,250 |
| Nidwalden | 37,400 |
| Uri | 34,700 |
| Obwalden | 32,480 |
| Appenzell Inner Rhodes | 14,700 |

1. For statistics, *see* Swiss Federal Statistical Office at http://www.statistik.admin.ch.
2. For statistics, *see* Swiss Federal Statistical Office at http://www.statistik.admin.ch.

## § 3. Languages

*54.* 63.9 per cent of the population is German-speaking, 19.5 per cent French-speaking, 6.6 per cent Italian-speaking and 0.5 per cent Romansh/Rhaeto-Romanic speaking, while 9.5 per cent speaks other languages (all data of 2000).[1] Note that Rhaeto-Romanic is the generic name for several related dialects of the Romance group of the Italic subfamily of the Indo-European family of languages. These dialects are now considered sufficiently similar to form a single unit in the Romance group. The principal Rhaeto-Romanic dialects are Romansh (with, again, several sub-families), Ladin (Italian Tyrol), and Friulian (Northeastern Italy). In this monograph, we will use the terms 'Romansh' and 'Rhaeto-Romanic' interchangeably.

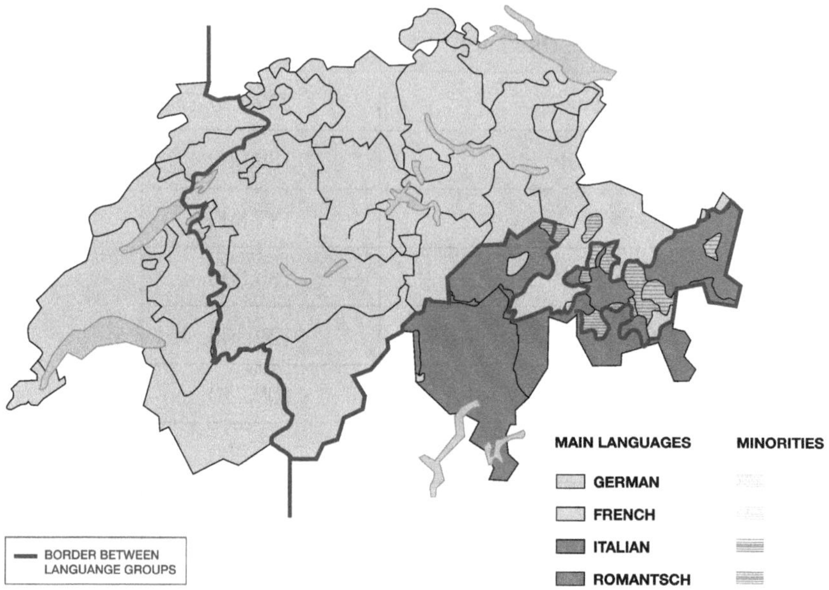


*Figure 2. Languages*

1. For statistics, *see* Swiss Federal Statistical Office at http://www.statistik.admin.ch.

## § 4. Religion

*55.* 44.1 per cent of the population is Catholic, 36.6 per cent Protestant, 4.5 per cent Muslim, 1.2 per cent Orthodox, 0.2 per cent Jewish, and 11.7 per cent do not adhere to a religious group (all data of 2000).[1]

1. For statistics, *see* Swiss Federal Statistical Office at http://www.statistik.admin.ch.

## § 5. Cities

*56.* In 2001, 68 per cent of the population lived in cities. The fifteen most populated cities are Zurich (340,873), Geneva, Basle, Berne, Lausanne, Winterthur, St. Gallen, Lucerne, Biel (Bienne), Thun, Köniz, La Chaux-de-Fonds, Schaffhausen, Fribourg (Freiburg) and Neuchâtel (Neuenburg) (31,739).[1]

1. For statistics, *see* Swiss Federal Statistical Office at http://www.statistik.admin.ch.

§ 6. UNEMPLOYMENT

*57.* In 2001, there was an unemployment rate of 1.9 per cent with the highest unemployed segments being foreigners (3.8 per cent), women (2.3 per cent) and people in the average age group of 25–49 (2.0 per cent).

§ 7. FOREIGNERS

*58.* By the end of 2001, 1,419,095 foreigners lived in Switzerland. In other words, 19.7 per cent of the population consists of non-Swiss citizens. The Canton of Geneva has the highest percentage of immigrants with 34.5 per cent, with most of them originating from Italy (about 300,000), Slovenia, Croatia, Bosnia-Herzegovina, Serbia and Montenegro, and the FYR of Macedonia (about 200,000), Portugal (about 150,000), Germany, Spain, Turkey and France. In 2001, 20,633 persons requested asylum, 2,253 were admitted and 29,429 foreigners were granted Swiss citizenship.[1]

1. For statistics, *see* Swiss Federal Statistical Office at http://www.statistik.admin.ch.

# Chapter 5. Selected Bibliography

*59.* Note: This selected bibliography contains the relevant treaties and monographies on Swiss constitutional and administrative law. When it seemed appropriate, further references for in-depth research are indicated directly in the footnotes.

Aubert Jean-François, *Traité de droit constitutionnel suisse*, 2 vol., Edition Ides et Calendes, Paris/Neuchâtel 1967. Supplément 1967–1982, Edition Ides et Calendes, Neuchâtel 1982.

Aubert Jean-François *et al.* (eds.), *Kommentar zur Bundesverfassung der Schweizerischen Eidgenossenschaft* vom 29. Mai 1874, 4 vol., Zurich/Berne 1987–1996 (cited as Author, in: Kommentar BV1874).

Aubert Jean-François & Mahon Pascal, *Petit commentaire de la Constitution fédérale de la Confédération suisse* du 18 avril 1999, Schulthess, Zurich 2003.

Auer Andreas & Malinverni Giorgio & Hottelier Michel, *Droit constitutionnel suisse*, 2 vol., Stämpfli, Berne 2000 (cited as Auer/Malinverni/Hottelier).

Auer Andreas, *Die schweizerische Verfassungsgerichtsbarkeit*, Helbing & Lichtenhahn, Basle/Frankfurt a.M. 1984.

Basta Fleiner Lidija R. & Fleiner Thomas (eds.), *Federalism and Multiethnic States: The Case of Switzerland*, PIFF 16, 2nd ed., Helbing & Lichtenhahn, Basle 2000 (cited as Basta Fleiner & Fleiner).

Bundeskanzlei, *The Swiss Confederation: a brief guide*, Berne 2002.

Burckhardt Walther, *Kommentar der schweizerischen Bundesverfassung* vom 29. Mai 1874, 3rd ed., Stämpfli, Berne 1931.

Ehrenzeller Bernhard/Mastronardi Philippe/Schweizer Rainer J./Vallender Klaus A., *Die schweizerische Bundesverfassung: Kommentar*, Schulthess, Zurich 2002 (cited as St. Galler Kommentar, Author ad Article).

Fleiner Fritz & Giacometti Zaccaria, *Schweizerisches Bundesstaatsrecht*, Polygraphischer Verlag, Zurich 1949.

Fleiner Thomas & Basta Fleiner Lidija R., *Allgemeine Staatslehre*, 3rd ed., Springer, Berlin 2004 (cited as Fleiner & Basta, Staatslehre).

Fleiner-Gerster Thomas, *Grundzüge des allgemeinen und schweizerischen Verwaltungsrechts*, 2nd ed., Schulthess, Zurich 1980.

Fleiner Thomas/Peter Forster/Alexander Misic/Urs Thalmann (eds.), *BV 2000: Die neue schweizerische Bundesverfassung: Föderalismus, Grundrechte, Wirtschaftsrecht und Staatsstruktur*, PIFF 26, Helbing und Lichtenhahn, Basle/Geneva/Munich 2000 (cited as Fleiner *et al.*).

Gauch Peter & Thürer Daniel (eds.), *Die neue Bundesverfassung – Analysen, Erfahrungen*, Ausblick, Helbing & Lichtenhahn, Zurich/Basle/Geneva 2002.

Gächter Thomas & Bertschi Martin (eds.), *Neue Akzente in der 'nachgeführten' Bundesverfassung*, Schulthess, Zurich 2000.

Giacometti Zaccaria, *Allgemeine Lehren des rechtsstaatlichen Verwaltungsrechts*, Vol. 1, Schulthess, Zurich 1960.

Grisel André, *Traité de droit administratif*, 2 vol., Edition Ides et Calendes, Neuchâtel 1984.

Gygi Fritz, *Bundesverwaltungsrechtspflege*, 2nd ed., Stämpfli, Berne 1983.

Gygi Fritz, *Verwaltungsrecht*, Stämpfli, Berne 1986.

Hangartner Yvo, *Grundzüge des schweizerischen Staatsrechts*, Vol. 1: *Organisation*, Schulthess, Zurich 1980, Vol. 2: *Grundrechte*, Schulthess, Zurich 1982.

Häfelin Ulrich & Haller Walter, *Schweizerisches Bundesstaatsrecht*, 5th ed., Schulthess, Zurich 2001 (cited as Häfelin & Haller).

Häfelin Ulrich & Müller Georg, *Allgemeines Verwaltungsrecht*, 4th ed., Schulthess, Zurich 2002 (cited as Häfelin & Müller).

Hänni Peter (ed.), *L'homme et l'Etat, Mélanges offerts par la Faculté de droit de l'Université de Fribourg pour Thomas Fleiner à l'occasion de son 65ème anniversaire*, Fribourg 2003 (cited as Festschrift Fleiner)

Imboden Max & Rhinow René, *Schweizerische Verwaltungsrechtsprechung*, 2 vol., 6th. ed., Helbing & Lichtenhahn, Basle/Frankfurt a.M. 1986.

Kälin Walter, *Das Verfahren der staatsrechtlichen Beschwerde*, 2nd ed., Stämpfli, Berne 1994.

Klöti Ulrich/Knoepfel Peter/Kriesi Hanspeter/Linder Wolf/Papadopoulos Yannis (eds.), *Handbuch der Schweizer Politik*, 3rd ed., NZZ Verlag, Zurich 2002 (cited as Klöti *et al.*).

Knapp Blaise, *Précis de droit administratif*, 4th ed., Helbing & Lichtenhahn, Basle/Frankfurt a.M. 1991.

Kölz Alfred & Häner Isabelle, *Verwaltungsverfahren und Verwaltungsrechtspflege des Bundes*, 2nd ed., Schulthess, Zurich 1998 (cited as Kölz & Häner).

Linder Wolf, *Swiss Democracy: Possible Solutions to Conflict in Multicultural Societies*, 2nd ed., Macmillan Press, Houndmills 1998 (cited as Linder, Swiss Democracy).

Linder Wolf, *Schweizerische Demokratie: Institutionen, Prozesse, Perspektiven*, Paul Haupt, Berne 1999 (cited as Linder, Schweizerische Demokratie).

Moor Pierre, *Droit administratif*, 3 vol., Stämpfli, Berne 1988/2002/1992.

Müller Jörg Paul, *Elemente einer schweizerischen Grundrechtstheorie*, Stämpfli, Berne 1982 (cited as Müller, Grundrechtstheorie).

Müller Jörg Paul, *Grundrechte in der Schweiz*, 3rd ed., Stämpfli, Berne 1999 (cited as Müller, Grundrechte).

Rhinow René, *Die Bundesverfassung* 2000, Helbing & Lichtenhahn, Basle/Geneva/Munich 2000 (cited as Rhinow).

Rhinow René, *Grundzüge des schweizerischen Verfassungsrechts*, Helbing & Lichtenhahn, Basle/Geneva/Munich 2003 (cited as Rhinow, Verfassungsrecht.)

Rhinow René A./Koller Heinrich/Kiss Christina, *Öffentliches Prozessrecht und Justizverfassungsrecht des Bundes*, Basle/Frankfurt a.M. 1996 (cited as Rhinow *et al.*).

Saladin Peter, *Das Verwaltungsverfahrensrechts des Bundes*, Helbing & Lichtenhahn, Basle/Stuttgart 1979.

St. Galler Kommentar, *see* Ehrenzeller *et al.*
Sitter-Liver Beat (ed.), *Herausgeforderte Verfassung: Die Schweiz im globalen Kontext*, Universitätsverlag Freiburg, Freiburg i.Ue.1999 (cited as Sitter-Liver).
Steinberg Jonathan, *Why Switzerland?*, 2nd ed., Cambridge University Press, New York 1996 (cited as Steinberg).
Thürer Daniel/Aubert Jean-François/Müller Jörg Paul (eds.), *Verfassungsrecht der Schweiz – Droit constitutionnel suisse*, Schulthess, Zurich 2001 (cited as Thürer *et al.*).
Tschannen Pierre/Zimmerli Ulrich/Kiener Regina, *Allgemeines Verwaltungsrecht*, Stämpfli, Berne 2000 (cited as Tschannen *et al.*).
Zimmerli Ulrich/Kälin Walter/Kiener Regina, *Grundlagen des öffentlichen Verfahrensrechts*, Stämpfli, Berne 1997 (reprint 2004) (cited as Zimmerli *et al.* [of the 1997 edition]).
Zimmerli Ulrich (ed.), *Die neue Bundesverfassung, Konsequenzen für Praxis und Wissenschaft*, Stämpfli, Berne 2000.

# Part I. Sources of Constitutional Law

## Chapter 1. Treaties

### § 1. In General

*60.* For Switzerland, the role of international treaties is especially important, particularly in view of its small size and its non-integration into the European Union, which led to the conclusion of a series of bilateral treaties between Switzerland and the European Union. Article 2(1)(a) of the Vienna Convention of 23 May 1969, on the Law of Treaties, defines the term *treaty* as 'an international agreement concluded between States in written form and governed by international law, whether embodied in a single or in two or more related instruments and whatsoever its particular designation.'[1]

1. Arnold Pascal, 'Ius cogens als materielle Schranke der Verfassungsrevision', in: Fleiner *et al.*, 53 *et seq.*; Balmelli Tiziano, *La Suisse saisie par l'Union européenne*, Fribourg 2003; Biaggini Giovnni, 'Das Verhältnis der Schweiz zur internationalen Gemeinschaft', in: AJP/PJA 1999, 722 *et seq.*; Cottier Thomas *et al.* (eds.), *Der Staatsvertrag im schweizerischen Verfassungsrecht: Beiträge zu Verhältnis und methodischer Angleichung von Völkerrecht und Bundesrecht*, Berne 2001; Cottier Thomas & Hertig Maya, 'Das Völkerrecht in der neuen Bundesverfassung: Stellung und Auswirkungen', in: Zimmerli *et al.*, 1 *et seq.*; Cottier Thomas *et al.*, *Die sektoriellen Abkommen Schweiz – EG, Ausgewählte Fragen zur Rezeption und Umsetzung der Verträge vom 21. Juni 1999 im schweizerischen Recht*, Berne 2002; Kälin Walter & Epiney Astrid, *Völkerrecht*, Stämpfli, Berne 2002; Müller Georg, 'Rechtssetzung und Staatsverträge', in Thürer *et al.*, § 70; Müller Jörg Paul & Wildhaber Luzius, *Praxis des Völkerrechts*, 3rd ed., Stämpfli, Berne 2001; Rhinow, Verfassungsrecht, 561 *et seq.*; Sägesser Thomas, 'Die vorläufige Anwendung völkerrechtlicher Verträge durch den Schweizerischen Bundesrat', in: recht 2003, 85 *et seq.*; Tschannen, § 9.

### § 2. Monistic System

*61.* Switzerland relies on the monistic system: International treaties, duly entered into force (*infra*, Part V, Chapter 1, § 2), are regarded as an integral part of the national legal system. Since Switzerland has adopted the monistic system, further transformation of the treaty into the national statutory system is not required (Decision of the Federal Court 127 II 177, 181; 120 Ib 360, 366; VPB 2000 Nr. 20; VPB 1989 Nr. 54). As a rule, international treaties must be published in the Official Register of Federal Laws (Article 2 of the Federal Publication Act) and, subsequently, in Section Zero of the Systematical Register of Federal Laws. Upon publication, the self-executing provisions of the international treaty gain binding force for the individual (Article 10 of the Federal Publication Act). The Federal Court has affirmed the self-executing character of international treaty provisions under two conditions: (1) the provision must directly regulate rights and duties of the individual, *and* (2) the provision must be sufficiently concretized in order to constitute an appropriate legal basis for authoritative adjudication (Decisions of the Federal Court 120 Ia 1, 11 and 124 III 90, 91; VPB 2000 Nr. 20).[1]

1. *See* Auer/Malinverni/Hottelier, Vol. I, 431 *et seq.*; Cottier Thomas *et al.*, *Der Staatsvertrag im schweizerischen Verfassungsrecht*, Berne 2001; Häfelin & Haller, 4; Müller Georg, 'Rechtssetzung und Staatsverträge', in: Thürer *et al.*, § 70, 1113–1116; Rhinow, Verfassungsrecht, 561 *et seq.*; Tschannen, § 9.

## § 3. The Relationship between Treaties and National Law

*62.* Under Article 5(4) of the Constitution, the Confederation and the Cantons shall respect international law. Note the vagueness of the formulation by the use of the term 'respect' in the constitutional text. Thus, although the State is bound to act in good faith according to Article 5(3) of the Constitution, it is not entirely clear whether this provision may be considered as the constitutional basis for the supremacy of international law over national law. In order to reduce the complexity of the relationship between international treaties and national law, the Federal Court and Swiss doctrine have identified three basic constellations and proposed the following solutions to remedy the normative conflicts:

*63.* *First*, the relationship between international treaties and constitutional provisions is unclear. It is commonly agreed upon that *ius cogens* takes precedence over constitutional law. In respect to other international law provisions, a balancing test is applied in order to give precedence to the more important norm, such as fundamental rights and liberties in comparison to purely international administrative agreements. Since the provisions regarding fundamental rights and liberties of the new Swiss Constitution and the provisions of the European Convention on Human Rights and the UN-Pacts I and II do not essentially differ from each other (*see* Part IV, Chapter 2, § 1, I., D.), Swiss doctrine has put them on equal footing.

*64.* *Second*, the relationship between international treaties and federal statutory law has led to a complex case law of the Federal Court. As a general rule, international law takes precedence over federal statutory law. However there are two exceptions to the rule:

(1) the relationship of international law to prior federal law; and
(2) the relationship of federal law to prior international law.

*65.* *Ad* (1): The Court held that newly adopted international law takes precedence over *prior* federal law (the *lex posterior* rule).

*66.* *Ad* (2): In a series of important cases, e.g., in *Schubert* (Decision of the Federal Court, 99 Ib 39), the Court clarified the relationship between a newly adopted federal statute in contradiction to prior international treaty provisions. In the cited case, the Court decided that the new federal statutory provision would prevail if Parliament intentionally deviated from international law. The *Schubert* doctrine was widely criticized and partly overruled in *Propaganda Material PKK* (Decision of the Federal Court 125 II 417). The Court has emphasized in *PKK* that conflicts shall be – to the extent possible – avoided through the interpretation of federal law in conformity with international law (*verfassungskonforme Auslegung*). Furthermore, if the normative conflict cannot be remedied through constitutional interpretation, the Court held that international law would always prevail at least in cases of a conflict between international human rights and newly adopted federal statutory law (no *lex posterior* rule; *see* Decision of the Federal Court 122 II 485, 487). However, parts of the ruling in *Schubert*, according to which newly adopted federal statutory provision prevail over international law *if Parliament intentionally deviated from international law*, are still good law (Decision of the Federal Court 112 II 1, 13 and 118 Ib 277, 281, reaffirming *Schubert*). But *PKK* clarified, that *Schubert* laws are *per se* void if they violate ius cogens or international human rights.

*67.* *Finally*, international law takes precedence over federal ordinances and contrary cantonal law.[1]

1. *See* Häfelin & Haller, 563–565; Schindler Diedrich, 'Der Vorrang des Völkerrechts und des Völkerrechts vor dem nationalen Recht als Problem der demokratischen Legitimation des Rechts', in: *'Rechtskollisionen', Festschrift für Anton Heini*, Zurich 1995, 321 *et seq.*, 323; Michel Nicolas, 'L'imprégnation du droit étatique par l'ordre juridique international', in: Thürer *et al.*, § 4, 63–75; Rhinow, Verfassungsrecht, 566 *et seq.*; Thürer Daniel, 'Verfassungsrecht und Völkerrecht', in: Thürer *et al.*, § 11.

## § 4. Important Treaties

*68.* Important international treaties are: The European Convention on Human Rights of 4 November 1950 (in force in Switzerland since 1974; SR 0.101), the UN-Pact I and II (SR 0.103.1 and SR 0.103.2) (in force in Switzerland since 1992), and the Bilateral Treaties I between the Swiss Confederation and the European Union (SR, in force since June 2002). The Bilateral Treaties I regulate the economic relationship with the European Union in such areas as personal freedom of movement, air and land traffic, reduction of technical trade barriers, and research. The Bilateral Treaties II still are in the process of negotiation: they will mainly deal with the 'left-overs' of the Bilateral Treaty I (such as education, agriculture, services and pensions, media, and environment). However, the Bilateral Treaties II will also focus on hard topics such as the closer cooperation in the fields of police, justice, asylum and migration (Dublin/Schengen), the taxation of savings, and fight against fraud. Furthermore, other important international treaties consider the areas of taxation, citizenship, neutrality, energy, traffic, health, finances, and economy.

# Chapter 2. Constitution

*69.* Switzerland has a written Federal Constitution and 26 written Cantonal constitutions.

## § 1. Federal Constitution

*70.* The Federal Constitution of 1999 is the supreme law of Switzerland. The Constitution of 1874 has been totally revised in order to enhance its readability and structure of the constitutional text, although it did not bring any fundamental contextual changes.[1]

1. *See* Auer/Malinverni/Hottelier, Vol. I, 455 *et seq.* (with further references); for further information on the notion and function of the Constitution, *see* Aubert Jean-François, 'Notion et fonction de la Constitution', in: Thürer *et al.*, § 1; Rhinow, Verfassungsrecht, § 1.

### I. System

*71.* The Federal Constitution is divided into titles, chapters, sections, and articles. The division into titles and chapters is the following:

Title 1: General Provisions
Title 2: Fundamental Rights, Civil Rights, and Social Goals
    Chapter 1: Fundamental Rights
    Chapter 2: Citizenship and Political Rights
    Chapter 3: Social Goals
Title 3: Confederation, Cantons, and Municipalities
    Chapter 1: Relationship between the Confederation and the Cantons
    Chapter 2: Powers
    Chapter 3: Finances
Title 4: People and Cantons
    Chapter 1: General Provisions
    Chapter 2: Initiative and Referendum
Title 5: Federal Authorities
    Chapter 1: General Provisions
    Chapter 2: Federal Parliament
    Chapter 3: Federal Council and Federal Administration
    Chapter 4: Federal Court and Other Judicial Authorities

Title 6: Revision of the Federal Constitution and Transitory Provisions
Chapter 1: Revision
Chapter 2: Transitory Provisions

## II. Constitutional Revision

*72.* The Swiss Federal Constitution can be revised *totally* or *in part* at any time (Article 192(1) of the Constitution).[1] However, the mandatory provisions of international law may not be violated (Article 193(4) of the Constitution).

1. *See* St. Galler Kommentar, Lombardi Aldo ad Article 192, 1985–1987; Rhinow, Verfassungsrecht, 448 *et seq.*; Tschannen, § 44.

*73.* A *total revision* of the Constitution can be proposed by the People by means of the constitutional initiative, (*infra* Part II, Chapter 2, § 3, I.) by one of the Chambers or by Federal Parliament. If the initiative emanates from the People or if the two Chambers of Parliament disagree on the total revision, the People shall decide in a popular vote whether a total revision shall be undertaken. Should the popular vote be successful, both Chambers of Parliament are newly elected (Article 193 of the Constitution). With respect to the Constitution of 1999, both Chambers agreed upon the project of a total revision. Therefore, no *popular vote on the principle* of the revision was needed, so it was unnecessary to newly elect two Parliamentary Chambers.[1]

1. *See* Häfelin & Haller, § 60; St. Galler Kommentar, Lombardi & Hangartner ad Article 193, 1988–1992; Rhinow, Verfassungsrecht, 449 *et seq.*; Tschannen, § 44.

*74.* A *partial revision* of the Federal Constitution may be proposed through a constitutional initiative or by Federal Parliament (Article 194(1) of the Constitution).[1]

1. *See* Häfelin & Haller, § 60; St. Galler Kommentar, Lombardi & Hangartner ad Article 194, 1993–1996; Rhinow, Verfassungsrecht, 450 *et seq.*; Tschannen, § 44.

*75.* The Constitution, revised in total or in part, enters into force only after acceptance by both the People and the Cantons through popular vote (Article 195 of the Constitution).[1]

1. *See* Häfelin & Haller, § 60; St. Galler Kommentar, Biedermann Dieter ad Article 195, 1997–2000; Tschannen, § 44.

### § 2. Cantonal Constitutions

*76.* The cantonal constitutions differ considerably from each other depending on the cantonal traditions and the time of their adoption. Several Cantons totally reformed their Constitution recently (e.g., the Cantons of Berne and Zurich).[1]

| Cantonal Constitution of the Canton of | Date of Adoption (as of 2002) |
|---|---|
| Zurich | 1869; new Const. (2005) valid as of January 2006 |
| Berne | 1993 |
| Lucerne | 1875 |
| Uri | 1984 |
| Schwyz | 1898 |
| Obwald | 1968 |
| Nidwald | 1965 |
| Glarus | 1988 |
| Zug | 1894 |
| Fribourg | 1857; new Const. (2004) valid as of 2005 |
| Solothurn | 1986 |
| Basle-City | 1889 |
| Basle-Land | 1984 |
| Schaffhausen | 1876 |
| Appenzell Outer Rhodes | 1995 |
| Appenzell Inner Rhodes | 1872 |
| St. Gallen | 1890; new Const. (2001) valid as of January 2003 |
| Grisons | 1892 |
| Aargau | 1980 |
| Thurgau | 1987 |
| Ticino | 1997 |

| | |
|---|---|
| Vaud | 1885 |
| Valais | 1907 |
| Neuchâtel | 2000 |
| Geneva | 1847 |
| Jura | 1977 |

1. *See* Auer/Malinverni/Hottelier, Vol. I, 561 *et seq.*; Ehrenzeller Bernhard, 'Reformprozesse im Verfassungsrecht von Bund und Kantonen', in: Thürer *et al.*, § 12; for a list of reform projects, *see* Germann Raimund E., 'Die Kantone: Gleichheit und Disparität', in Klöti *et al.*, 387–388.

# Chapter 3. Legislation

## § 1. Forms of Legislation

*77.* According to Article 164(1) of the Constitution, all important provisions establishing rules of law must be enacted in the form of Federal Statutes or Acts (here used interchangeably) which include fundamental provision on the exercising of political rights, the restriction of constitutional rights, the rights and obligations of persons, the subject (the object and the calculation of taxes), the duties and services of the Confederation, the obligations of the Cantons when implementing and executing federal laws, as well as the organization and structure of federal authorities. Thus, federal legislation is of great importance to Swiss constitutional law. The most important Federal Acts in the area of Constitutional Law are:

- The Federal Act on the Organization of the Federal Judiciary of 16 December 1943 (SR 171.11; hereafter referred to as the Federal Judicial Act).
- The Federal Administrative Procedure Act of 20 December 1968 (SR 172.021).
- The Federal Act on the Organization of the Federal Council and the Federal Administration of 21 March 1997 (SR 172.010).
- The Federal Act on the Proceedings of Federal Parliament and the Form, Publication, and Entry into Force of its Acts of 23 March 1962 (SR 171.111).
- The Federal Political Rights Act of 17 December 1976 (SR 161.1).
- The Federal Swiss Citizenship Act of 29 September 1952 (SR 141.0).

*78.* In some cases, Federal Parliament legislates by means of *decrees*, which, in the hierarchy of laws, is a lower form of legislation. In contrast to Federal statutes, the possibilities to instigate a referendum against a federal decree are limited, as it is only permitted to the extent that the Constitution or statute foresees it (Article 141(1)(c) of the Constitution). For example, territorial modifications between Cantons have to be approved by a federal decree (Article 53(3) of the Constitution). The lowest form of federal legislation is the *ordinance*, which is not submitted to a referendum.[1]

1. *See* Auer/Malinverni/Hottelier, 491 *et seq.*; Häfelin & Haller, 5; Müller Georg, 'Rechtssetzung und Staatsverträge', in: Thürer *et al.*, § 70, 1006–1112; Rhinow, Verfassungsrecht, § 27; Tschannen, § 45.

§ 2. LAW MAKING PROCEDURE

79. The process for the adoption of a new law is complex and takes a minimum of twelve months. Especially in complex or contested cases it may even take up to twelve years. The lawmaking procedure consists of fifteen steps:

(1) Law making procedures can be *started* by individual voters, interest groups, members of Parliament, the Federal Council, the Administration.
(2) In order to establish a *first draft*, the Federal Council normally institutes a commission wherein experts and persons interested in the new law are represented.
(3) The draft is then submitted to the *consultation procedure*. In this preliminary procedure the Cantons, parties, associations and other groups with a particular interest in the subject are invited to state their position and to propose modifications.
(4) The Federal Administration revises the draft and *submits it to the Federal Council*.
(5) The Federal Council can refer the text back for further consideration or *pass it on to Parliament* for the Parliamentary debate.
(6) The Presidents of the two Chambers of Parliament decide which Chamber shall debate the proposal first. A *preparatory committee* of the chosen Chamber (1st Chamber) discusses the text and presents conclusions to the Chamber.
(7) The *first Chamber* may then decide that the law is not needed, in which case the matter is closed or it can refer the text back to the Federal Council or the committee for further revisions, for preparation of a new draft, or it may debate the law in detail and take a decision.
(8) Steps 6 and 7 are repeated in the *second Chamber*.
(9) If the decisions of the two Chambers differ, a *conciliation procedure* takes place. The committee of the first Chamber assesses the differences and makes a proposal to their Chamber. This proposal can be to adopt all or some of the modifications proposed by the second Chamber, and/or choose to retain its own version.
(10) Following discussions in the first Chamber, the committee of the second Chamber considers the remaining differences and makes proposals to the second Chamber.
(11) If after three debates, differences still exist a *conference of conciliation* constituted of members of the committees from both Chambers is convened in order to seek a compromise.
(12) Which is then submitted to both Chambers for a *final vote*.
(13) The new law, adopted by the two Chambers of Parliament, can then enter into force unless a *referendum* is demanded within 100 days (*see infra* Part II Chapter II, § 4).
(14) If a referendum was successfully demanded, a *popular* vote is scheduled.
(15) If a majority of the voters agree to the new law, it is included in the official register and implemented.[1]

1. *See, inter alia*, Häfelin & Haller, 525 *et seq*. (with further references); Rhinow, Verfassungsrecht, § 27; Tschannen, § 45.

# Chapter 4. Jurisprudence

*80.* The status of the Federal Court and its jurisprudence is not comparable to that of the court in the Common Law system, e.g., the US Supreme Court, although, the Federal Court did perform an important function in solidifying the development of the Constitution of 1874, e.g., with respect to the equal protection clause (Article 4 of the Constitution of 1874) as well as to the fundamental rights and liberties (*infra*, Part IV, Chapter 2). Decisions are taken by the Court or its Chambers; there are no dissenting opinions.[1] *See* for more details Part II, Chapter 5, § 3.

1. *See* Biaggini Giovanni, 'Rechtsprechung', in: Thürer *et al.*, § 73; Rhinow, Verfassungsrecht, § 29; Tschannen, §§ 40–43.

# Chapter 5. Customary Law

*81.* Swiss constitutional law recognizes customary law under the following three conditions:

(1) there must be evidence of a continuous, uninterrupted and coherent practice;
(2) there must be an *opinio iuris* of the law-applying agency and the concerned individual (or legal entity); and
(3) there must be a lacuna in the written law.[1]

1. *See* Häfelin & Haller, 5–6.

# Chapter 6. Administrative Ordinances and Orders

*82.* Federal Acts often delegate considerable discretionary powers to the Federal Council or the Federal Administration, which usually act through administrative ordinances (synonymous to regulations), which are the lowest rules of law in the hierarchy of norms. In fact, however, they play an important role in constitutional practice (on the Federal Council *see infra* Part II, Chapter 4).

*83.* Article 5 of the Federal Administrative Procedure Act provides a legal definition of the administrative order, according to which it is the final and unilateral decision of an agency, in a concrete and individual case, imposing upon the individual a set of obligations or granting a set of rights, based on federal public law (for administrative orders, *infra* Part II, Chapter 5).

# Chapter 7. Interpretation and Publication

## § 1. Interpretation

*84.* The famous Article 1 of the Swiss Civil Code emphasizes that legal rules can never regulate all facts of life and that legal texts must be interpreted in order to establish their true meaning.

*85.* Switzerland relies on a plurality of methods for the interpretation of legal texts. None of the methods necessarily takes precedence (relativity of methods). *See* Decisions of the Federal Court 128 I 34, 40 *et seq.*; 124 III 266, 268; 123 III 24, 26. The Court usually takes a balancing approach combining the different elements of interpretation, which are as follows:

(1) The starting point of every interpretation is the *grammatical interpretation* of legal norms in which the ordinary use of language, including the meaning of terms, grammar and syntax is relevant. Switzerland publishes its legal texts in the three official languages – German, French and Italian, of which all versions carry the same normative weight. If their meaning in the translations differs, the text, which – according to other interpretation techniques – reflects the true meaning, receives precedence.
(2) The *systematical interpretation* interprets the norm in light of the systematic context with other legal provisions within the concerned Act. Compared to the Constitution of 1874, the Constitution of 1999 is characterized by a high degree of systematization. Thus the systematical interpretation could gain new relevance under the new Constitution and the Federal Court case law.
(3) The *historical interpretation* establishes the meaning of the norm at the time of its creation. In general, a norm should either be interpreted according to the historical will of the framers of the Constitution (*subjective* interpretation) or according to the general understanding of the norm by the People at the time of the adoption (*objective* interpretation).
(4) In contrast to the historical interpretation – with its inherent potential for ossification of the legal order – the *contemporaneous interpretation* relies on the public understanding of the norm under contemporaneous circumstances.
(5) The *teleological interpretation* establishes the meaning of the norm by considering the aims that the legislator wanted to achieve. The norm must imply the goal. It is not permissible to subsume a non-implied goal from the norm.

*86.* As a consequence of the hierarchy of norms and the unity of the legal order, statutes and ordinances are interpreted in light of the values expressed in the

Constitution. Through this interpretation in conformity with the Constitution, the legal system can be harmonized. Furthermore, in the proceeding of the Public Law Action (*infra*, Part IV, Chapter 2, § 4) the Court will only declare a cantonal decision or act as unconstitutional when an interpretation in conformity with the constitution is not possible.

*87.* Probably the most famous example of such an interpretation in conformity with the Federal Constitution was the introduction of female suffrage in the Canton of Appenzell Inner Rhodes (Decision of the Federal Court, *Theresa Rohner*, 116 Ia 359). The cantonal constitution that attributed the right to vote to all Swiss citizens (Schweizer) was interpreted by the Federal Court to include men and women (Schweizer und Schweizerinnen), contrary to a historical, grammatical, systematic or teleological interpretation of the Constitutional text.

*88.* Similarly, legal texts including constitutional provisions are interpreted in conformity with international law, in particular the European Convention on Human Rights. In such cases, Swiss Courts have to rely on the interpretation given by the highest authorities responsible for the application of the Convention.[1]

1. *See* Häfelin & Haller, 25–50; Tschannen, § 4; Rhinow, Verfassungsrecht, 79 *et seq.*; Tschannen Pierre, 'Verfassungsauslegung', in: Thürer *et al.*, § 9.

## § 2. Publication

*89.* All Swiss federal law, including each cantonal constitution, is published in two official registers. Firstly, the legal text is published in a chronological register of federal law, which is updated weekly. According to Article 10 of the Federal Publication Act, the publication in the chronological register is a prerequisite for the validity of the legal text. Secondly, several months later the legal text is introduced in the systematic register of federal law (hereafter referred to as SR). These texts are published in the three official languages – German, French, and Italian – and each version being equivalent to the other. The most important legal texts are additionally translated into Rhaeto-Romanic.

A version of the federal legal texts is also available on the Internet (www.admin.ch); however, it is not binding.

*90.* Cantonal laws are also published in official cantonal registers, most of which are available on the Internet. The Institute of Federalism provides access to cantonal laws based on a standardized index (*see* www.federalism.ch).

*91.* A selection of decisions by the Federal Court is published in an official register. A case is usually cited with the volume number (starting 1874), followed by the indication in Roman letters of the deciding chamber of the Federal Court, the page number of the beginning of the case, and the page numbers of the cited part of the case. It is upon the discretion of the Federal Court to publish its most important cases, which are presented in different volumes:

Volume 1: Constitutional Law (including conflicts of competencies and delegated powers)
Volume 2: Administrative Law and International Public Law
Volume 3: Civil Law and Bankruptcy Law
Volume 4: Criminal Law
Volume 5: Social Security Law

*92.* Therefore, as an example, the abbreviation BGE 126 I 1, 5 means: Decision of the Federal Court, in the year 2000, in the field of constitutional law, the case starts on page one, the relevant portion is on page five. All recent cases of the Federal Court are accessible on the Internet at (www.bger.ch) and are published in the national language in which the parties addressed the Court. Therefore, no official translation of the decisions is provided.

# Part II. State Organization

## Chapter 1. General

### § 1. A Form sui generis

*93.* The Swiss political system can neither be easily qualified as a Parliamentary nor as a presidential or a semi-presidential system.[1]

1. For a short overview over the political system, *see* e.g., Fleiner Thomas, 'Switzerland: Constitution of the Federal State and the Cantons', in: Basta Fleiner & Fleiner, 103–144; Kriesi Hanspeter, *Le système politique suisse*, Paris 1995; Linder Wolf, 'Grundzüge des politischen Systems', in: Thürer *et al.*, § 64, 995–1010.

### § 2. Consensus-Oriented Democracy

*94.* The Swiss political system is characterized by a *consensus-oriented democracy*, eschewing a majoritarian system similar to the Westminster Model but tries to generate, as much as possible, consensus and compromise. Consensus driven democracy not only results from the design of the institutions, but also from their operation. Swiss governmental institutions aim to institutionalize diversity by representing its entire spectrum of citizens; they operate in favour of compromises, or at least to accommodate the constantly changing majorities. Consensus-oriented democracy developed out of respect for the pre-existing diversity or because of pragmatic attempts to avoid making any group in Switzerland feel like a perpetual loser. Compromise driven democracy, which allows even small communities the possibility to pursue their legitimate interests effectively within the political system can prevent the adoption of extra-political means and the alienation of a part of the population. Consensus-oriented democracy was and still is a crucial element of peaceful coexistence in multicultural Switzerland.[1]

1. *See* Basta Fleiner Lidija R., 'Minority and Legitimacy of a Federal State: An Outsider Perception of the Swiss Model', in: Basta Fleiner & Fleiner, 77–102; Linder, Schweizerische Demokratie; 51–52; Töpperwien Nicole, *Nation-State and Normative Diversity*, Helbing & Lichtenhahn, Basle/Geneva/Munich 2001, 249–255.

# Chapter 2. The People

## § 1. Supreme Power and Opposition

*95.* The People, together with the Peoples of the Cantons, are the supreme power in Switzerland because these two can establish and revise the constitutional order. Thus, they form the constituent power as the Swiss state is based on a double legitimacy as clarified by Article 142 of the Constitution: proposals submitted to the vote of the People and the Cantons shall be accepted if the majority of the People (Swiss citizens) an the majority of the cantonal electorates (cantonal voters) approves it.[1]

1. Rhinow, Verfassungsrecht, § 3 (with further references).

*96.* In addition, the Swiss People fulfils the function of an opposition. Swiss institutions are designed so as to include the largest part of the Swiss population. In the executive, legislature, and the judiciary all the stronger political parties are represented, thus disabling them to act as an effective opposition force. Consequently, this function was taken over by the Swiss People, whereby direct democratic instruments empowered them to control the political agenda (initiative) and to supervise the legislating activity (referendum).

*97.* In § 2 the elections as a means of representative democracy will be regarded, followed by the initiative (§ 3) and the referendum (§ 4) as means of direct democracy which will be depicted.

## § 2. Elections

### I. Types of Elections

*98.* The citizens may participate in federal, cantonal, and local elections. On the *federal level*, the Swiss citizens elect the members of the House of Representatives, which is the chamber of Swiss Parliament representing the Swiss People. In the *Cantons*, the citizens of the Cantons elect the members of the Senate, which is the chamber of Federal Parliament that represents the Cantons. Depending on the various cantonal systems, the citizens of the canton elect a cantonal Parliament, the cantonal executive, and in some Cantons the judges. In *municipalities* with Parliaments, the citizens of the municipality elect the municipal Parliament as well as the municipal executive. In some municipalities, they may even elect higher civil servants and teachers. The right to participate in elections normally encompasses the right to vote and to stand for election. The *members of the Federal Parliament* elect the Federal Council, which is the Swiss executive, and the judges of the Federal Court.

## II. Constitutional Provisions

### *A. Distribution of Powers*

*99.* According to Article 38 of the Swiss Federal Constitution of 1999, which regulates the *distribution of powers* concerning the political rights in general, including the right to participate in elections, the Confederation shall regulate the execution of political rights in federal matters, while the Cantons are empowered only to regulate the execution of political rights in cantonal and municipal matters.[1]

1. *See* St. Galler Kommentar, Hafner Felix & Buser Denise ad Article 38, 506–509.

### *B. Access to Political Rights for Federal Matters*

*100.* The *access to political rights for federal matters* is directly regulated in Article 136 of the Constitution, which defines the holder of political rights, guarantees the equality of Swiss citizens in respect to political rights and obligations, and lists the areas of political participation at the Federal level. All Swiss citizens who are 18 years or older, and who are not under guardianship because of mental illness or weakness, have equal political rights and obligations in federal matters (Article 136(1) of the Constitution). The citizens may participate in elections to the House of Representatives, in federal voting, and may launch, as well as sign popular initiatives and referenda in federal matters (Article 136(2) of the Constitution).

*101.* While Article 136(2) of the Constitution establishes who has the right to elect the House of Representatives, Article 143 of the Constitution regulates the right to stand for election to the House of Representatives, the Federal Government and the Federal Court. The latter two are elected by the assembly of both Chambers of Parliament. Every Swiss citizen who is entitled to vote for federal matters is also eligible to these three institutions.

*102.* The elections to the Senate, the second chamber of federal Parliament, are regulated by cantonal law. Since the Senate represents the Cantons, it is therefore left to the Cantons to decide on the mode of election (Article 150(3) of the Constitution).[1]

1. *See* Mahon Pascal, 'La citoyenneté active en droit politique suisse', in: Thürer *et al.*, § 20, 335–347; St. Galler Kommentar, Kley Andreas ad Article 136, 1426–1431; St. Galler Kommentar, Lüthi Ruth ad Article 143, 1516–1518; St. Galler Kommentar, Lanz Christoph ad Article 150, 1547.

*C. Principles for the Exercise of Political Rights*

*103.* In addition to the distribution of tasks and the enumeration of principles for the access to political rights for federal matters, the Constitution establishes some *principles for the exercise of political rights.* According to Article 39(2) of the Constitution, the Swiss citizens cast their vote at their *place of domicile*, which must not necessarily be in the canton or municipality of which they have citizenship. However, while the Confederation and the Cantons can create exceptions, persons shall not exercise political rights in more than one canton (Article 39(3) of the Constitution). The Cantons can provide that persons who have recently established their domicile in the respective canton may exercise political rights in cantonal and municipal matters only after a waiting period of no more than three months (Article 39(4) of the Constitution).[1]

1. *See* Häfelin & Haller, 385–390; Mahon Pascal, 'La citoyenneté active en droit politique suisse', in: Thürer *et al.*, § 20, 335–347; St. Galler Kommentar, Kley Andreas ad Article 39, 510–517.

*D. Non-Discrimination Principle*

*104.* Article 37 of the Constitution states a *non-discrimination principle*, according to which, Swiss citizens who are not citizens of the canton or municipality in which they live may not be discriminated against because of their cantonal or municipal citizenship. No Swiss citizen living in the canton shall be entitled to any privilege or suffer prejudice because of his or her origin.

*E. Swiss Citizens Living Abroad*

*105.* Finally, the Constitution mandates the Confederation to legislate concerning the political rights of *Swiss citizens living abroad.* According to Article 40(2) of the Constitution, the Confederation shall legislate the rights and obligations of Swiss citizens who have their domicile abroad. This mandate mainly concerns the exercise of political rights at the federal level, the duty to render military or alternative service, assistance to needy People, and social security (Article 40(2) of the Constitution). Today, Swiss citizens who are registered at a Swiss embassy or consulate abroad can vote in federal elections by mail.[1]

1. *See* Mahon Pascal, 'La citoyenneté active en droit politique suisse', in: Thürer *et al.*, § 20, 335–347; Rhinow, Verfassungsrecht, 60 *et seq.*

§ 3. INITIATIVE

*106.* The initiative gives the People the possibility to act by allowing them to influence and control the political agenda.[1] In order to place an initiative, a certain number of signatures must be collected. When the requested amount of valid signatures has been attained and there is no procedural or substantial reason for the invalidity of the initiative, a popular vote (referendum) on the content will take place. The initiative exists at the federal and at the cantonal levels.

1. *See* Linder Wolf, 'Verfassung als politischer Prozess', in: Sitter-Liver, 543–562.

## I. At the Federal Level

### *A. Forms of Federal Initiatives: Constitutional Initiative*

*107.* The constitutional initiative is only recognized by Federal law (*see* the reform *infra* I, C.). By attaining the required 100,000 citizen signatures, a partial (Article 139 of the Constitution) or a complete (Article 138 of the Constitution) constitutional revision can be demanded.[1]

1. For the constitutional initiative, *see*, *inter alia*, Auer/Malinverni/Hottelier, Vol. I, 233–247; Grisel Etienne, 'Les droits populaires au niveau fédéral', in: Thürer *et al.*, § 24, 383–390; Linder, Swiss Democracy, 84–137, St. Galler Kommentar, Lombardi Aldo, Vorbemerkungen zu Artikel 138–142, 1437–1447; St. Galler Kommentar, Lombardi Aldo ad Article 138, 1448–1454; St. Galler Kommentar, Lombardi Aldo/Hangartner Yvo ad Article 139, 1455–1478; Rhinow, Verfassungsrecht, § 22; Tschannen, § 44.

*108.* Initiatives can be handed in as a general proposition or as a formulated draft (Article 139(2) of the Constitution).

#### 1. General Proposition

*109.* The general proposition of the partial and the total revision of the Constitution can be distinguished.

*110.* In the event of general propositions for the *partial revision* of the Constitution, the Parliament will concretize the proposition when it approves of it. If Parliament is opposed to the general proposition, a popular vote on the proposition will take place. If approved through the vote, the Federal Parliament must then formulate a corresponding draft (Article 139(4) of the Constitution).

*111.* When the proposition involves a *total revision* of the Constitution, it is then presented to the People in a popular vote (Article 138(2) of the Constitution).

#### 2. Formulated Draft

*112.* Formulated drafts will be put to a popular vote in their original form. Parliament can introduce a counterproposal (Article 139(5) of the Constitution). In the popular vote, the project must receive a majority of the overall votes cast, and a majority in more than half of the Cantons (Article 139(6) of the Constitution).

*B. Procedure*

1. List Preparation for Signature Collection

*113.* When an individual wishes to start an initiative, he or she must first prepare a list for the collection of signatures, which has to include the following.

*114.*

(1) The text of the initiative;
(2) the name and addresses of at least seven drafters of the initiative;
(3) an unconditional escape clause;
(4) the warning that any fraud in the collection of signatures and/or the falsification of the collection of results is a crime under the Swiss Federal Criminal Code; and
(5) the name of the canton and community in which the signatories have the right to vote.

*115.* The list is sent to the Federal Chancery, which undertakes preliminary control of it and publishes the initiative title and text in an official publication.

2. Collection of Signatures

*116.* The collection of signatures starts only after publication. The proponents have eighteen months to collect the requested 100,000 signatures. Any citizen who signs the initiative must give all necessary information to verify his or her identity i.e. name, address, and date of birth.

3. Verification of Signatures

*117.* Before the end of the eighteen-month period, the lists must be sent to the respective cantonal authorities who verify that the signatories have the right to vote on federal matters in the indicated municipality. They are then immediately returned to the framers, who depose them at the Federal Chancery no later than eighteen months after being published in the official publication. The Federal Chancery then determines whether the necessary 100,000 signatures have been collected.

4. Validity of the Initiative

*118.* Within a year, the Federal Council must present a report to the Parliament on the validity and the chances of success. When the Federal Council would like the Parliament to introduce a counterproposal, the delay is extended to eighteen months during which the Federal Council can prepare and submit a counterproposal to the Parliament.

*119.* The Federal Parliament verifies the legal validity of the initiative. Pursuant to the procedural requirements, the initiative must fulfil certain criteria which directly concern the form and content of the initiative:

(1) The initiative must be consistent in its form. It must be either formulated as a concrete project or as a general proposition.
(2) The initiative must be consistent in its subject matter. Only matters that are interconnected can be regulated in one initiative so as to guarantee that the citizens can clearly express their opinion in the vote.[1]
(3) The initiative must be in accordance with international *ius cogens*. If this is not the case, the Federal Parliament can refuse a popular vote on the said initiative. Initiatives that are opposed to international agreements, which are not part of the ius cogens, must be presented to the People and to the Cantons. Its text interpretation must be as consistent with international law as possible. However, when such an interpretation is not possible, the approval of the initiative in the popular vote is understood as the implicit mandate to the Federal Council to terminate the international treaty.[2] Up to now, initiatives that have been opposed to international law were clearly rejected by the People. Further, if Switzerland were to join the European Union, an initiative would have to be declared invalid if it was opposed to European Union law.
(4) Finally, it must be possible to execute the initiative. The impossibility of its execution must be manifest and clear.

1. *See*, e.g., Tschannen, § 52; Rhinow, Verfassungsrecht, § 22; Zen-Ruffinen Piermarco, 'L'expression fidèle et sûre de la volonté du corps électoral', in: Thürer *et al.*, 349–362.
2. *See* Arnold Pascal, 'Ius cogens als materielle Schranke der Verfassungsrevision', in: Fleiner *et al.*, 53–69 (with further references).

### 5. Decision on Support

*120.* After the validity of the initiative is declared, Parliament will decide whether to support it and whether they want to make a counter proposition. This decision must be taken within two years for general propositions, and within thirty months for concrete proposals.

### 6. Referendum

*121.* Thereafter, the Federal Council will set a date for the referendum. Up to this point the framers can withdraw the initiative. Under normal circumstances, it takes about five years from the framing of the initiative until the popular referendum takes place.

*122.* When a counterproposal is introduced, the citizens can cast a 'double yes' for the initiative and counterproposal, and can state their preference should it occur that both versions are approved. Before the possibility of a 'double yes' was introduced, Parliament used the counterproposal to split the votes of those who wanted a change of the status quo.

*C. Reform of the Right to Initiative: Introduction of a General Initiative*

*123.* A general initiative proposal was introduced by Parliament in which it could decide whether an initiative should be considered as statutory or as a constitutional initiative depending on the nature and importance of the subject matter concerned in the initiative. The People and the Cantons accepted the reform in a constitutional referendum on 9 February 2003, and Parliament set most of the provisions into force on 1 August 2003:[1]

1. *See, inter alia*, Auer/Malinverni/Hottelier, 734 (new); Rhinow, Verfassungsrecht, § 22; Tschannen, § 2 VI 1. and the critical remarks in § 44 I 4.

*124.* This new form of initiative complements the means of direct democracy and will be available in addition to the constitutional initiative. A general initiative should prevent subject matters that could be regulated on a statutory level to be introduced in the Constitution, as is presently allowed because the People can only initiate constitutional amendments but not statutory amendments. In the Constitution of 1874, there was, for example, a provision on the prohibition of a certain type of alcohol (Absinth) that could have been regulated by statute or even by decree.

*125.* According to the new Article 139(a) of the Constitution, general initiatives must be introduced in the form of a general proposition. If Parliament accepts the proposed amendment, it then changes the Constitution or statutory law accordingly. However, if Parliament is opposed to the content of the general proposition, the initiative is then presented to the People in a popular vote. Should the initiative be accepted in the vote, Parliament must then amend the Constitution or statutes. The new Article 189(1bis) of the Constitution guarantees a remedy to the Federal Court if Parliament does not adequately take into account the content or aim of the initiative.

## II. At the Cantonal Level

*A. Forms of Cantonal Initiatives*

*126.* All Cantons provide for constitutional and legislative initiatives. Under a constitutional initiative, the cantonal constitution can be revised in total or in part. With a legislative initiative, changes to cantonal ordinary law can be initiated. In addition, the Cantons allow for administrative initiatives, which are directed at a specific project like the building of a school or the construction of an electricity plant.[1]

1. *See* Auer/Malinverni/Hottelier, Vol. I, 262–277; Grisel Etienne, 'Les droits populaires au niveau cantonal', in: Thürer *et al.*, § 25, 397–405; Tschannen, § 18 N 16–18.

*B. Requirements and Procedure*

*127.* The Canton regulates the number of signatures necessary and the procedure for pursuing an initiative. The Federal Constitution provides that each cantonal constitution must be subject to revision if a majority of the People in the canton so wishes (Article 51 of the Constitution). All Cantons, however, set lower signature requirements. Otherwise, aside from this minimum requirement established by the Federal Constitution, the Cantons are free to determine how, in what cases, and under what conditions an initiative may be sought. The regulations differ decisively from Canton to Canton.

### *C. Legal Validity*

*128.* When the necessary amount of signatures have been collected in accordance with the necessary procedure, the *legal validity* of an initiative depends on five criteria which apply to all Cantons (and that are similar to the four criteria needed for federal initiatives, *supra* Part II, Chapter 2, § 3, I.):

(1) The initiative must be limited to one subject matter and the suggested provisions must be general in their application. Should the initiative have several parts, the different parts must be intrinsically connected.
(2) The initiative must either be formulated as a concrete project or as a general proposition. Initiatives that are formulated as a general proposition must then be made concrete by Parliament. For initiatives that are formulated as concrete proposals, Parliament can make a counterproposal.
(3) The initiative must either be conceived as a constitutional initiative or as a legislative initiative, taking caution not to mix either form. When an initiative is formulated as a legislative initiative but deals with constitutional matters, the cantonal authorities must treat it as a constitutional initiative.
(4) The constitutional initiative can not be in contradiction or violation of higher (federal and international) law or infringe upon the rights of other Cantons. Legislative initiatives must additionally respect the cantonal constitution and intercantonal concordats. Administrative initiatives additionally must respect cantonal ordinary law.
(5) The initiative must be possible to execute. Impossible initiatives are not valid. However, an initiative may not be defeated merely because it is irrational.

*129.* If an initiative is introduced successfully, a cantonal vote will take place in which the citizens of the canton can approve or reject the proposal.

## III. Importance of the Initiative

*130.* Since the introduction of the constitutional initiative at the federal level in 1891 about 220 initiatives have been successful in so far as the necessary number of signatures was collected and the initiative was declared valid. Fewer than half of them were withdrawn before the date of the popular vote was set. Approximately twenty percent of the initiatives were put to the popular vote. Against those initiatives, Parliament introduced counterproposals of which a clear majority were accepted. Only about five percent of the successful initiatives, that is of initiatives that were supported by 100,000 valid signatures, were later approved by popular vote.

*131.* While, the statistics may suggest that the initiative is only of minor importance, in reality they are quite important. Initiatives that are withdrawn (even though successfully introduced) are normally withdrawn after negotiations with the Swiss Parliament and government. Therefore, it can be a means to bring politicians to the negotiation table. In many instances, the politicians prefer the introduction of some of the demands in order to avoid having the initiative be accepted in the popular vote.

*132.* Even initiatives that do not succeed in the popular vote normally have repercussions on the political agenda. When an initiative manages to win the support of a major part of the population, the Executive and the Parliament will normally take up the demands in a more moderate way.[1]

1. *See* e.g., Linder Wolf, Schweizerische Demokratie, 268–278; Linder Wolf, 'Direkte Demokratie', in: Klöti *et al.*, 115–126.

## § 4. Referendum

### I. In General

*133.* The referendum accords the People the possibility to react. In a popular vote the People can approve or reject constitutional and legislative proposals introduced by Parliament or through a popular initiative.

### II. At the Federal Level

*134.* There are two types of referenda: mandatory and optional referenda. For certain issues the Constitution prescribes that a referendum must take place – e.g., for constitutional amendments (mandatory referendum). In other issues the People must specifically demand the referendum (optional referendum).[1]

1. For the referendum, *see* among many Auer/Malinverni/Hottelier, Vol. I, 247–255; Grisel Etienne, 'Les droits populaires au niveau fédéral', in: Thürer *et al.*, § 24, 390–396; Linder, Swiss Democracy, 84–137, St. Galler Kommentar, Lombardi Aldo, Vorbemerkungen zu Artikel 138–142, 1437–1447; St. Galler Kommentar, Lombardi & Thürer ad Article 140, 1479–1490; St. Galler Kommentar, Lombardi & Thürer ad Article 141, 1491–1502; St. Galler Kommentar, Kley Andreas ad Article 142, 1503–1505; Rhinow, Verfassungsrecht, § 22; Steinberg, 103–113.

#### *A. Mandatory Referendum*

*135.* As is regulated in Article 140 of the Constitution, the mandatory referendum assures the legitimacy of certain types of decisions and Federal statutes that are deemed most important from a constitutional law perspective.[1] There are two categories of mandatory referenda:

1. *See* St. Galler Kommentar, Lombardi & Thürer ad Article 140, 1479–1490; Rhinow, Verfassungsrecht, § 22.

*136.* (1) The first category of mandatory referenda always requires a *double majority*. These referenda must be approved by the majority of the Swiss People and by the majority of the Peoples in a majority of the Cantons (Articles 140(1) and 142(2, 3, 4) of the Constitution).

*137.* The most important case of this type of mandatory referendum is the constitutional referendum. All revisions of the constitution must be submitted to the vote by the People and the Cantons. Furthermore, this category of mandatory referenda requiring a double majority encompasses as well:

(1) the entry into organizations for collective security;
(2) the entrance into supranational organizations; and
(3) Federal Statutes declared urgent and adopted without constitutional basis by Parliament, and whose validity exceeds one year.

*138.* (2) The second category of mandatory referenda requires a *simple majority* of the People. This category includes:

(1) the popular initiative for the total revision of the Constitution;
(2) the popular initiative for the partial revision of the Constitution in the form of a general suggestion which has been rejected by Federal Parliament; and
(3) the question whether a total revision of the Constitution should be carried out if the two Chambers of Parliament disagree.

*130.* For most cases of mandatory referenda, a positive result in the popular vote is a prerequisite for the subject matter of the referendum to enter into force. In the case of urgent legislation, the referendum has a dissolving effect. Once the urgent legislation has been rejected in the popular vote, it loses its binding force.

*B. Optional Referendum*

*140.* The optional referendum confers to the People a veto power, insofar as the People can veto decisions taken by Federal Parliament. This was introduced in the Constitution of 1874 as a compensation for the stronger federal centralization. Within thirty years (1970–2000), about sixty statutes or statutory revisions had to be submitted to the vote of the People, who rejected about one third of them. The optional referendum has a strong influence on Swiss law-making procedure. It creates pressure upon Parliament to find a compromise in order to prevent the People to demand and introduce a referendum. Although a referendum may run the risk of discrediting the policy of Parliament, a negative referendum result has no direct personal consequences for the Parliamentarians or for the Federal Councillor who suggested or promoted a legislative draft.[1]

1. *See* e.g., Linder Wolf, 'Direkte Demokratie', in: Klöti *et al.*, 115–126.

*141.* In the case of the optional referendum, (1) 50,000 Swiss citizens with their signature or (2) eight Cantons may demand a popular vote (Article 141 of the Constitution).[1] The optional referendum can be used for:

(1) federal statutes; for
(2) federal statutes with a constitutional basis that have been declared urgent with a validity exceeding one year;
(3) federal decrees, insofar as the possibility of referendum is especially foreseen in the Constitution or in the statute; and
(4) international treaties which are:
    (a) of unlimited duration and
    (b) may not be terminated, which
    (c) provide for the entry into an international organization or
    (d) which contain important provisions that require a nomotechnical transformation into Federal statutes. In order to enhance the legitimacy of international treaties, Federal Parliament may submit – even if not required to do so – further international treaties to the optional referendum.

1. In 2003, for the first time in Swiss constitutional history, eleven Cantons decided to make use of the optional referendum against a Federal taxation scheme decided by Federal Parliament. The opposing Cantons (Basle-City, Berne, Glarus, Jura, Obwalden, St. Gallen, Schaffhausen, Solothurn, Vaud and Valais) won and the Federal taxation scheme was successfully rejected by the People, *See* St. Galler Kommentar, Lombardi & Thürer ad Article 141, 1491–1502.

*142.* In most cases, a negative result following a popular vote prevents the parliamentary act from entering into force. If a piece of urgent legislation with a constitutional basis is rejected in a popular vote, then it becomes invalid no later than one year after its adoption, and it cannot be renewed.

## *C. Organization*

*143.* Every year, several weekends are reserved for federal popular votes in which the citizens may vote on various issues at the time.[1] In most cases, cantonal votes are also held on these dates. The federal popular votes are organized by the Cantons on specified weekends. The federal level prepares a leaflet including a short summary on the subject matter to be voted on, a statement of the referendum respectively the initiative committee, and the recommendations of the Federal Council. These are then distributed to the citizens in advance to the vote. The citizens can either vote directly on the weekend in which the voting is taking place, or they can vote by correspondence beforehand. Some Cantons plan to introduce the option of voting via the Internet.[2]

1. For the dates until the year 2020, *see* http://www.admin.ch.
2. *See* the different critical approaches concerning e-voting in Muralt Müller Hanna *et al.*, *E-Voting, Journée 2001 d'informatique juridique*, Berne 2001; Auer Andreas & Trechsel Alexander H. (eds.), *Voter par Internet? Le projet e-voting dans le canton de Genève dans une perspective socio-politique et juridique*, Basle 2001; Auer Andreas & Von Arx Nicolas, 'La légitimité des procédures de vote: les défis du e-voting', in: AJP/PJA 2002, 491 *et seq.*

*144.* The Cantons organize the counting of the votes, and in some Cantons electronic counting machines have been introduced. However, electronic counting is only allowed with permission from federal authorities. In cases of violation of the voting rules, the votes must be recounted in the concerned Cantons or municipalities.

## III. At the Cantonal Level

### *A. Mandatory Referendum*

*145.* As prescribed by federal law, the revision of the cantonal constitution necessitates a referendum (Article 51 of the Constitution). Thirteen Cantons also allow mandatory referenda for the adoption and revision of statutes, and one canton also allows them for directives issued by Parliament. In seventeen Cantons, public expenses exceeding a certain amount must be approved in a referendum (financial referendum). Six Cantons may demand a referendum for intercantonal conventions and treaties.[1]

1. For the referendum at the cantonal level, *see*, *inter alia*, Auer/Malinverni/Hottelier, Vol. I, 277–282; Grisel Etienne, 'Les droits populaires au niveau cantonal', in: Thürer *et al.*, § 25, 405–411.

### *B. Optional Referendum*

*146.* The thirteen Cantons that do not have a mandatory referendum for the adoption of statutes foresee an optional referendum. Twenty Cantons provide for an optional financial referendum, and nine Cantons demand an optional referendum for intercantonal conventions and treaties.[1]

1. *See*, *inter alia*, Auer/Malinverni/Hottelier, Vol. I, 277–282; Grisel Etienne, 'Les droits populaires au niveau cantonal', in: Thürer *et al.*, § 25, 405–411.

## IV. Importance of the Referendum

*147.* The referendum accords the majority of the People the right to veto legislation. In cases of constitutional revisions both the majority of the People and of the Cantons can veto constitutional changes. Although this seems contrary to the consensus-oriented approach of Swiss democracy, in reality, the right to referendum does not introduce elements of competitive democracy. On the contrary, it further enhances consensus-driven democracy and promotes the legitimacy of decisions. Proposals are normally rejected in a popular vote when a basic consensus of the political elite is lacking.

*148.* There are several probable reasons for this phenomenon. When the major political parties and politicians are divided, the population tends to prefer to remain with the existing rule they already know. In addition, the crossing over of party lines emphasizes that the minority and majority opinions need not be the same on all issues. So as not to have a perpetual minority and loser on a particular issue, one might choose to vote with a minority on that issue even while normally belonging to the political majority. Between 1948 and 1978, one quarter of the political actions were in favour of a minority to which the political majority did not belong to.[1] In order to avoid referenda and a possible negative outcome in the popular vote, the parties usually try to find a consensus in advance.

1. *See* Linder Wolf, 'Politische Kultur', in: Klöti *et al.*, 22.

*149.* Recently, however, there has been a noticeable development in the French- and German-speaking Swiss populations as their voting behaviour has become increasingly more divided or at least the media has analyzed the voting results by stressing the differing voting patterns of different linguistic communities. In some cases, these patterns have also become apparent and even more exaggerated when comparing the countryside to the cities. There were several referenda where, for example, the German-speaking part of Switzerland was strongly opposed while the French-speaking part was in favour (e.g., on 26 September 2004, a new proposal to facilitate the naturalization of foreigners living in Switzerland for the second and third generation was clearly rejected by the German-speaking population and clearly accepted by the French-speaking population). Because of the larger German-speaking population, as well as the larger number of Cantons dominated by German speakers, they were in the position to dominate the voting in these referenda.

*150.* A relatively small number of popular vote proposals have been rejected even though a majority of the Swiss People has been in favour of it due to the negative vote of a majority of the Cantons (e.g., a proposal on the facilitated naturalization of foreigners in 1994). Up to now only one constitutional change failed in the popular vote even though a majority of the Cantons were in favour. In November 2002, an initiative that was aimed at the restriction of the rights of asylum seekers was rejected by the People but adopted by the majority of the Cantons.

*151.* An additional *albeit indirect* reason that safeguards the interests of minorities is the low turnout at ballots. However, low turnout is problematic from a democratic point of view. Since referendum voting often attracts only 30 per cent of the overall population, this means a strongly concerned minority of 16 per cent can win the vote.[1]

1. *See* e.g., Fleiner & Basta Fleiner, Staatslehre, 470 *et seq.*; Fleiner Thomas, 'Switzerland: Constitution of the Federal State and the Cantons', in: Basta Fleiner & Fleiner, 116–119; Fleiner Thomas, 'Legal Instruments and Procedures to Prevent and Solve Ethnic Conflicts: Experiences of the Swiss Constitution', in: Basta Fleiner & Fleiner, 154–155; Linder Wolf, 'Direkte Demokratie', in Klöti *et al.*, 115–130; Linder Wolf, Schweizerische Demokratie, 242–259.

# Chapter 3. The Legislature

## § 1. Organization

### I. The Status of Federal Parliament as Highest Authority

*152.* According to Article 148(1) of the Constitution, Federal Parliament is the highest authority of the Swiss Confederation. Nevertheless, it is limited by the rights of the People and the Cantons that form together the constituent power (*pouvoir constitutant*).

*153.* A special feature of Swiss democracy is the militia system (*Milizsystem*). In congruence with the militia system, Members of Parliament are only part-time politicians who continue to work in their professions in order to prevent the emergence of a political caste.[1]

1. On Federal Parliament, *see* e.g., Auer/Malinverni/Hottelier, Vol. I, 29–43; Häfelin & Haller, 416–464; Lüthi Ruth, 'Parlament', in: Klöti *et al.*, 131–158; St. Galler Kommentar, Mastronardi Philippe, Vorbemerkungen ad Articles 148–173, 1534–1536; Rhinow, Verfassungsrecht, § 24; Tschannen, § 30.

### II. Bicameral Parliament

*154.* Similar to the American system and based upon its direct influence, Swiss Parliament is bicameral.[1]

- In the House of Representatives, the Swiss citizens are represented proportionally in accordance with the democratic principle. However, if proportionality were applied in its purest form, some of the smaller Cantons would not be represented at all in this Chamber. Therefore, based on the principle of federalized democracy, each canton is guaranteed at least one seat (Article 149(4) of the Constitution).
- In the Swiss Senate, similar to the Senate in the United States of America, the Cantons are equally represented in accordance with the federal principle.

1. Kölz Alfred, 'Geschichtliche Grundlagen', in: Thürer *et al.*, § 7 IX ('the Atlantic circular flow of modern state ideas').

*155.* The House of Representatives and the Senate have equal powers, e.g., in order to be adopted, all legislation must pass both Chambers.[1]

1. *See inter alia*, Zimmerli Ulrich, 'Bundesversammlung', in: Thürer *et al.*, § 66 (with further references).

## III. Composition

### *A. House of Representatives*

#### 1. Distribution of Seats

*156.* The House of Representatives has been composed of two hundred members since 1963 (Article 149(1) of the Constitution). Every four years, the Representatives are elected by the People (Article 149(2) of the Constitution). Each Canton forms a constituency (Article 149(3) of the Constitution).

#### 2. Procedure for the Distribution of Seats

*157.* According to Article 17 of the Political Rights Act, the procedure for the distribution of seats per canton is the following:

- In the first round, the total number of all inhabitants is divided by 200. Cantons that have a population of less than the determined number receive one seat. These Cantons and their share in the Swiss population are excluded from the further procedure.
- In the second round, the remaining population is divided by the remaining seats. Again, the Cantons whose population is less than the determined number receive one seat and they and their populations are, from then on, excluded from the procedure. This procedure is repeated until all remaining Cantons have populations higher than the determined number.
- In the third round, for the distribution of the remaining seats, the population of each remaining canton is divided by the last determined number.[1]

1. *See* Poledna Tomas, 'Wahlrecht im Bund', in: Thürer *et al.*, § 22, 364–368.

#### 3. Outcome

*158.* This procedure led to the following distribution of seats (for the period between 2003–2011):

> Zurich (34), Berne (26), Lucerne (10), Uri (1), Schwyz (4), Obwalden (1), Nidwalden (1), Glarus (1), Zug (3), Fribourg (7), Solothurn (7), Basle-City (5), Basle-Land (7), Schaffhausen (2), Appenzell Outer Rhodes (1), Appenzell Inner Rhodes (1), St. Gallen (12), Grisons (5), Aargau (15), Thurgau (6), Ticino (8), Vaud (18), Valais (7), Neuchâtel (5), Geneva (11), and Jura (2).

*159.* As a result of the census of 2000, the distribution of seats had to be re-adjusted. The Cantons of Berne, Basle-City and Appenzell Outer Rhodes lost each a seat in favour of the Cantons Vaud, Fribourg and Schwyz.

*B. The Senate*

*160.* The Senate is composed of forty-six members (Article 150(1) of the Constitution). Each canton elects two representatives, except for the so-called half Cantons (Obwalden, Nidwalden, Basle-City, Basle-Land, Appenzell Outer Rhodes, Appenzell Inner Rhodes), which each elect one representative (Article 150(2) of the Constitution).

## IV. Elections

*A. The House of Representatives*

*161.* The Constitution prescribes only that the members of the House of Representatives shall be elected directly by the People according to the system of proportionate representation. Each canton forms a constituency (Article 149(2) and (3) of the Constitution). Therefore, owing to the disproportionate demographic size of the Cantons, the actual procedures for the election in each canton differ decisively. In Cantons that are entitled to elect one representative, the proportional system is *de facto* replaced by the majority principle, which favours bipolarization among voters. As a consequence, the smaller Cantons are rather dominated by the influential conservative political parties. In contrast, e.g., in the Canton of Zurich, a political party can gain a seat in Parliament with less than 3 per cent of the cantonal votes. Therefore, a much more diversified political landscape can be observed.

*162.* For the election to the House of Representatives the citizens can propose candidate lists. These lists are in most cases proposed by political parties (party lists), and must not include more candidates than the number of representatives the concerned canton is attributed. The lists must be signed by one hundred to four hundred citizens of the concerned constituency, depending on the size of the constituency.

*163.* The election is limited to the candidates included on the lists and voters can (but need not) give as many votes as the number of representatives attributed to the canton. Voting citizens are provided with the proposed lists and with a blank list of which and they can either use a prepared list as proposed by the citizens, they can modify the lists or they can fill in a blank list. There are three permissible modifications to the prepared lists:

(1) Voters can add names to lists that contain less than the maximum number of candidates;
(2) They can strike out one or more names on the list; or
(3) They can modify the lists so as to include candidates of different parties on one list (*panachage*). If a voter wants to increase a candidate's probability of being elected, he or she can *cumulate* – in other words, he or she can put the name of a candidate down twice.

*164.* In tallying the results, each candidate receives as many votes as he or she received on the voted-for lists. In addition to these individual votes, the party vote is established as well. A vote for a candidate counts as a vote for that candidate's political party. In addition, the party receives votes for the blank spaces on the voted-for party lists in those cases in which the citizens did not fill in the maximum amount of names.

*165.* The distribution of seats is based on a formula taking into account the individual votes and the party votes.[1]

1. *See* Poledna Tomas, 'Wahlrecht im Bund', in: Thürer *et al.*, § 22, 364–368; Steinberg, 260–265.

### *B. The Senate*

*166.* Whereas federal law regulates the election to the House of Representatives, the elections to the Senate are mainly a cantonal matter (Article 150(3) of the Constitution). The Cantons have to respect the one man, one vote principle, the right to free formation of opinion by the citizens, and citizens' right to the unaltered expression of their will (Article 34(2) of the Constitution).

*167.* All Cantons, except for the Canton of Jura, rely on the majority principle. As a rule, in the first round, the candidate must receive an absolute majority of votes; in the second round, a relative majority is sufficient. However, the Canton of Geneva forms an exception: In the first round, a relative majority of more than a third of the votes suffices.

*168.* In most of the Cantons, the representatives are elected by secret ballot. The half Cantons of Obwalden and Appenzell Inner Rhodes, however, still follow the practice of voting for their Senate representatives in the so-called *Landsgemeinde* (a publicly held assembly of all citizens).[1]

1. *See* Poledna Tomas, 'Wahlrecht im Bund', in: Thürer *et al.*, § 22, 369–370.

## V. Session Period

*169.* The provisions of the Constitution concerning session periods of Parliament are rather rudimentary. Article 151(1) of the Constitution prescribes that the Chambers shall only meet regularly for ordinary sessions, which take place in spring, summer, autumn, and winter for a period of three weeks. Any further regulation is left to statutory law. According to Article 151(2) of the Constitution, extraordinary sessions must be called when one quarter of the members of a Chamber or Federal Parliament so request.

## VI. Presidency

*170.* Both Chambers elect their own Presidents, as well as first and second Vice-Presidents. The mandate of the President and the Vice-Presidents is non-renewable and limited to one year (Article 152 of the Constitution).

*171.* Officially, the President of the House of Representatives is the highest-ranking politician in Switzerland. The Presidents chair the sessions of their respective Chambers of Parliament. In the case of joint sessions, the President of the House of Representatives acts as chairperson. Apart from purely representative functions, this is the only additional power accorded to the President.

## VII. Parliamentary Commissions and Groups

*172.* The influence of the Parliamentary Commissions on the decision-making process in Parliament cannot be underestimated. According to Article 153 of the Constitution, each Chamber shall appoint commissions, most of which have been designed to be permanent. In order to fulfil their task, commissions have the right to obtain information, to consult documents, and to conduct inquiries to which the limits of these rights are defined by statute. In addition to commissions in each Chamber, there are also joint commissions of both Chambers (Article 153(2) of the Constitution). The most important case of a joint commission is the so-called Parliamentary Investigation Commission. This commission is instituted by Parliament when there are signs of major state irregularities.

*173.* According to Article 154 of the Constitution, the members of Parliament may form parliamentary groups, which normally include party members of both Chambers and can include members of several parties as long as the parliamentary group has at least five members in one of the Chambers.

## VIII. Parliamentary Services

*174.* Parliament can rely on parliamentary services which plan and coordinate the sessions of Parliament and the meetings of commissions, and which equally act as a secretariat, take the protocol, and undertake translations (Article 155 of the Constitution). They also counsel the presidents of the commissions on substantive and procedural questions. Parliament can also request the support of the services of the federal administration.

### § 2. Procedures

## I. Separate and Joint Deliberations

*175.* In most cases, the House of Representatives and the Senate deliberate separately. Decisions of Federal Parliament require the approval of both Chambers

(Article 156 of the Constitution). The House of Representatives and the Senate deliberate jointly only for elections, to rule on jurisdictional disputes between the highest federal authorities, and to rule on petitions for pardon. In addition, both Chambers will assemble jointly for special occasions, and to hear declarations of the Federal Council (Article 157 of the Constitution). These meetings are open to the public (Article 158 of the Constitution).[1]

1. Rhinow, Verfassungsrecht, § 24.

## II. Quorum and Majority

*176.* Deliberations in the Chambers are valid if the majority of their members are present (Article 159(1) of the Constitution). The President of each Chamber presides over the quorum. In both Chambers and in joint sessions, the decisions are taken by the majority of those voting (Article 159(2) of the Constitution). An absolute majority of the members of each Chamber is required for the declaration of urgency of federal statutes, for provisions granting subsidies, authorizing credit lines, and establishing spending ceilings, which cause new one-time expenditures exceeding 20 million Swiss Francs, or new recurrent expenditures exceeding 2 million Swiss Francs (Article 159(3) of the Constitution).[1]

1. Rhinow, Verfassungsrecht, § 24.

## III. Rights to Initiatives and Motions

*177.* According to Article 160(1) of the Constitution, every Member of Parliament, every parliamentary commission or group, and every Canton is entitled to submit initiatives to Federal Parliament. (For the initiative of the Federal Council *see infra* Part II, Chapter 4, § 2 II., A.). With the parliamentary initiative – not to be confused with the popular initiative – the initiator or the initiators can submit a draft for a new Act of Parliament, or the initiator can make a general proposition.

*178.* In a preliminary phase, after deliberations in the parliamentary commission, the concerned Chamber of Parliament decides whether to follow the initiative. In cases of rejection – contrary to the procedure of the popular initiative – the matter is put *ad acta.*

*179.* In those rare cases in which a canton introduces a parliamentary initiative, the concerned commission in *each* Chamber deliberates. Otherwise, the procedure and the effects are the same.[1]

1. Rhinow, Verfassungsrecht, § 24.

## IV. Prohibitions of Instructed Mandates

*180.* The members of both Chambers are not instructed on how to vote by individuals, the Cantons, or by any interest groups (Article 161(1) of the Constitution).

However, the militia system implicates that the politicians are deeply rooted in civil society. Therefore, the Constitution mandates that they reveal their links with interest groups (Article 161(2) of the Constitution).

*181.* Recently, controversy arose over whether the Cantons should receive the right to instruct their representatives in the Senate. However, it is not likely that the Constitution will be amended in this respect.

## V. Immunity

*182.* Article 162(1) of the Constitution provides for absolute immunity for the members of Parliament, as well as for the members of the Federal Council and for the Federal Chancellor. The absolute immunity applies for statements in Parliament and before parliamentary organs – e.g., the parliamentary commissions and groups. For these statements, immunity cannot be lifted. Statutory law may provide for further forms of immunity and can extend immunity to other persons (Article 162(2) of the Constitution).

*183.* In contrast to the American model, members of Parliament and of the Government cannot be prosecuted for criminal offences *during sessions*, even if not connected with their office.

*184.* Outside of sessions, relative immunity applies for criminal acts in connection with the political office. In these cases prosecution is allowed only upon authorization of both Chambers. The consent of the accused does not suffice because the relative immunity is supposed to safeguard the functioning of political institutions and is therefore within the exclusive power of Parliament. When in doubt, the Parliament assumes there was a connection between the criminal act and the political office and normally rejects the lifting of immunity.[1]

1. *See* Häfelin & Haller, § 52; Tschannen, § 33; Rhinow, Verfassungsrecht, § 24; St. Galler Kommentar, Von Wyss Moritz ad Article 162, 1592–1598.

## § 3. Powers

## I. Legislation

*185.* Concerning the rules of law, a distinction can be drawn between federal statutes and decrees (Article 163(1) of the Constitution). The distinction is mainly relevant with respect to the rights of direct democracy, to judicial remedies, and to the rules of delegation. Provisions of importance, which establish rules of law, must be enacted in the form of statutes. These include the fundamental provisions on the exercise of political rights, the restrictions of constitutional rights, the rights and obligations of persons, the circle of taxpayers, and the object and the calculation of taxes, the tasks and services of the Confederation, the obligations of Cantons when implementing and executing federal law, and the organization and the procedure of federal authorities (Article 164 of the Constitution). Other acts shall use the form of a federal decree (Article 163(2) of the Constitution). A federal decree not subjected to referendum is called a simple federal decree.

*186.* According to Article 164(2) of the Constitution, Parliament can delegate, within a federal statute, the power to legislate unless the Federal Constitution prohibits the delegation.

*187.* When the coming into force of a statute does not tolerate delay, the statute may be *declared urgent* by the absolute majority of the members of each Chamber of Parliament and can be put into force immediately. A federal statute that shall be declared urgent must be limited in time (Article 165(1) of the Constitution). Urgent statutes lapse one year after their adoption unless they are approved in a popular vote before that date. Depending whether the statute has a constitutional basis, the statute must be approved by the People or by the People and the Cantons. Urgent Federal Statutes that have not been approved by the People may not be renewed by Parliament (Article 165(2)–(4) of the Constitution).[1]

1. *See inter alia*, with further references, St. Galler Kommentar, Sutter-Somm Karin ad Articles 163 (1599–1607), 164 (1608–1617) 165 (1618–1624); Tschannen, § 45.

## II. Further Tasks of Parliament

*188.* Aside from its powers in the fields of legislation, the Federal Parliament shall deal with all subjects that are within the powers of the Confederation and that are not attributed to another federal authority (Article 173(2) of the Constitution).

*189.* In addition to this general power, the Constitution enumerates some further tasks of Federal Parliament (Article 173(2) of the Constitution):

(1) Foreign relations are mainly a task of the Federal Council. However, Federal Parliament shall participate in the shaping of foreign policy and shall supervise foreign relations. Additionally, it has the right to approve international treaties unless a statute or an international treaty declares the treaty within the power of the Federal Government (Article 166 of the Constitution).
(2) Federal Parliament decides on the spending, adopts the budget, and approves the federal accounts (Article 167 of the Constitution).
(3) Federal Parliament elects the members of the Federal Council, the Federal Chancellor and the judges of the Federal Supreme Court. In case of war, Parliament would elect the general of the Swiss army (Article 168 of the Constitution).
(4) Federal Parliament supervises the Federal Government, the Federal Administration, the Federal Courts, and the other organs entrusted with tasks of the state (Article 169 of the Constitution), and evaluates the efficacy of measures taken by the Confederation (Article 170 of the Constitution).
(5) Federal Parliament may confer mandates to the Federal Government.

(6) Federal Parliament maintains the relations between the Confederation and the Cantons, it approves the cantonal constitutions and decides whether to approve intercantonal treaties or treaties between Cantons and foreign countries, should the Federal Government or a canton raise objections against the treaty.

(7) Parliament must fulfil tasks in the area of security in order to safeguard the inner and external security, the independence, and the neutrality of Switzerland. For these tasks Federal Parliament can issue ordinances or simple federal decrees (that are not submitted to popular referendum). Federal Parliament can order active military service and, to this end, can mobilize the army (Article 173(1)(a)–(d) of the Constitution).

(8) Federal Parliament takes measures to enforce federal law, it decides on the validity of popular initiatives that meet the formal requirements, decides on individual acts in cases especially foreseen in a Federal Statute, decides conflicts of jurisdiction between the highest federal authorities; and it decides on petitions for pardon and can declare amnesties. For instance, Federal Parliament granted general tax amnesties in which persons could declare tax frauds without being punished.

# Chapter 4. The Executive

*190.* In Switzerland, the Federal Council forms the Executive and it is the most distinctive of the Swiss Federal institutions. Its composition and functioning is representative of the Swiss stance towards diversity and Switzerland's compromise driven way of decision-making.[1]

1. *See* Fleiner & Basta Fleiner, Staatlehre, 466 *et seq.*; Mader Luzius, 'Bundesrat und Bundesverwaltung', in: Thürer *et al.*, § 67; Rhinow, Verfassungsrecht, § 25; Tschannen, § 36.

## § 1. Organization and Procedure

### I. Federal Government as Highest Governing and Executive Authority of the Confederation

*191.* According to Article 174 of the Constitution, the Federal Government is the highest governing and executive authority of the Confederation.

### II. The Government as Federal Council

*192.* The Federal Government is organized as a Federal Council. The French directorate inspired this institution.[1]

1. On the Federal Council *see* for instance Altermatt Urs, *Die Schweizer Bundesräte, Ein biographisches Lexikon*, Artemis & Winkler, Zurich 1991; Auer/Malinverni/Hottelier, Vol. I, 43–54; Fleiner & Basta Fleiner, Staatlehre, 466 *et seq.*; Häfelin & Haller, 465–488; Linder, Schweizerische Demokratie, 219–234; Klöti Ulrich, 'Die Regierung', in: Klöti *et al.*, 159–185; Mader Luzius, 'Bundesrat und Bundesverwaltung', in: Thürer *et al.*, § 67, 1047–1056.

### III. Composition and Election

*193.* The Federal Government consists of seven members, called Federal Councillors, who concurrently serve as head of state and ministers. In a joint session of both Chambers of Parliament, Federal Parliament elects the Federal Councillors for a four-year term among the Swiss citizens eligible for membership in the House of Representatives after each full renewal of the House of Representatives (Article 175(1)–(3) of the Constitution), or after a Federal Councillor vacated his or her seat. The candidate must receive an absolute majority of the votes. The political parties normally propose candidates. In the first two rounds of voting, however, elections are free and the Parliamentarians can vote for every eligible person. From the third round onwards, only candidates receiving at least ten votes in the previous round are eligible; after every new round the candidate with the smallest amount of votes is excluded from the coming rounds.

*194.* In the past, with one exception in 2003, Federal Councillors have always been re-elected by Federal Parliament as long as they stood for re-election. There is no official maximum term for Federal Councillors. The Federal Council, therefore, has remained an institution that guarantees continuity in politics, considering that since 1848 there has never been a complete renewal of the Federal Council.

*195.* According to the Constitution, Parliament shall consider in the selection of the Councillors that the various geographical and language regions be adequately represented (Article 175(4) of the Constitution). In accordance with this provision, the Federal Council normally includes two or three French- or Italian-speaking Councillors. The rule that all Councillors have to originate from different Cantons has been abolished in the elections of 7 February 1999.

*196.* In addition to these constitutional requirements, the most important political parties agreed on the so-called 'magic formula' for the composition of the Council. According to this formula, the four major parties shall be represented in the Government. Since 1956, the Free Democratic Party, the Social Democratic Party and the Christian Democratic Party have each been represented by two Federal Councillors. The Swiss People's Party proposes the remaining Councillor. However, in the elections of 2003, due to a sharp increase of popularity of the Swiss People's Party (SPP) in the last eight years, the SPP won 55 seats in the House of Representatives. Consequently, on 10 December 2003, the new Parliament denied the re-election of Federal Councillor Ruth Metzler, the representative of the Christian Democratic Party, in favour of Mr. Christoph Blocher, the representative of the Swiss People's Party. Whether the magic formula has just been re-adjusted – two seats for the Swiss People's Party, one seat for the Christian Democratic Party – or sacrificed in terms of 'anything goes' is difficult to predict.

*197.* On 2 October 1984, the first woman, Mrs. Elisabeth Kopp from the Free Democratic Party, was elected to the Federal Council. However, in 1990, Mrs. Kopp decided to resign when it became notorious that she had informed her husband, who was vice-president of the board of directors of the Shakarchi Inc., about a criminal money-laundering investigation against the company. The Federal Court did not classify the famous telephone call as a violation of an official secret in the sense of Article 320 of the Criminal Code and the sentence was one of acquittal (Decision of the Federal Court 116 IV 56 *et seq.*) Since then, three women representatives were elected to the Federal Council: Mrs. Ruth Dreifuss from the Social Democratic Party (1993–2002), Mrs. Ruth Metzler from the Christian Democratic Party (1998–2003), and Mrs. Micheline Calmy-Rey from the Social Democratic Party (elected in 2002 and still in office.)

*198.* The constitutional and informal requirements for the composition of the Federal Council have the effect in that the political system loses its opposition and thus including all main political forces and groups in the government.[1]

1. *See* especially Altermatt Urs, *Die Schweizer Bundesräte, Ein biographisches Lexikon*, Artemis & Winkler, Zurich 1991; Linder, Schweizerische Demokratie, 219–234; Klöti Ulrich, 'Die Regierung', in: Klöti *et al.*, 162–178; Mader Luzius, 'Bundesrat und Bundesverwaltung', in: Thürer *et al.*, § 67, 1047–1056.

## IV. Presidency

*199.* Parliament elects the President and the Vice-President of the Confederation from among the Federal Councillors. The term of the presidency and of the vice-presidency are limited to one year and are not renewable (Article 176 of the Constitution). The president is *primus inter pares*. The presidential office does not confer additional powers, but includes representative duties. The Swiss presidency is therefore a very weak one, and decisions are taken by the Federal Council *in corpore*.

## V. Principle of Collective Authority

*200.* In order to ensure continuity, consistency and stability within the executive branch of government, the Federal Council takes its decisions as a collective body (Article 177(1) of the Constitution) by majority vote. Thus, in practice, decisions must at least be based on the consensus of two political parties. According to Article 4 and 12 of the Federal Act on the Organization of the Federal Council and the Federal Administration of 21 March 1997, all members of the Federal Council have the same legal status and their decisions are taken as a collective body and represented as such uniformly towards the public regardless of the personal opinion of the Federal Councillor (duty of identification with collective decision). Consequently, to the extent possible, the voting behaviour of the individual Federal Councillors shall be kept secret.[1]

1. *See*, *inter alia*, Rhinow, Verfassungsrecht, 409 *et seq.*; Tschannen, § 36 III.

## VI. Federal Administration

*201.* According to Article 178 of the Constitution, the Federal Council directs the Federal Administration with the duty to insure its efficient administration and the effective fulfilment of its tasks.

*202.* The Federal Administration is divided into Departments and each member of the Federal Council is head of a Department (Article 178(2) of the Constitution). The distribution of departments is based on free choice and not necessarily on qualification. In practice, the Federal Council members gather behind closed doors and – not bound by any rule of law – decide who will head which Department. The seven Departments are the following: Federal Department of Foreign Affairs, the Federal Department of Home Affairs, the Federal Department of Justice and Police, the Federal Department of Defence, Civil Protection and Sports, the Federal Department of Finance, the Federal Department of Economic Affairs, and the Federal Department of Environment, Transport, Energy and Communications.

*203.* Influenced by the current New Public Management trend in public administration, Article 178 of the Constitution provides the general basis for the delegation of administrative tasks to organizations and persons of public or private law outside of the Federal Administration.[1]

1. *See* Koller Heinrich, 'Regierung und Verwaltung', in: Thürer *et al.*, § 72; Mader Luzius, 'Bundesrat und Bundesverwaltung', in: Thürer *et al.*, § 67, 1056–1059; Rhinow, Verfassungsrecht, 413 *et seq.*; Tschannen, § 39 VIII.

## VII. Federal Chancery

*204.* Central services are provided by the Federal Chancery. The Chancery is directed by a Chancellor who is elected in a joint session of both Chambers of Parliament for a period of four years (Article 179 of the Constitution). Although the Constitution is silent on the tasks of the Federal Chancery, its importance should not be underestimated.

*205.* The Chancellor attends the weekly sessions of the Federal Council in an advisory capacity and may table motions. The Chancery organizes the sessions of Parliament including the setting up of the agenda for deliberation. It draws up Federal Council decisions and ensures the timely internal distribution of information. A legal division of the Chancery advises the Federal Council in its legislative process and supports the law-drafting committees of the two Chambers of Parliament. Further, a language division ensures that legislation is drafted in a language that can be easily understood by the public. A political division advises initiative and referendum committees, verifies the submitted lists of signatures, organizes federal votes and elections and deals with complaints concerning votes and elections.

*206.* As part of the Federal Chancery, a Federal Data Protection Commissioner and a Federal Data Protection Commission work to safeguard the privacy of individuals whose data are processed by federal bodies or by private individuals and organizations. The Commissioner can conduct investigations, issue recommendations, and counsel private individuals as well as government agencies on questions concerning data protection. The Federal Data Protection Commission presides over appeals against decisions of most federal bodies and of the Commissioner's office, and it acts as arbitration commission for recommendation of the Commissioner in the private sphere. Judgments of the Commission can be brought before the Federal Court.

*207.* In addition, the Chancery is involved in public relations and communication, in the publication and distribution of laws, and in personnel matters concerning training, equal opportunities, logistics and budget, payments and auditing.[1]

1. *See* Adam Elisabeth, 'La chancellerie fédérale dans l'histoire: aperçu sur les origines d'une institution bientôt bicentenaire', in: Mélanges François Couchepin, Schlieren 1995, 163 *et seq.*; Rhinow, Verfassungsrecht, 415; Tschannen, § 39 VII.

## § 2. Powers

### I. Government Policy

*208.* The Federal Council is responsible for the strategic planning and coordination of all governmental activity. It determines the goals and the means of its government policy (Article 180 of the Constitution). Transparency of governmental activity shall be assured by timely information to Parliament (Article 187(1)(b) of the Constitution) and to the public, whenever not opposed by preponderant public interests. In order to guarantee this principle, Federal Parliament exercises the high supervision over the Federal Council (Article 169 of the Constitution).

### II. Powers in Respect to Legislation Issued by Parliament

#### *A. Initiative*

*209.* The Federal Council can submit parliamentary initiatives to Parliament. (For the discussion on parliamentary initiatives, *see supra* Part II, Chapter 3, § 2, 3.).

#### *B. Draft Legislation*

*210.* In nearly all cases, drafts for legislation are prepared by the Federal Council based on its own initiative or the request of Parliament. The Federal Council submits these drafts to Parliament (Article 181 of the Constitution).[1]

1. *See* e.g., St. Galler Kommentar, Biaggini Giovanni ad Article 181, 1813–1818 (with further references); Rhinow, Verfassungsrecht, 405 *et seq.*; Tschannen, § 38.

#### *C. Preliminary Procedure (Consultation Procedure)*

*211.* The Federal Council directs the preliminary procedure of the legislative process, including the consultation of the Cantons, of associations and of economic, social, environmental and other interest groups (Article 147 of the Constitution). The preliminary procedure is a specific feature of Swiss law making which aims at creating consensus in a very early stage of the legislative procedure. The Federal Council selects experts and organizes hearings in order to accomplish this goal.[1]

1. *See* St. Galler Kommentar, Lüthi Ruth ad Article 147, 1530–1533 (with further references); Rhinow, Verfassungsrecht, 405 *et seq.*

*D. Entry into Force of Acts of Parliament*

*212.* Many acts of Parliament foresee that the Federal Council shall determine the date for the entry into force of the act.

## III. Own Legislative Powers

*213.* The separation of powers is based more on an *institutional separation* than on a functional separation of powers. While the Federal Council has important legislative powers and can issue ordinances, it cannot legislate on the level of the Constitution or of statutes. Two types of ordinances can be distinguished: the dependent and the independent ordinance.

*A. Dependent Ordinances*

*214.* Usually, the Federal Council issues dependent ordinances, which are based upon an express delegation in a Federal Statute (Articles 164(2) and 182(1) of the Constitution).[1]

1. *See*, *inter alia*, Rhinow, Verfassungsrecht, 406 *et seq.*

*B. Independent Ordinances*

*215.* Independent ordinances are based upon a Constitutional provision, such as ordinances for the implementation of statutes (Article 182(2) of the Constitution), ordinances concerning the safeguards of the interests of the country (Article 184(3) of the Constitution), and police ordinances in case of imminent danger of public order (Article 185(3) of the Constitution).

## IV. Judicial Powers of the Federal Council

*See infra*, Part IV, Chapter 4, § 4.

## V. Further Tasks

*216.* Additional tasks of the Federal Council include the preparation of the financial plan, the budget, the federal accounts, and the supervision of the financial management (Article 183 of the Constitution). Other important tasks include foreign relations (Article 184 of the Constitution, *infra* Part V, Chapter 1, § 3), external and national security (Article 185 of the Constitution, *infra* Part V, Chapter 1, § 1), and the relation between the Confederation and the Cantons (Article 186 of the Constitution, *infra* Part III, Chapter 1).

# Chapter 5. The Judiciary

## § 1. Independence of the Judiciary and the Principle of Impartiality of the Judge

### I. Independence of the Judiciary as Fundamental Right

*217.* The principle of independence of the judiciary derives from the *Rechtsstaat* principle (*supra* General Introduction, Chapter 2, § 4). Article 30(1) of the Constitution contains the *fundamental right to impartiality* of the judge. According to this provision, influenced by Article 6 of the European Convention on Human Rights, every person, whose case must be judged in judicial proceedings, has the right to have this done by a court that is established by law, has jurisdiction, and is independent and impartial (Decision of the Federal Court 126 I 228, 230–231; *infra*, Part IV, Chapter 2, § 2, IV., B., 1.).[1]

1. *See* Häfelin & Müller, 386–387; St. Galler Kommentar, Hotz Reinhold ad Article 30, 427 *et seq.*, Kiener Regina, *Richterliche Unabhängigkeit*, Berne 2001; Rhinow *et al.*, 29 *et seq.*; Haller Walter, in: Kommentar BV1874 ad Article 106, N 30 *et seq.*; Müller, Grundrechte, 574 *et seq.*; Rhinow, Verfassungsrecht, 484 *et seq.*; for a thorough analysis of the functional, organizational and personal elements of the independence of the judiciary (and its limits) *see* Tschannen, § 40 II 3.

### II. Independence of the Judiciary as Institutional Principle

*218.* As an institutional principle, Article 191(c) of the Constitution grants independence to *every* judicial authority of the Confederation (Article 191(a) of the Constitution) and of the Cantons (Article 191(b) of the Constitution).

*219.* As an institutional principle, the independence of the judiciary is 'defensive' in character.[1] It is directed against any form of dependencies and requires the judge to be *impartial* and *independent*, especially from the parties in a case or controversy.

1. *See* Rhinow, 200–201; Rhinow *et al.*, 31–33; Rhinow, Verfassungsrecht, 484 *et seq.*; Kiener Regina, Richterliche Unabhängigkeit, Berne 2001, 235 *et seq.*; Haller Walter, in: Kommentar BV1874 ad Article 106, N 30 *et seq.*; Tschannen, § 40 II 3.

*220.* As a derivate of the principle of separation of powers, the institutional aspects of Article 191c of the Constitution also demand *independence of the judiciary from other branches of government.* The judge shall not receive directives from other branches of government, nor be influenced by political parties or other interest groups.

*221.* Furthermore, the constitutional guarantee of independence of judges includes the *autonomy* of the judicial decision-making process. The judge shall not be influenced by other parts of the judiciary in her decisions.

## § 2. Judicial Organization

### I. Overview

*222.* The following paragraph gives a short overview of the organization of the administrative, civil, and criminal law judiciary at both the cantonal and federal levels.

*223.* The organizational structure may be compared to a pyramid. Generally, in civil and criminal cases, there are – on the cantonal level – *trial courts* at the bottom of the pyramid, followed by the courts of appeal, both applying federal and cantonal civil and/or criminal law. Generally, Swiss courts are competent both in criminal and civil matters. From an organizational perspective, the courts are mainly subdivided into chambers, which are only competent in criminal or civil matters (e.g., the three criminal chambers of the Zurich superior court). Additionally, there are special criminal instances competent for grave criminal cases, e.g., jury courts with a special criminal procedure. 'Pure' criminal courts constitute the exception (Lucerne, Basle City, Basle Land, Schwyz, Valais).

*224.* Based upon the public/private law distinction, a different regime applies to the administrative law judiciary (*see infra* Part II, Chapter 5, § 2, II., A., 1.). In order to facilitate the comprehensibility of the administrative law judiciary, three cases can be distinguished:

(1) federal law applied by federal agencies;
(2) federal law applied by cantonal agencies; and
(3) cantonal law applied by cantonal agencies. In many cases, the cantonal agency simultaneously applies federal and cantonal law. For the relevancy of the distinction, *see infra* Part IV, Chapter 5, § 4, II., B.

*225.* The *Federal Court,* which shall be discussed *infra* in § 3, operates as highest judicial instance. *See also infra,* Part IV, Chapter 5, § 4.

## II. The Administrative Law Judiciary

### *A. Cantonal Administrative Law Courts*

#### 1. Original Hostility Towards the Creation of Cantonal Administrative Courts

*226.* The process to introduce independent administrative courts took more time to be realized within the Cantons than within the Confederation. One of the main reasons for this reluctant evolution was that the 19th century was dominated by the *doctrine of the supremacy of the democratic principle over the Rechtsstaat principle* (*see supra* General Introduction, Chapter 2, § 1 and § 4). Important parts of the population were rather hostile to the 'aristocratic and elitist idea' of creating administrative courts in order to control the administration.[1]

1. *See* Kölz & Häner, 63–66 (with further references).

#### 2. The Creation of Cantonal Administrative Courts

*227.* The first administrative tribunal with very limited jurisdiction, however, was created in the Canton of Valais in 1877. The Administrative Court Act in the Canton of Basle City created the first genuine administrative court with general jurisdiction in 1905, followed by the Canton of Berne in 1907. A second round followed, with the creation of the Zurich administrative court in 1959, in Basle-Land (1959), Solothurn (1960) and St. Gallen (1965).[1]

1. *See* Hafelin & Müller, 387, 388–389.

#### 3. Article 98(a) of the Judicial Act

*228.* Due to the fact that some Cantons were reluctant to institute independent administrative courts with general jurisdiction, the Confederation decided to amend the Judicial Act in 1991 (in force since 1992). The new Article 98(a) of the Judicial Act declared that the Cantons shall create administrative courts as a last judicial instance for those cases that can be remedied under an Administrative Court Action before the Federal Court (*see infra*, Part IV, Chapter 5, § 4).

*229.* This reluctance was due to the fact that cantonal administrations were (and still are) integrated in a small democratic community giving the individuals a democratic possibility to defend themselves against arbitrary and capricious actions of their government. The local government, which is politically responsible to the People, does not want to surrender its authority to a court, which is composed of lawyers and does not have the legitimacy of politicians elected by the People. In the Canton of Zurich, for example, the People rejected the creation of an administrative court in 1933, with the concern in mind it would get in the way of governmental endeavours.[1]

1. *See* Kölz & Häner, 64–65.

*230.* The above discussion includes the main reasons why it was difficult to establish administrative courts within the cantonal court system. However, a great majority of the Cantons have followed the federal example and introduced courts, which differ substantially mainly because of their different competencies.

### *B. Organizational Structure of the Administrative Judiciary*

#### 1. Complex Structure of the Judiciary

*231.* The structure of administrative judicial organization is complex and attempts are being made to change it. Owing to the fact that 19th century Switzerland gave priority to the democratic principle rather than to the *Rechtsstaat* principle, the administrative court system is still not complete (*supra*, General Introduction, § 2, D.). The following discussion depicts the structure of the cantonal and the federal court systems.

#### 2. The Cantonal System

*232.* Prior to the introduction of Article 98(a) of the Judicial Act, not all administrative cases and controversies could be brought before a cantonal court. Rather, they were heard only by a political body. In some cases, after the accomplishment of the administrative procedure, the order could be *appealed before an internal administrative body.* This administrative body did not constitute a court but was normally a superior administrative instance. After their verdict, one could only appeal – in cases of cantonal law – before the *Council of the Canton*, a political body. In cases of federal law applied by cantonal administrations, appeal was open to the *Federal Court* or the *Federal Council.* With time, the Federal Court got broader and extended jurisdiction over most federal administrative law cases. However, even under the new Article 98(a) of the Judicial Act, some cases, which cannot be remedied with the Administrative Court Action, cannot be brought before court.[1]

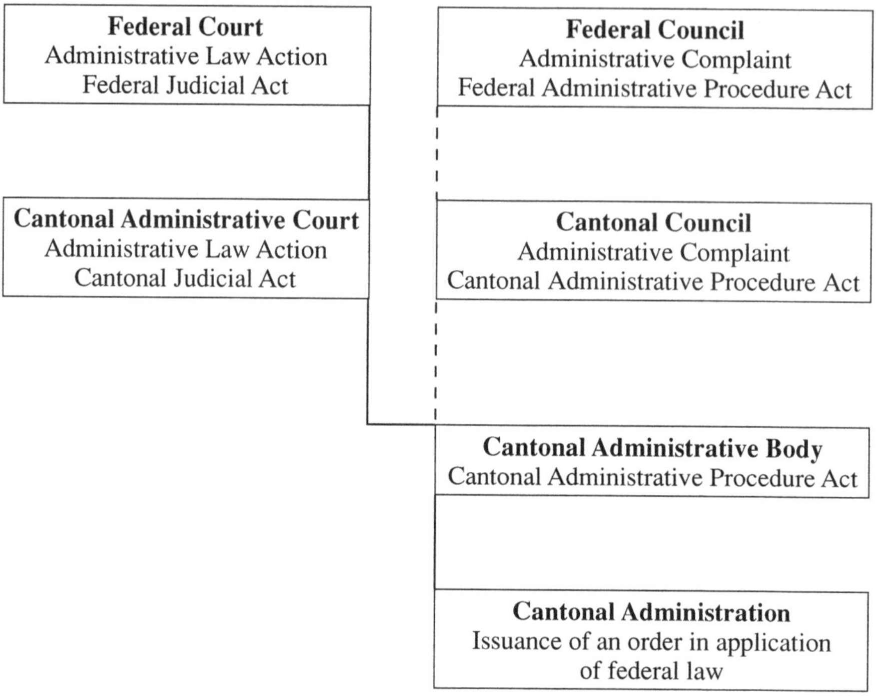


1. *See* Zimmerli *et al.*, Grundlagen des öffentlichen Verfahrensrechts, 72–74.

## 3. The Federal System

*233.* In cases of federal law applied by federal agencies, after the termination of the administrative process, one could appeal against an order before an internal administrative body and then before the Federal Court or the Federal Council. *See* for the administrative process and the control of its regularity, *infra*, Part IV, Chapter 5, § 3 and 4.

*234.* With Article 98(a) of the Judicial Act, the Confederation instituted so-called *Independent Federal Tribunals*, for instance in the field of asylum and refugee law, competition law or broadcasting law.[1] These Tribunals decide either as last instance (asylum and refugee law) with no appeal to the Federal Court, or as first judicial instance with the possibility to appeal before the Federal Court.

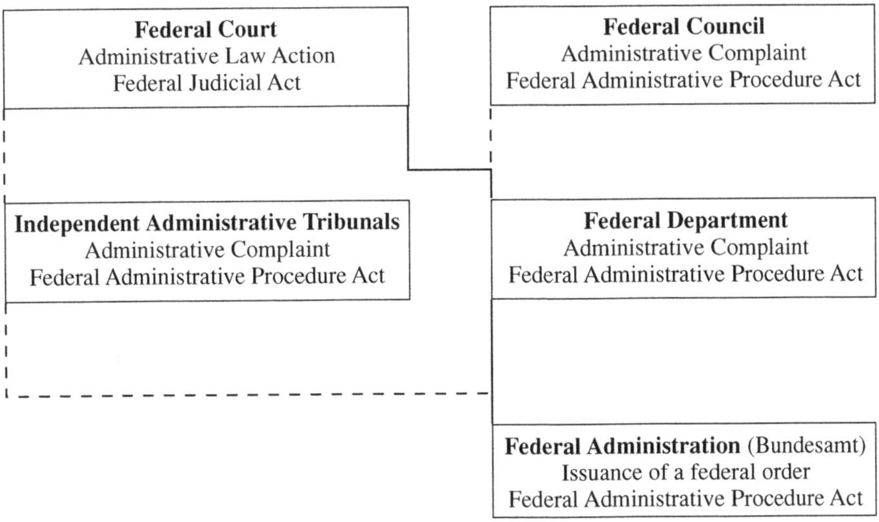


1. *See* Rhinow *et al.*, 82–85.

### 4. The Reform

*235.* The reform of the Judicial Act (*see supra* General Introduction, § 2, IV., C.) will change the administrative judicial system and its organizational structure considerably.[1]

1. *See* Hafelin & Müller, 413 *et seq.*; Rhinow, Verfassungsrecht, 475 *et seq.*; Tschannen, § 2, IV. 2.

*236.* *First*, according to Article 29(a) of the Constitution, in *all* administrative matters there shall be access to an independent and impartial court. Therefore, the problem that one could only appeal before a political body will disappear.

*237.* *Second*, as a consequence to the heavy caseload of the Federal Court, there shall be a new *Federal Administrative Court* in St. Gallen. The Federal Administrative Court will replace the twenty-two *Independent Administrative Tribunals* (*see infra* Part IV, Chapter 2, § 4, IV.).

*238.* *Third*, the reform is aimed at *abolishing the internal appeal before an administrative body* (e.g., the Federal Departments or the superior cantonal administrative body). However, this proposal is very controversial.

## III. The Civil Judiciary

*239.* According to Article 122(2) of the Constitution, the organization of the judiciary is within the competence of each canton.[1] Note that a draft for a Federal

Code of Civil Procedure is at the stage of elaboration. The schema below shows the organizational structure of the civil courts in the Canton of Zurich. Note that in some cases the procedure before the Justice of Peace is not mandatory (§§ 103–105 of the Zurich Code of Civil Procedure.)

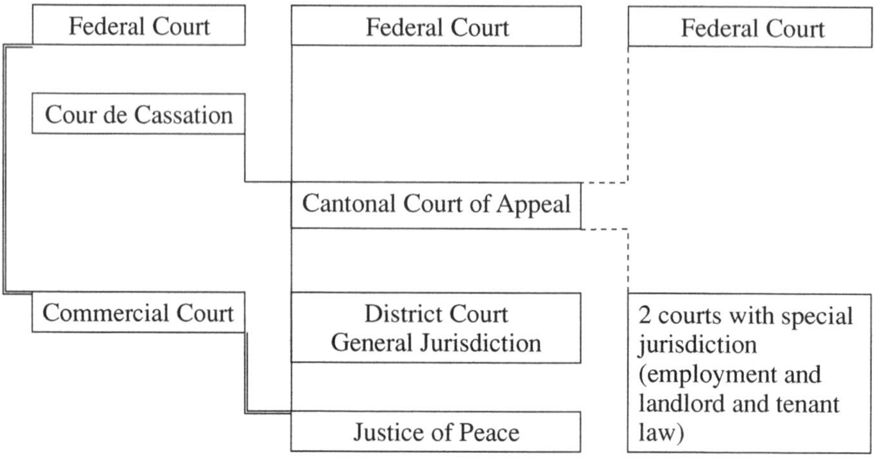


1. For details about the judiciary reform in civil matters *see* St. Galler Kommentar, Leuenberger Christoph, ad Article 122, 1260 *et seq*. *See*, for the Canton of Zurich, Hauser Robert & Schweri Erhard, Kommentar zum zürcherischen Gerichtsverfassungsgesetz vom 13. Juni 1976 mit den seitherigen Änderungen, Schulthess, Zurich 2002.

## *A. Trial Courts in Civil Cases*

*240.* Due to the self-rule principle of Swiss federalism, the organization of the civil law courts varies considerably from one Canton to another.[1]

1. *See*, with further references, Guldener Max, Schweizerisches Zivilprozessrecht, 3rd ed., Zurich 1979; Hohl Fabienne, Procédure civile, tome II, Berne 2002; Vogel Oscar/Spühler Karl, *Grundriss des Zivilprozessrechts*, 7th ed., Berne 2001; Walder Hans-Ulrich, Zivilprozessrecht, 4th. ed., Zurich 1996.

*241.* Some territorially smaller Cantons are not subdivided into court districts. In these smaller Cantons, the first instance is a trial court with general jurisdiction for the whole of the cantonal territory, while in bigger Cantons, the first instance trial court with general jurisdiction over civil matters corresponds to the territory of each district. In Cantons with large populations, judges are professional lawyers working on a full-time basis, while in Cantons with smaller populations, judges (esp. Justices of Peace) are often laymen and work part-time.

*242.* Trial Courts in civil cases are usually composed as a collegiate. However, trials with a small litigation value, up to CHF 8000.-, are often confined to a single trial judge who decides definitely with no possibility of appeal (unless an extraordinary remedy is available).

*B. Appeal in Civil Cases*

*243.* Depending on the litigation value, most Cantons have instituted a second instance of appeal – the cantonal superior courts. They have general jurisdiction over all factual and legal questions that arose before the cantonal trial court. Grave mistakes of procedure of those cantonal or superior courts of appeal can be invoked before the same court with other personal composition, although in rare situations the Cantons have created a special court of appeal (cour de cassation or Kassationsgericht). For the role of the Federal Court in civil law cases, *see infra* § 3.

*C. Courts with Limited Jurisdiction*

*244.* The aim of courts with limited jurisdiction in civil law cases is to combine expertise and speedy procedure, especially in the field of labour law, commercial law, and landlord & tenant law. Special statutes regulate their organization. The expertise of the judge shall increase the parties' confidence in the judicial process. However, not all Cantons have courts with limited jurisdiction in civil law cases.[1]

1. *See*, with further references, Hohl Fabienne, *Procédure civile*, tome II, Berne 2002; Vogel Oscar/Spühler Karl, *Grundriss des Zivilprozessrechts*, 7th ed., Berne 2001; Walder Hans-Ulrich, *Zivilprozessrecht*, 4th ed., Zurich 1996.

## IV. The Criminal Law Judiciary

*A. Overview*

*245.* According to Article 123(1) of the Constitution, legislation in the field of criminal law and criminal procedure are federal matters, whereas the organization of the judiciary is a cantonal concern (Article 123(2) of the Constitution).[1] Note that a draft for a Federal Code of Criminal Procedure is at the stage of elaboration.

1. For details about judiciary reform in criminal matters *see* Vest Hans, St. Galler Kommentar, ad Article 123, 1268 *et seq.*

*B. The Federal Criminal Judiciary*

*246.* Based upon the delegation in Article 190(a)(1) of the Constitution, Parliament has instituted a *Federal Criminal Court* (Bundesstrafgericht) in Bellinzona

(Ticino) consisting of 15–35 Federal Judges (Article 1(3) of the Federal Criminal Court Act). The Federal Criminal Court is the general criminal court of the Confederation. Appeals to the Federal Court are possible as far as not excluded by statute (Article 1(1) and (2) of the Federal Criminal Court Act). The substantive jurisdiction of the Federal Criminal Court is defined by Article 340 and 340bis of the Criminal Code (Article 26 of the Federal Criminal Court Act): Cases that can be heard by the Federal Criminal Court are, for example, (1) crimes against persons protected by international public law, (2) attacks against an embassy and a consulate, (3) crimes with explosives (Articles 224–226 of the Criminal Code), (4) forgery of Federal documents (Articles 251–253 of the Criminal Code), (5) crimes and felonies against the state and the military defence (Article 265 *et seq.* of the Criminal Code), and (6) felonies against the will of the People in federal elections, referenda and initiatives (Article 279 *et seq.* of the Criminal Code).[1]

1. *See* Hauser Robert/Schweri Erhard, *Schweizerisches Strafprozessrecht*, 5th ed., Basle/Geneva/ Munich 2002, 42–43 (with further references).

*247.* The crimes listed above indicate that the Federal Criminal Court is an *institution for exceptional cases*. Furthermore, Article 18 of the Federal Criminal Procedure Act contains a delegation clause with the possibility to delegate the cases to the Cantons, which is common practice. In the last twenty-five years before the creation of the Federal Criminal Court in Bellinzona in 2004, the Federal Court judged only nine, but important cases.

## *C. Cantonal Criminal Courts*

*248.* According to Article 343 of the Criminal Code, the Cantons are responsible for all matters not subject to federal jurisdiction. As indicated above, the jurisdiction of the Federal Criminal Court is exceptional. On the whole, criminal justice is a cantonal matter, as stipulated by Article 123(2) of the Constitution. A distinction must be drawn between original and delegated jurisdiction of the Cantons.

*249.* The Cantons have *original jurisdiction* in most criminal matters, such as murder, homicide, and manslaughter (Article 111 *et seq.* of the Criminal Code), crimes against property (Article 137 *et seq.* of the Criminal Code), crimes against the honour of a person (Article 173 *et seq.* of the Criminal Code), crimes against privacy and liberty (Article 179 *et seq.* of the Criminal Code), and crimes against sexual integrity (Article 187 *et seq.* of the Criminal Code). Furthermore, contraventions in the field of street and traffic law fall within the original jurisdiction of the Cantons.[1]

1. *See* Hauser Robert/Schweri Erhard, *Schweizerisches Strafprozessrecht*, 5th ed., Basle/Geneva/ Munich 2002, 45–46.

*250.* According to Article 18 and 18bis of the Federal Criminal Procedure Act, the Federal Attorney General can fully *delegate* federal jurisdiction cases of minor importance to the Cantons.

*D. Organization of the Criminal Courts*

*251.* According to Article 30(1) of the Constitution, *exceptional tribunals* acting outside the constitutional order and instituted just for a single case are prohibited. *Ordinary criminal courts* dispose of a general jurisdiction and hear all cases that are not delegated by statute to a court with special jurisdiction. *Courts with special jurisdiction,* for example military courts, juvenile courts, or economic crime courts, are only permitted if their competencies and organizational structure have been created by statute and if there is an objective reason for their creation.

*252.* During the 19th century and the beginning of the 20th century, all members of the court usually heard criminal cases. Nowadays, criminal courts are subdivided into *chambers* upon which all incoming cases are distributed. All larger cantonal district courts, cantonal superior courts and the Federal Court have adopted the system of subdividing the criminal court into chambers. In order to guarantee a consistent case law among the chambers, Article 16 of the Judicial Act provides that a chamber needs the approbation of another chamber or an affirmative decision of the united chambers in order to set a new precedent.[1]

1. For an overview *see* Hauser Robert/Schweri Erhard, *Schweizerisches Strafprozessrecht*, 5th ed., Basle/Geneva/Munich 2002, 26–27.

§ 3. The Federal Court

## I. The Federal Court as Supreme Federal Judicial Authority

*253.* The Federal Court in Lausanne in the Canton of Vaud was founded in 1874. It is the supreme federal judicial authority of the Swiss Confederation (Article 188(1) of the Constitution). According to the *organizational* element of the principle of separation of powers, the Federal Court is independent in its jurisprudential function and free of interferences from other branches of government (*see supra* Part II, Chapter 5, § 1). Only the law binds the Federal Court. The high supervision of Parliament over the Federal Court in Article 169(1) of the Constitution is not intended to constitute an instrument to influence the decision-making process of the Federal Court. Generally, the high supervision is limited to the formal control of the regularity of judicial affairs and the organizational and financial management of the Court.[1]

1. *See* Häfelin & Haller, 489–503; Kiss Christina & Koller Heinrich, St. Galler Kommentar, ad Article 188, 1887 *et seq.*; Rhinow, Verfassungsrecht, § 29; Schubarth Martin, 'Bundesgericht', in: Thürer *et al.*, § 68; Tschannen, § 40.

## II. Election of the Federal Judges

*A. Eligibility*

*254.* All Swiss citizens who are eighteen years or older and are not under custody because of mental illness or weakness are eligible for membership in the

Federal Court (Articles 143 and 136 of the Constitution). Even though not constitutionally required, the Court is composed of distinguished judges, lawyers or law professors. Furthermore, Article 1(2) of the Judicial Act demands that all official languages shall be represented.

### *B. Incompatibilities*

*255.* Judges of the Federal Court may not at the same time be members of the Houses of Representatives, of the Senate or of the Federal Government (Article 144(1) of the Constitution). They are not entitled to undertake another function of the Confederation or a Canton, nor may they exercise another remunerative private activity (Article 144(2) of the Constitution, Article 3 of the Federal Judicial Act and Federal Court Directive of 22 February 1993 [SR 173.311.1]). Express authorization of the Federal Court is needed if a Federal Court Judge is acting in the function of an arbitral referee, expert or legal counsel (Articles 3 and 3(a) of the Federal Judicial Act and the Federal Court Directive of 22 February 1993 [SR 173.311.1]).

### *C. Election*

*256.* The members of the Federal Court are elected by the *united* Federal Parliament (*Vereinigte Bundesversammlung*) (Article 168(1) of the Constitution) with its judges being elected for six years term (Article 145 of the Constitution) at the end of which most are always re-elected. As a customary rule, Federal Court judges retire at the age of sixty-seven.

## III. Organization of the Federal Court

### *A. Personal Composition of the Federal Court*

*257.* According to Article 1(1) of the Judicial Act, the Federal Court is composed of thirty Federal Judges and fifteen part-time judges. In practice, due to the heavy caseload of the Federal Court, the number of part-time judges has been increased to thirty.

### *B. The President and the Vice-President of the Federal Court*

*258.* The *President* and the *Vice-President* of the Federal Court are elected for two years by the united Federal Parliament (Article 6(1) of the Judicial Act). The main function of its President is the general conduct of the judicial business and supervision of the administration and of the staff of the Federal Court (Article 6(2) and (3) of the Judicial Act).

*C. The Chambers of the Federal Court*

*259.* The Federal Court is divided into two or three chambers dealing with public law matters, two chambers dealing with private law, a bankruptcy chamber and a chamber of accusation. Furthermore, it incorporates the Federal Criminal Court and the cour de cassation in criminal matters.

*D. The Federal Insurance Court*

*260.* According to Article 122 of the Judicial Act, the Federal Insurance Court in Lucerne constitutes, from an organizational perspective, the independent social security department of the Federal Court. It consists of each nine to eleven full- and part-time judges (Article 123 of the Judicial Act). The revision of the judiciary will enable the integration of the Federal Insurance Court into the Federal Court.

# Part III. The State and its Subdivisions

## Chapter 1. Switzerland as a Federal State

### § 1. Federalism as Legitimizing Element of State Organization

#### I. Historical Development

*261.* Swiss Federalism can only be understood from a historical perspective (*see supra* General Introduction, Chapter 1, § 1), as it is the pragmatic answer to internal and external developments in the 19th century. Swiss history is characterized by a slow centralization without cultural homogenization. Switzerland adopted its first federal Constitution in 1848. This Constitution, as well as the Constitutions of 1874 and 1999, enabled a compromise between centralization and decentralization. While the Constitutions included elements of centralization, they also maintained the sovereignty of the Cantons.

*262.* The modernization of Switzerland was not complete. Switzerland applied the paradigms of the French Revolution – *Equality, Liberty and Fraternity* – only in part, stressing not only the equality of the individual, but also the equality of the Cantons.

#### II. Diversity Promotion in the Constitution

*263.* The limited modernity of the Swiss nation-state is visible mainly in the emphasis placed on maintaining and promoting diversity, which is one of the prime constitutional values.

*264.* The Preamble of the Constitution of 1999 relies on a concept of diversity in unity: 'We, the Swiss People and the Cantons . . . are determined to live our diversity in unity respecting one another.' Article 2 of the Constitution, which states the purpose of the Swiss Confederation goes further by declaring that the 'Swiss Confederation . . . shall promote . . . the cultural diversity of the country.'

*265.* However, the value of diversity is not universal. Rather, it is limited to the indigenous diversities.[1] For minority issues, *see infra* Part IV, Chapter 3.

1. *See* Basta Fleiner, Lidija R., 'Minority and Legitimacy of a Federal State: An Outsider Perception of the Swiss Model', in: Basta Fleiner & Fleiner, 99–102; Fleiner Thomas, 'Legal Instruments and Procedures to Prevent and Solve Ethnic Conflicts: Experiences from the Swiss Constitution', in: Basta Fleiner & Fleiner, 145–164; Linder, Swiss Democracy, 38–79; Töpperwien Nicole, *Nation-State and Normative Diversity*, Helbing & Lichtenhahn, Basle 2001, 241–283.

### III. Federalized Democracy

*266.* Federalism and participatory democracy are the means to promote diversity. Federalism was not introduced as a corrective to a majoritarian democracy, but unites the participatory democracies of the Cantons under a common federal government. Federalism enables a multi-level democracy through which decisions can receive multilevel legitimacy. Decisions can be left to the democratic decision-making of the level that is most concerned by the decision. Local and group interests can be channelled into the democratic decision-making process so as to enable political solutions to ethnic problems. Understood in this way, federalism can facilitate the democratic self-determination of different groups.[1]

1. *See* Basta Fleiner, Lidija R., 'Minority and Legitimacy of a Federal State: An Outsider Perception of the Swiss Model', in: Basta Fleiner & Fleiner, 94–99; Fleiner Thomas, 'Die schweizerische Verfassung im Kontext eines gemeinsamen europäischen Verfassungsrechts', in: Sitter-Liver, 431; Linder, Swiss Democracy, 73–77.

## § 2. Elements of Federalism

### I. Definition

*267.* Federalism can be defined as constitutionally guaranteed self and shared rule. A federal state can be understood as a state with sub-entities (in the case of Switzerland: the Cantons), each of which has a constitutionally guaranteed right to these forms of rule. Self-rule is understood here as a substantive decision-making and self-governing power. Shared rule does not necessarily mean shared competencies, but rather presupposes an institutionalized and guaranteed special input from the subunits in the decision-making process of the federal level. In Switzerland, this special input is guaranteed, for example, through the representation of the Cantons in the second Chamber of Parliament (*see supra* Part I, Chapter 3).[1]

1. *See* Auer/Malinverni/Hottelier, Vol. I., 295–303; Fleiner Thomas & Basta Fleiner Lidija R., 'Federalism, Federal States and Decentralization', in: Basta Fleiner & Fleiner, 1–40; Fleiner Thomas & Misic Alexander, 'Föderalismus als Ordnungsprinzip der Verfassung', in: Thürer *et al.*, § 27; Häfelin & Haller, §§ 32–43; Kägi-Diener Regula, *Brevier des Föderalismus: Eine Einführung in den Föderalismus aufgrund der Erfahrungen im schweizerischen Bundesstaat*, Berne 2000; Linder, Schweizerische Demokratie, 135–189; Stauffer Thomas & Töpperwien Nicole, 'Balancing Self-Rule and Shared Rule', in: Lidija R. Basta Fleiner & Fleiner, 41–74; Rhinow, Verfassungsrecht, §§ 5–10; Tschannen, §§ 15–26.

### II. Constitutionally Guaranteed Self-Rule

#### *A. Principle*

*268.* According to Article 3 of the Constitution, the Cantons have original or residual powers: They exercise all rights that are not constitutionally transferred to the Confederation. *E contrario*, the Confederation has only those powers which are explicitly attributed to it by the Constitution (Article 42(1) of the Constitution).

Title III, Chapter 2 of the Constitution contains the enumeration of federal powers (*see infra* 2.).

*269.* Article 42(2) of the Constitution states that the Confederation shall assume the tasks that require uniform regulation. This provision is in conflict with the above stated principle of enumerated powers unless it is interpreted as an additional requirement for the distribution of powers. The subsidiarity principle, when understood in this way, serves only as a guideline for the makers of the Constitution.[1]

1. *See* Rhinow, Verfassungsrecht, § 6 and § 8; Rhinow, 75–77; Thalmann Urs, 'Subsidaritätsprinzip und Kompetenzverteilung', in: Fleiner *et al.*, 162–169 (with further references).

*270.* Even when executing federal powers, the Confederation shall respect the autonomy of the Cantons (Article 47 of the Constitution).

*271.* In the following section, the constitutionally guaranteed distribution of powers between the Federation and the Cantons shall be depicted.

## *B. Distribution of Powers*

*272.* Due to the shared rule principle and the increased interdependency of tasks, a clear-cut distinction between federal and cantonal matters often cannot be drawn.[1]

1. For the distribution of powers, *see*, *inter alia*, Auer/Malinverni/Hottelier, 323–351; Häfelin & Haller, 299–341; Knapp Blaise, 'Kompetenzverteilung und Zusammenwirken der Kantone', in: Thürer *et al.*, § 29, 457–472; Tschannen, §§ 19–22.

### 1. Relations with Foreign Countries

*273.* Foreign relations are one of the prerogatives of the sovereign state and are a federal matter (Article 54(1) of the Constitution). However, the Cantons shall participate in the preparation of decisions of foreign policy, which concern their powers or their essential interests. Furthermore, the position of the Cantons shall have particular weight where their powers are concerned. In these cases, the interested canton shall participate in international negotiations as appropriate (Article 55 of the Constitution).

*274.* As a rule, the relations of the Cantons with foreign countries are conducted by the Confederation on behalf of the Cantons. However, within the scope of their powers, the Cantons have a limited treaty-making power with foreign countries and they may deal directly with lower ranking foreign authorities. These treaties may neither be contrary to the law and the interests of the Confederation nor to the laws of other Cantons. In order to guarantee this, the Cantons must inform the Confederation before concluding a treaty. This is an improvement of the position of the Cantons in comparison to the situation under the Constitution of 1874, which required that the Cantons not only must inform the Federal level, but also ask for federal approval.

2. Security, National and Civil Defence

*See infra* Part V, Chapter 1.

3. Education, Research and Culture

*275.* The Constitution states that education and culture are cantonal matters (Articles 62(1) and 69(1) of the Constitution). The Federal level, however, can run technical universities (Article 62(2) of the Constitution), grant subsidies to the Cantons for scholarships and other measures to encourage education (Article 66 of the Constitution). The Confederation also encourages scientific research (Article 64 of the Constitution) and may support cultural activities, which are of national interest (Article 69 of the Constitution).

4. Environment and Zoning

*276.* The Preamble of the Constitution expresses the growing respect for the environment by stressing the People's responsibility towards life and all creation. Furthermore, sustainable development is now understood as one of the responsibilities of the Confederation as such (Article 2 of the Constitution). The importance of sustainable development is repeated in Article 73 of the Constitution, which states: 'The Confederation and the Cantons shall strive to establish a durable equilibrium between nature, in particular its capacity to renew itself, and its use by man.'

*277.* In the areas of environmental protection, zoning, water, forestry, nature and cultural heritage, fishery and hunting, as well as the protection of animals, the Confederation's only competencies are for framework legislation. There is an intertwining of the principles and basic rules established by the Confederation and cantonal legislation. However, especially in zoning regulation, the density of norms differs from very vague principles, which leave any important discretion for implementation and further legislation to the Cantons to detailed provisions that must be applied directly by the Cantons (Article 24 of the Federal Zoning Act, SR 700).

5. Public Works and Transportation

*278.* Switzerland has an extensive road and rail network. Even the smallest villages are connected to the road system and public transportation.

*279.* The Confederation legislates on road and rail traffic, cable cars, navigation, aviation and space travel (Articles 82 and 87 of the Constitution). It is mandated to supervise roads of national importance (Article 82 of the Constitution) and establish a network of national highways. While the national highways are constructed and maintained by the Cantons, the costs are shared among federal and cantonal governments (Article 83 of the Constitution). All cantonal and municipal roads are cantonal matters.

Due to Switzerland's important geo-strategic position in Middle Europe, most of Europe's heavy north-south traffic runs through Switzerland, with the Alps forming a natural barrier between the north and south. The Gotthard tunnel is one of the few throughways as well as the shortest connection. Nevertheless, improved mobility created a nuisance mainly for the alpine region. As a result, an initiative that aimed at limiting trans-alpine border-to-border transit on the roads by mandating rail transportation was introduced and finally approved by popular referendum in the 1990s (Article 84 of the Constitution).

6. Energy and Communication

*280.* Switzerland has vast energy resources, mainly from water. The Confederation and the Cantons shall strive to insure a sufficient, diversified, reliable, and economical energy supply compatible with the protection of the environment as well as an economical and efficient use of energy. Furthermore, the Confederation is entitled to establish principles for the use of domestic and renewable energy, while measures concerning the use of energy in buildings are primarily a cantonal matter. Article 89(5) of the Constitution stresses the need for coordination between the measures taken by the Confederation, the Cantons, municipalities and economic interest groups. Nuclear legislation, legislation on the transport of energy, postal and telecommunication laws, legislation on radio and television and other forms of public telecasting fall within competence of the Confederation (Articles 90, 91, 92, and 93 of the Constitution).

*281.* With the promulgation of the Electricity Market Act of December 2000, *rejected* in a popular referendum in 2002, Parliament had opted for a moderate liberalization of the energy market. In order to facilitate the competitiveness of Swiss energy providers in Europe, this Act was intended to respond to the harmonization of rules concerning the electricity market in the European Union (Directive 96/92 of 19 December 1996).

7. Economy

*282.* The Confederation and the Cantons must respect the principle of economic freedom, as stipulated by Article 94 of the Constitution. They shall safeguard the interests of the national economy and, together with the private sector, contribute to the welfare and economic security of the population. The Confederation may specifically support economically weak regions and subsidize certain branches of their economy when reasonably expected measures of private self-help turn out to be insufficient to ensure the economic existence of those regions (Article 103 of the Constitution).

*283.* Alcohol, gambling and lotteries as well as weapons and military equipment are exclusively federal matters (Articles 105–107 of the Constitution). The Confederation also has legislative competencies in the following fields: private economic activity (Article 95 of the Constitution), competition policy in order to fight against economically or socially damaging effects of cartels, and other restrictions of competition (Article 96 of the Constitution); consumer protection (Article 97 of the Constitution), banking, stock exchange, and insurance (Article 98 of the Constitution).

*284.* According to Article 95(2) of the Constitution, the Confederation shall strive to create a unified Swiss economic area. It shall guarantee that university degrees as well as federal and cantonal educational certificates, or certificates recognized by one canton, permit the holder to exercise his or her profession throughout Switzerland.

*285.* Furthermore money and currency, including monetary policy, are federal matters. The Confederation has the exclusive right to coin money and to issue bank notes. As an independent central bank, the Swiss National Bank shall follow a monetary policy that serves the general interest of the country. The Bank is also charged with creating sufficient money reserves from its profits; a part of these reserves shall be held in gold. At least two thirds of the net profits of the Swiss National Bank shall be credited to the Cantons (Article 99 of the Constitution).

*286.* According to Article 100 of the Constitution the Confederation shall take measures to ensure a balanced economic development and, in particular, to prevent and fight unemployment and inflation. Additionally, the Confederation shall safeguard the interests of the Swiss economy abroad (Article 101 of the Constitution).

*287.* Introduced as part of neutrality and in reaction to food shortage during World War II, the supply of essential goods and services is still an important issue in Swiss politics. Thus, the Confederation shall ensure the country's supply of essential goods and services in the event of threats of military or economic war, or in cases of severe shortage to which the economy cannot counteract itself (Article 102 of the Constitution).

*288.* State interventions and derogations from the principle of economic freedom are most frequent with respect to agriculture. The Constitution foresees six measures designed to ensure provision of enough agricultural goods for the population, to conserve natural resources and the rural scenery, and to provide decentralized forms of settlement. The measures are (Article 104(3)(a–f) of the Constitution):

- direct payments to secure a fair and adequate remuneration for the services rendered, provided that compliance with ecological requirements is proven;
- economic incentives, in order to promote forms of production which are close to nature and friendly to environment and livestock;
- legislation on the declaration of origin, quality, production and food processing methods;
- protection of the environment against pollution due to excessive use of fertilizers, chemicals and other auxiliary substances;
- encouragement of agricultural research, counselling, and education, and subsidies for investments;
- legislation on the consolidation of rural property.

## 8. Housing, Work, Social Security, and Health

*289.* Even though some contest that Switzerland qualifies as a social state, the Preamble proclaims that 'the strength of a People is measured by the welfare of the weakest of its members.'

*290.* The overwhelming majority of the Swiss People hold property by lease or rent (nearly 70 per cent). The Constitution promotes the construction and ownership of housing and aims to prevent abuses in the field of landlord and tenant law, particularly with respect to abusive rent practices (Articles 108 and 109 of the Constitution).

*291.* The Confederation has limited powers concerning labour regulations. It may legislate on the protection of employees, the relationship between employees and employers, and placement services. According to Article 110(2) of the Constitution, the Confederation can confer a binding effect on collective labour contracts if justified minority interests and regional differences are taken into account and the principle of equality before the law (Article 8(1) of the Constitution) as well as the freedom to unionize (Article 28 of the Constitution) are respected.

*292.* Federal and cantonal competencies are intertwined in most social security areas. Swiss social security covers the following areas:

- old age, survivors' and disability insurance (Article 112 of the Constitution);
- employee pension plans (Article 113 of the Constitution);
- unemployment insurance (Article 114 of the Constitution);
- assistance to needy persons, which is a cantonal matter (Article 115 of the Constitution);
- family allocation and maternity insurance (Article 116 of the Constitution). Although foreseen in the Constitution for more than 50 years, a federal maternity insurance was finally introduced on 26 September 2004 by popular vote; and
- health and accident insurance (Article 117 of the Constitution). As a rule, health and accident insurance are mandatory.

*293.* The Confederation is further responsible for taking measures for the protection of health, protection against the abuse of medically assisted procreation, and in all aspects of gene technology (Articles 118–120 of the Constitution).

## 9. Residence and Domicile of Foreigners

*See infra* Part IV, Chapter 4, § 3.

## 10. Civil and Criminal Law, Weights and Measures

*294.* Legislation in the area of civil and criminal law is a federal matter (Articles 122 and 123 of the Constitution).

*295.* As set out *supra* in Part II, Chapter 5, § 2, III. and IV., the organization of the judiciary in civil and criminal matters is within the competencies of the Cantons. However, as of Spring 2000, criminal and civil procedure are determined at the federal level. Drafts for a Federal Code of Civil and Criminal Procedure are at the stage of elaboration.

*296.* Legislation on weights and measures also is also considered to be a federal matter.

## Table 1: Distribution of Powers according to different fields of state activity (for abbreviations see the special list at the end of the table)

**Basic Features and Financial System**

| Field | Power | CO | SP | EF | Federal and Cantonal | | | | | | P | EC |
|---|---|---|---|---|---|---|---|---|---|---|---|---|
| | | | | | Legisl. | | Implement. | | | FC | | |
| | | | | | EF | SH | EF | SH | EC | | | |
| ***Basic Features*** | | | | | | | | | | | | |
| | Residual Power | Art. 3 | CA | N | N | N | N | N | N | N | N | Y |
| | Subsidiarity | Art. 42 | FR | N | N | Y | N | Y | N | N | N | N |
| | Implementation of Federal Law | Art. 46 | CA | N | N | Y | N | N | Y | Y | N | Y |
| | Supremacy of Federal Law | Art. 49 | FR | Y | Y | Y | Y | Y | Y | Y | Y | Y |
| | Cantonal Constitutions | Art. 51 | DE | N | N | N | N | Y | N | Y | N | Y |
| | Communes | Art. 50 | AU | N | N | N | N | N | Y | N | N | Y |
| | Cantonal Existence | Art. 52 | PO | N | N | Y | N | Y | N | N | Y | N |
| Financial System | | CH3 | | | | | | | | | | |
| | Financial Management | Art. 126 | BA | N | Y | N | N | N | N | N | Y | N |
| | Taxing Principles | Art. 127 | N | N | Y | N | N | N | N | N | N | N |
| | Direct Taxes | Art. 128 | N | Y | YL | N | N | Y | N | Y | Y | N |
| | Harmonization of Taxes | Art. 129 | N | N | N | YP | N | Y | N | N | N | N |
| | Value Added Tax | Art. 130 | N | Y | YL | N | Y | N | N | N | N | N |
| | Consumption Tax | Art. 131 | N | N | YC | N | Y | N | N | N | N | N |
| | Stamp and Withholding Taxes | Art. 132 | N | Y | Y | N | Y | N | N | N | N | N |
| | Customs | Art. 133 | FR | Y | Y | N | Y | N | N | N | N | N |
| | Financial Equalization | Art. 134 | FR | Y | Y | N | N | Y | N | N | N | N |

**Foreign Affairs, Security, Education and Culture**

| Field | Power | CO | SP | EF | Federal and Cantonal | | | | | | P | EC |
|---|---|---|---|---|---|---|---|---|---|---|---|---|
| | | | | | Legisl. | | Implement. | | | FC | | |
| | | | | | EF | SH | EF | SH | EC | | | |
| ***Relations with Foreign Countries*** | | S1 | | Y | | | | | | | | |
| | Foreign Affairs. | Art. 54 | A | Y | N | N | N | Y | N | N | n | n |
| | Cantonal Relations with Foreign Countries | Art. 56 | N | N | N | N | N | Y | N | Y | Y | N |
| ***Security National and Civil Defence*** | | Art. S2 | | | | | | | | | | |
| | Security | Art. 57 | CR | N | N | Y | N | Y | N | Y | Y | N |
| | Army | Art. 60 | N | N | Y | N | N | Y | N | Y | N | N |
| | Civil Defence | Art. 61 | FR | | Y | N | N | Y | N | Y | N | N |
| ***Education Research Culture*** | | S3 | | | | | | | | | | |
| | Education | Art. 62 | CA | N | YG | N | N | N | Y | N | N | Y |
| | Universities | Art. 63 | CR | N | YG | N | N | Y | N | Y | P | N |
| | Professional Education | Art. 63 | N | N | N | Y | N | Y | N | N | N | N |
| | Research | Art. 64 | N | N | N | Y | N | Y | N | Y | Y | N |
| | Statistics | Art. 65 | N | N | N | Y | N | Y | N | Y | Y | N |
| | Educational Needs of Adults and young People | Art. 67 | SU | N | N | yc | N | y | Y | Y | N | (Y) |
| | Sport | Art. 68 | PR | N | N | Y | N | Y | N | N | N | N |
| | Culture | Art. 69 | CA | N | N | PR | N | (y) | N | Y | N | Y |
| | Languages | Art. 70 | RU | N | N | YO | N | N | N | Y | O | Y |
| | Cinema | Art. 71 | EN | N | N | Y | N | Y | N | Y | N | N |
| | Church and State | Art. 72 | CA | N | N | RU | N | N | Y | N | N | Y |

**Environment and Public Transport**

| Field | Power | CO | SP | EF | Federal and Cantonal | | | | | | P | EC |
|---|---|---|---|---|---|---|---|---|---|---|---|---|
| | | | | | Legisl. | | Implement. | | | FC | | |
| | | | | | EF | SH | EF | SH | EC | | | |
| ***Environment and Land Use Planning*** | | S4 | | | | | | | | | | |
| | Sustainable Development | Art. 73 | CP | N | N | Y | N | Y | N | Y | N | N |
| | Environment Protection | Art. 74 | RP | N | N | Y | N | Y | N | Y | N | N |
| | Land Use Planning | Art. 75 | CR | N | N | YP | N | N | Y | Y | N | N |
| | Water | Art. 76 | RP | N | N | Y | N | Y | N | Y | N | N |
| | Forests | Art. 77 | RP | N | N | Y | N | Y | N | Y | N | N |
| | Nature and Cultural Heritage | Art. 78 | CA | N | N | YP | N | Y | N | Y | N | N |
| | Hunting and Fishing | Art. 79 | N | N | N | YP | N | Y | N | Y | N | N |
| | Protection of Animals | Art. 80 | RP | N | N | YP | N | Y | N | Y | N | N |
| ***Public Work and Transport*** | | S5 | | | | | | | | | | |
| | Public Work | Art. 81 | CI | N | N | Y | N | Y | N | Y | Y | N |
| | Road Traffic | Art. 81 | N | N | Y | N | N | Y | N | Y | N | N |
| | National Highways | Art. 83 | CP | NE | N | Y | N | Y | N | Y | N | BU |
| | Alpine Transit | Art. 84 | RP | N | Y | N | N | Y | N | N | N | N |
| | Transport | Art. 87 | N | FR | Y | N | N | Y | N | N | N | N |
| | Foot Path and Hiking Trails | Art. 88 | N | N | N | YP | N | Y | N | N | N | N |

**Energy Communication and Economy**

| Field | Power | CO | SP | EF | Federal and Cantonal | | | | | | P | EC |
|---|---|---|---|---|---|---|---|---|---|---|---|---|
| | | | | | Legisl. | | Implement. | | | FC | | |
| | | | | | EF | SH | EF | SH | EC | | | |
| ***Energy and Communications*** | | S6 | | | | | | | | | | |
| | Energy Policy | Art. 89 | CP | N | YP | Y | N | Y | N | Y | N | N |
| | Nuclear Energy | Art. 90 | N | N | Y | N | N | Y | N | Y | N | N |
| | Energy Transport | Art. 91 | N | N | Y | N | N | Y | N | Y | N | N |
| | Postal and Telecommunication Services | Art. 92 | FR | y | Y | N | Y | N | N | N | N | N |
| | Radio, Television | Art. 93 | CR | Y | Y | N | Y | N | N | N | N | N |
| ***Economy*** | | S7 | | | | | | | | | | |
| | Gainful Private Econ. Activity | Art. 95 | N | N | N | Y | N | Y | N | N | N | N |
| | Competition Policy. | Art. 96 | N | Y | Y | N | Y | N | N | N | N | N |
| | Consumer Protection | Art. 97 | CR | N | N | Y | N | Y | N | N | N | N |
| | Banking Insurance | Art. 98 | N | Y | Y | N | N | Y | N | N | N | N |
| | Monetary Policy | Art. 99 | N | Y | Y | N | N | Y | N | N | N | N |
| | Cyclical Economic Policy | Art. 100 | FR | N | Y | N | N | Y | N | N | N | N |
| | Foreign Trade | Art. 101 | FR | Y | Y | N | N | Y | N | Y | N | N |
| | Maintaining Stocks of Essential Goods and Services | Art. 102 | FR | Y | Y | N | N | Y | N | Y | N | N |
| | Structural Policy | Art. 103 | FR | N | N | Y | N | Y | N | N | N | N |
| | Agriculture | Art. 104 | FR | N | N | Y | N | Y | N | N | N | N |
| | Alcohol | Art. 105 | FR | Y | Y | N | N | Y | N | N | N | N |
| | Games of Chance | Art. 106 | FR | Y | Y | N | N | Y | N | Y | N | N |
| | Weapons and Military Material | Art. 107 | N | Y | Y | N | N | Y | N | Y | N | N |

**Social Security, Health, Foreigners Civil and Criminal Law**

| Field | Power | CO | SP | EF | Federal and Cantonal | | | | | | P | EC |
|---|---|---|---|---|---|---|---|---|---|---|---|---|
| | | | | | Legisl. | | Implement. | | | FC | | |
| | | | | | EF | SH | EF | SH | EC | | | |
| ***Housing, Work, Social Security Health*** | | S8 | | | | | | | | | | |
| | Promotion: Construction, Access to Ownership | Art. 108 | FR | N | Y | N | N | Y | N | Y | N | N |
| | Leasehold | Art. 109 | N | N | N | Y | N | Y | N | Y | N | N |
| | Labour | Art. 110 | N | N | N | Y | N | Y | N | Y | N | N |
| | Old Age Survivors Disability Respons. | Art. 111 | FR | EN | Y | N | N | Y | N | Y | N | N |
| | Old Age Survivors, Disability Insurance | Art. 112 | FR | MI | Y | N | N | Y | N | Y | N | N |
| | Pension Plans | Art. 113 | FR | PE | Y | N | N | Y | N | Y | N | N |
| | Unemployment Ins. | Art. 114 | FR | Y | Y | N | N | Y | N | Y | N | N |
| | Assistance to those in Need | Art. 115 | CA | N | N | SU | N | Y | N | Y | N | Y |
| | Family Allowance and Maternity Insurance | Art. 116 | RP | N | N | RP | N | Y | N | Y | N | Y |
| | Health and Accident Insurance | Art. 117 | CR | Y | Y | N | N | Y | N | N | N | N |
| | Protection of Health | Art. 118 | CA | N | N | YT | N | Y | N | N | N | N |
| | Procreation, Genetic Engineering involving humans | Art. 119 | AP | RC | N | Y | N | Y | N | Y | N | RC |
| | Med. Transplant. | Art. 119(a) | N | N | N | Y | N | Y | N | Y | N | N |
| | Genetic Eng. | Art. 120 | AP | N | N | Y | N | Y | N | Y | N | N |
| ***Foreigners*** | Establishment and Residence | Art. 121 | N | FR | Y | N | N | Y | N | Y | N | N |
| ***Civil, Criminal L.*** | | S10 | | | | | | | | | | |
| | Civil Law | Art. 122 | N | FR | N | Y | N | Y | N | Y | N | N |
| | Criminal Law | Art. 123 | N | FR | N | Y | N | Y | N | N | N | N |
| | Aid to Victims of Criminal Acts | Art. 124 | RC | PO | N | Y | N | Y | N | N | N | N |
| | Weights, Measures | Art. 125 | N | FR | Y | N | N | Y | N | N | N | N |

**Abbreviations**

| | |
|---|---|
| A | Aims of Foreign Policy: Independence, prosperity, welfare, alleviate poverty, human rights, democracy, peace, natural resources |
| AP | Abuse Protection |
| AU | Guarantee of Autonomy |
| BA | Financial Balance |
| BU | Build and Construct |
| CA | Primary Cantonal Responsibility |
| CC | Civil and Criminal Law, Weights and Measures |
| CI | Common Interest |
| CI PR | Civil Law and Civil Procedure |
| CO | Constitution |
| CP | Cooperation Responsibility of Confederation and Cantons |
| CR | Coordination Responsibility |
| CR LA | Criminal Law and Procedure |
| CH | Chapter |
| CP | Federal Power only based on a constitutional provision |
| DE | Guarantee of Democratic System |
| EC | Exclusive Cantonal |
| EF | Exclusive Federal |
| EN | Ensure an adequate social security provision for elderly, survivors and disabled |
| FC | Implementing Administrative Decisions are controlled by cantonal administrative courts but finally under the jurisdiction of federal administrative courts |
| FR | Primary Confederal Responsibility |
| Genet. En. | Genetic Engineering in non Human Fields |
| MI | Pension must be sufficient to cover basic living expenses |
| NE | National Network |
| N | No |
| P | Parallel Powers of Confederation and Cantons |
| PE | Company Pensions Plans together wit the old age insurance should permit to maintain previous Standard of living |
| PO | Protection |
| PR | Responsibility to promote |
| PROF | Professional Education |
| RC | Common Responsibility of Cantons and Confederation |
| RP | Responsibility to protect |
| RU | Responsibility for common understanding |
| S | Section |
| SECU | Social Security (Age, Disability) |
| SH | Shared Power |
| SU | Supplement Cantonal Measures |
| SP | Special Obligation |
| SU DE | Sustainable Development |
| STA | Statistics |
| VI | Aid to Victims of Criminal Acts |
| Y | Yes |
| YC | Limited to specific products |
| YL | Limited to exact value |
| YP | Limited to principles |
| YO | Restricted to the use of the official languages |
| YT | Limit to its powers for food, drugs, organic material etc; fighting contagious diseases, protection against ionising radiation |
| yc | Only complement cantonal measures |
| YG | Limited to federal grant |

### III. Constitutional Guaranteed Shared Rule

*297.* The Cantons are accorded a special input in the decision-making of the federal level.[1] Because most aspects of shared rule have already been mentioned above, the following shall serve as a short summery:

1. *See* e.g., Häfelin & Haller, 271–274.

*298.* (1) The Cantons are included in the Constitution-making process. For the adoption of a new constitution or a constitutional amendment (as well as for entry into organizations for collective security entry into supranational communities and under certain conditions federal statutes declared urgent), it requires the approval of the vote of both, the People and the Cantons (Article 140(1) of the Constitution). In such cases, proposals shall be accepted if the overall majority of those voting at a national level and of those within the majority of the Cantons, vote in favour of the proposal (Article 142 of the Constitution). *See supra* Part I, Chapter 2, § 1, II. and Part II, Chapter 2, § 3, I. and § 4, II.

*299.* (2) The Cantons are represented in the second Chamber of Parliament (Senate), which has powers equal to those of the first Chamber of Parliament. Although Cantons regulate the election of their Councillors (Article 150(3) of the Constitution), the direct influence of the Cantons on the Senate is nevertheless limited. Furthermore, the Cantons may not instruct their Councillors (Article 161 of the Constitution). *See supra* Part II, Chapter 3.

*300.* (3) The Cantons are involved in the law making process and are included in the preliminary phase of legal drafting (Article 147 of the Constitution). In most cases it is the cantonal governments that participate in the preliminary procedure, whereas in other cases of cantonal involvement, the cantonal Parliament normally acts, as is the case in most Cantons for the parliamentary initiative and the referendum. Each canton can launch parliamentary initiatives (not to be confounded with the popular initiative, *see supra* Part II, Chapter 2, § 3). Eight Cantons are needed to initiate a referendum against federal statutes, federal statutes declared urgent with a validity exceeding one year, federal decrees when foreseen by the Constitution or the statutes, and international treaties which are (a) of unlimited duration and (b) may not be terminated, which (c) provide for the entry into an international organization or (d) which contain important provisions that require a nomotechnical transformation into Federal statutes (Article 141(1) of the Constitution).

*301.* (4) Article 55 of the Constitution introduces the participation of the Cantons in the preparation of foreign policy decisions, which concern cantonal powers or their essential interests. The Confederation shall inform the Cantons and consult them. The opinion of the Cantons shall particularly be taken into account when cantonal powers are concerned, as in such cases where the Cantons shall participate in international negotiations.

§ 3. Selected Aspects

## I. Supremacy Clause

*302.* According to European continental law systems, the legal order forms a unity in which the constitution, different treaties, statutes, and ordinances of federal, cantonal, and municipal governments are hierarchically classified. This is apparent both in the German Basic Law and in the system of the European Union.

*303.* The Swiss Constitution determines in Article 49 that all levels of federal law take precedence over contrary cantonal law. According to this principle, even ordinances of the Federal Council (*supra* Part II, Chapter 4, § 2, III.) take precedence over cantonal constitutional law. The Confederation has the duty to ensure that the Cantons respect federal law.

*304.* Federal law prevails irrespective of whether it is constitutional. The supremacy of constitutional federal law logically follows from the general rule of Articles 3 and 42 of the Constitution. Furthermore, unconstitutional federal law prevails over cantonal law because of Article 190 of the Constitution, which orders the Federal Court to apply federal law regardless of its constitutionality.

*305.* The supremacy clause is a recognized constitutionally guaranteed right of the citizen (verfassungsmässiges Recht; *see infra* Part IV, Chapter 2, § 1, I. C.). Contrary cantonal law is null and void – there is no need to engage further judicial proceedings. In case of doubt, a Public Law Action (*infra* Part IV, Chapter 2, § 4 III.) is available as a remedy in order to establish whether cantonal law contradicts federal law.[1]

1. *See* Auer/Malinverni/Hottelier, Vol. I, 353–372; Forster Peter, 'Eigenständigkeit der Kantone, Vorrang und Einhaltung des Bundesrechts und Bundesgarantien', in: Fleiner *et al.*, 133–134; Häfelin & Haller, 332–341; Rhinow, Verfassungsrecht, § 7; St. Galler Kommentar, Ruch Alexander ad Article 49, 603–610; Tschannen, § 22.

## II. Partnership between Confederation and Cantons

*306.* A federation can only exist on the basis of the solidarity of its partners. In addition to the constitutionally instituted cooperation, Swiss federalism finds a complementary balance in a network of informal cooperation at all levels of government, as well as between labour unions and economic entities (the so-called 'social partners') although, due to its informal character, this network may often not be apparent. It is this *comity* of different partners that contributes to the unity of Switzerland. Moreover, the complexity of state tasks and state obligations requires not only cooperation among magistrates and elected authorities, but also among civil servants of federal and cantonal administrations. This is the underlying philosophy of Article 44 of the Constitution. According to the constitutional provision, the Confederation and the Cantons shall cooperate and support each other in the fulfilment of their tasks.

*307.* Rather a political maxim than a normative principle (Decision of the Federal Court 125 II 152, 163), the moral duty to solidarity between the Cantons and the Confederation is anchored in Article 44(2) of the Constitution: The Cantons and the Confederation owe each other *mutual consideration and support*, and shall grant each other administrative and judicial assistance. The duty to solidarity is not limited to a duty of loyalty, as is the case according to the German Basic Law concerning the German Länder. It is a duty *to* solidarity that goes beyond loyalty in the sense that it is less hierarchical and more partnership driven. If partners – especially those representing the majority – are unwilling to sacrifice some of their interests for the sake of national unity, federalism will sooner or later disintegrate.[1]

1. *See* Tschannen, § 23 III 1: The 'duty to solidarity' is a moral term and inappropriate insofar as it presupposes a *conscience*, which is *per se* not a feature of legal entities. – Note the similar wording in Article 159(3) of the Civil Code regarding the effects of marriage between natural persons.

*308.* The duty of solidarity is further illustrated in Article 44(3), which states that disputes between Cantons, or between Cantons and the Confederation, shall whenever possible be resolved through mediation and negotiation.[1]

1. *See* Fleiner Thomas & Misic Alexander, 'Föderalismus als Ordnungsprinzip der Verfassung', in: Thürer *et al.*, § 27, 439; Häfelin & Haller, 314–315; Kölz Alfred, 'Bundestreue als Verfassungsprinzip?', in: *Schweizerisches Zentralblatt für Staats- und Verwaltungsrecht* (ZBl), 1980, 145 *et seq.*; Roberts Julian, 'Solidarität und Gerechtigkeit als Verfassungsinhalte', in: Sitter-Liver, 27–42; Tschannen, § 23 III.

## III. Cooperation v. Autonomy

*309.* In comparison to former constitutions, the Constitution of 1999 places more emphasis on the principle of cooperation than on the principle of self-rule as expressed by the autonomy of the Cantons. Although the constitutions of 1848 and 1874 placed clear priority on the autonomy of the Cantons, since 1874, as a result of approximately 150 constitutional amendments, the originally extensive powers of the Cantons have slowly shifted to the federal level. This process of centralization gradually diminished cantonal autonomy. Integration into the European Union would also have centralizing effects on Swiss federalism, which could be the most important reason why the new Constitution focuses more on the issues of cooperation than on autonomy. In this sense, Swiss federalism has been increasingly influenced by the German tradition, as can be seen by three major changes which were introduced with the Constitution of 1999:

(1) the right of Cantons to participate in foreign policy decisions of the federal government;
(2) the general right to participate in internal federal legislation; and
(3) the general possibility for Cantons to regulate matters of general concern through international or intercantonal treaties.

*310.* The strengthening of the shared rule principle has not led, as one might expect, to a strengthening and widening of the powers of the second Chamber. The shared rule principle has been implemented instead by strengthening the possibilities for cantonal executive bodies to participate in the decision-making processes of the federal government. In order to participate in the federal decision-making processes, cantonal executives ordered a new body, which represents all the cantonal governments. Thus, the widening of the shared rule principle at a federal level has caused the establishment of a presidential council of cantonal governments. This, in turn, has led to better cooperation between cantonal governments and enabled the Cantons to use new ways and means for cantonal and intercantonal partnership as well as cooperation. The newness of this cooperative federalism may lead Switzerland to a greater flexibility: For example, in the field of university education, the legislature has established a body – composed of representatives of cantonal governments and the Federal Council – who must plan and establish strategies for developing federal and cantonal universities. With this new 'superstructure', combining shared rule and self-rule in the field of higher education, Switzerland tries to meet the new challenge of a 'European Area of Higher Education,' proclaimed in the Bologna Declaration of 1999. There are also new tendencies that may lead to supra-cantonal cooperation on a regional basis, which as already partially realized in the field of professional education.

*311.* Presently there is discussion not only of direct partnership of executive bodies, but also of cantonal parliaments. It may well be that this new flexibility of intercantonal cooperation will lead to the establishment of real intercantonal bodies with specific democratic legitimacy, based on the citizens and united by a functional focus on areas such as school, hospital, or police region. Thus, Swiss federalism will face new administrative bodies, distinct regional parliaments, and new executive branches, all united to fulfil specific tasks in order to be more efficient. Federalism involving shared power in representative bodies will be supplemented by a shared power system of executive and administrative bodies. As far as the Constitution of 1999 is concerned, it seems clear that it does not only restrict federalism to the legislative branch and to representative bodies, but enlarges federalism to encompass the executive branches.[1]

1. *See* Abderhalden Ursula, 'Der kooperative Föderalismus', in: Fleiner *et al.*, 213–221 (with further references); Hänni Peter, 'Verträge zwischen den Kantonen und zwischen dem Bund und den Kantonen', in Thürer *et al.*, § 28; Rhinow, Verfassungsrecht, § 9; St. Galler Kommentar, Knapp Blaise ad. Article 48, 597–601.

## IV. Executive Federalism

*312.* Contrary to the American system of dual federalism, the Cantons implement federal law (executive federalism). Consequently, the federal administration is rather small in size and would be incapable of executing the federal law by itself. While federal law binds the Cantons in how they implement federal law, the Federation must leave them as much leeway of action as possible as well as take the financial burden and the particularities of the Cantons into account (Article 46 of the Constitution). Depending on federal regulation, the Cantons have varying degrees of discretion in the execution of federal norms. Due to the diversity among

Cantons with respect to size, topography, demography and other structural elements, it is nearly impossible for the Confederation to consider the particularities of the Cantons unless it grants the Cantons broad discretion.[1]

1. *See* St. Galler Kommentar, Knapp Blaise ad. Article 46, 585–592; for the consequences on the political culture *see* e.g., Linder, Schweizerische Demokratie, 177–179.

## V. Non-Promotion of Equal Living Conditions

*313.* Article 72(2) of the German Basic Law provides general federal legislative power should a standardization of law be necessary for the establishment of equal living conditions throughout the country. A similar provision is found in Article 130 of the Spanish Constitution, which provides that the 'public authorities shall attend to the modernization and development of all economic sectors, particularly of agriculture, livestock raising, fishing, and handicrafts, in order to equalize the standard of living of all Spaniards.' Modern constitutions generally require equal rights with regard to equal opportunities, but not with equal results.

*314.* The Swiss Constitution, however, guarantees neither equal opportunities nor equal results. Swiss federalism does *not* promote equality of living conditions among the Cantons. Diversity and autonomy can only be upheld if a certain degree of economic discrepancies among the different Cantons – and even among the different municipalities – is permitted. Swiss federalism has always accepted this inequality for the sake of the autonomy of the Cantons while equalization would mean centralization, and most of the Swiss People believe this would imperil diversity in Switzerland. (For financial equalization, *see infra* Part V, Chapter 2, § 2).

*315.* As noted above, with the possible integration in the European Union, which promotes an open market based on equal opportunities, Switzerland may have to face a new era of federalism. Therefore, Federal Parliament has already put into force a law guaranteeing equal opportunities with regard to the internal market in Switzerland (Federal Internal Market Act, SR 943.02). According to this Act, quite a number of cantonal legislative modifications would be required in order to eradicate intercantonal discrimination. However, according to evaluations, based on Article 170 of the Constitution, most Cantons have not followed these federal obligations, which shows how difficult it would be – even *within* Switzerland – to truly establish equal opportunities.

*316.* In a state with a fragmented society, the issue of equality pertains not only to individuals, but also to the status of different cultural communities and religions. Equality of communities may often have priority over equality of individuals, which may very well be the reason why the Constitution of 1874 did not – and the Constitution of 1999 still does not – have any provision guaranteeing equal opportunities among individuals or equal living conditions for the whole population. The words, equal rights, can be understood in two ways:

(1) the *right to be equal*; and
(2) the *right to equal rights*.

If persons belonging to the small indigenous Romansh community had only equal rights, they would always be considered or would consider themselves second-class citizens. In a society relying solely on the concept of individual equality, which reduces the citizen to a political person naked of any culture, the Romansh community would remain a tiny minority that could easily be outvoted and therefore feel *de facto* discrimination. If the Romansh community shall have the right to be equal, they must be accepted on equal terms as a cultural community. It is obvious that Switzerland is seeking a balance between equal individual rights and the right to be respected as equal even when belonging to a different cultural group.

# Chapter 2. The Cantons

## § 1. The Position of the Cantons in the Confederation

*317.* The Cantons formed the Confederation and later the Federation. Most Swiss citizens feel closely attached to their canton of origin.[1]

1. For the position of the Cantons in the Confederation, *see* e.g., Auer/Malinverni/Hottelier, Vol. I, 59–75; Fleiner Thomas & Misic Alexander, 'Föderalismus als Ordnungsprinzip der Verfassung', in Thürer *et al.*, § 27; Germann Raimund E., 'Die Kantone: Gleichheit und Disparität', in: Klöti *et al.*, 386–419; Jaag Tobias, 'Die Rechtsstellung der Kantone in der Bundesverfassung', in Thürer *et al.*, § 30, 473–489; Schenkel Walter & Serdült Uwe, 'Bundesstaatliche Beziehungen', in: Klöti *et al.*, 469–506 (with further references); Tschannen, § 16.

*318.* The Cantons are territorially based legal entities with a special public law status, whose rights and duties are equal, even though the status of the half Cantons is slightly inferior to the status of the other Cantons. Half Cantons have only one representative in the Senate, in contrast to the two seats of the other Cantons (Article 150(2) of the Constitution, *supra* Part II, Chapter 3, III. and IV.). Additionally, in cases of mandatory referendum for which the approval of the People and the Cantons is needed, the half Cantons are attributed only half a vote (Article 142(3) of the Constitution). In all other aspects – for instance in respect to their autonomy – the half Cantons are equal to the other Cantons.

*319.* Cantons have a relatively high degree of autonomy, particularly with respect to their own organization, legislation and finances, but their autonomy is also restricted by federal law. As a counterbalance to these restrictions, the federal level guarantees cantonal constitutional order and assures the existence and territorial integrity of the Cantons.

*320.* The discussions below focuses on the constitutionally established notion of cantonal sovereignty, cantonal autonomy and its restrictions, the federal guarantees, and the political organization of the Cantons.

## I. Cantonal Sovereignty

### A. Principle

*321.* According to Article 3 of the Constitution, the Cantons are sovereign insofar as their sovereignty is not limited by the Constitution.[1]

1. *See* instead of many, St. Galler Kommentar, Schweizer Rainer J. ad Article 3, 31–42; Rhinow, Verfassungsrecht, 108; Tschannen, § 16.

*B. Theory of Sovereignty*

*322.* Sovereignty is a disputed concept in relation to federal states and in the theory of federalism. While some argue that in federal systems, either the federal state or the subunits have undivided sovereignty (Laband, Jellinek), others argue for a sovereignty of the *Gesamtstaat*, encompassing the federal level and the subunits (Nawiasky), or for divided sovereignty between the federal state and the sub-entities (Tocqueville, Madision, Fleiner). Based on the difficulties of finding a concept of sovereignty which corresponds with the reality of the federal state, some do not rely on the sovereignty argument at all.[1]

1. *See* instead of many: Fleiner & Basta Fleiner, Staatslehre, 562 *et seq.*, St. Galler Kommentar, Schweizer Rainer J. ad Article 3, 33–35.

*C. Relative Sovereignty*

*323.* According to the prevailing European continental tradition, sovereignty is normally regarded as indivisible and absolute. In this understanding – contrary to the wording of the Constitution – the Cantons are not sovereign because cantonal powers are limited by the Constitution and are therefore not absolute. Sovereignty is also limited because cantonal constitutions must be approved by the Confederation (*see infra* Part III, Chapter 2, II.).

*324.* According to this view, the formulation in Article 3 of the Constitution was chosen mainly for historical reasons. The term 'sovereignty' was maintained as a reminder of Switzerland's foundation out of sovereign Cantons. The Cantons have only relative sovereignty.[1]

1. *See* Häfelin & Haller, 266, 269–270¸ St. Galler Kommentar, Schweizer Rainer J. ad Article 3, 33–35 (with further references).

*D. Missing Statehood-Quality According to International Law*

*325.* Based on the argument of missing absolute sovereignty, the statehood quality according to international law of the Cantons is normally also negated. According to the *Three-Element Theory* of Jellinek, a state exists when it has a territory, a People, and sovereignty.[1] While the Cantons have a cantonal territory and a cantonal People, they do not have absolute sovereignty. They lost their statehood quality when they adopted a federal constitution and transferred powers to the federal level.[2] Nevertheless, many Cantons call themselves a *State* or a *Republic* (e.g., the Cantons of Ticino, Neuchâtel, Geneva, and Jura).

1. *See* Jellinek Georg, *Allgemeine Staatslehre*, 3rd ed., O.Häring, Berlin 1919, 183.
2. *See* e.g., Jaag Tobias, 'Die Rechtsstellung der Kantone in der Bundesverfassung', in: Thürer *et al.*, 477–478 who stresses the limited statehood of the Cantons.

*E. Federation or Confederation?*

*326.* The official name of Switzerland is *Confoederatio Helvetica*. The Latin name, from which the official abbreviation of Switzerland *CH* derives, was maintained because consensus on a new name could not be reached in 1848.

*327.* Nevertheless, Switzerland is a federation, not a Confederation. According to MALINVERNI, a Confederation is a system of coordinated sovereign powers.[1] Sovereignty and statehood-quality according to international law of the sub-units is therefore a prerequisite for the existence of a Confederation. In accordance with the lacking this statehood quality, the Cantons are not direct addressees of international law.

1. Malinverni Giorgio, 'The Classical Notion of Confederation and of the Federal State', in: *The Modern Concept of Confederation, Science and technique of democracy*, No. 11, Council of Europe Publishing, Strasbourg 1995, 41.

*328.* In addition to the statehood quality of the subunits, the legal quality of the founding document is taken as an indicator in distinguishing federations from Confederations. The founding document of the federal state is a constitution and does not need unanimity of the subunits for revision. In the case of Confederation, the founding document is an international treaty that normally can only be revised when all parties consent, which further supports the notion that Switzerland is a federation, without even relying on the sovereignty theory.[1]

1. *See* e.g., Häfelin & Haller, 267–268.

*329.* In this monograph, the terms 'federation' and 'Confederation' are used interchangeably with respect to Switzerland. While the term 'federation' is technically speaking correct, the term 'Confederation' is commonly used due to the historical reasons.

## II. Cantonal Autonomy and its Restrictions

*A. Cantonal Autonomy*

*330.* The Cantons have maintained a relatively large amount of autonomy despite the strong trend towards centralization. They have the residual power – all powers that the Federal Constitution does not attribute to the federal level remain with the Cantons (Articles 3, 42 and 43 of the Constitution).[1]

1. On cantonal autonomy, *see* e.g., Auer/Malinverni/Hottelier, Vol. I, 60–64; Häfelin & Haller, 270–271; Fleiner Thomas & Misic Alexander, 'Föderalismus als Ordnungsprinzip der Verfassung', in Thürer *et al.*, § 27; Germann Raimund E., 'Die Kantone: Gleichheit und Disparität', in: Klöti *et al.*, 389–391; Jaag Tobias, 'Die Rechtsstellung der Kantone in der Bundesverfassung', in Thürer *et al.*, § 30, 473–489; Rhinow, Verfassungsrecht, § 8.

*331.* Cantonal autonomy includes the right to self-organization, under which the Cantons have adopted their own constitutions, their own coat of arms and in some cases even their own cantonal anthem. The Cantons decide on their form of government and the structure of cantonal institutions, although with some limitations. With the legislative autonomy, it is within the power of the Cantons to decide on what issues and how they want to legislate. Further, the Cantons maintain financial autonomy through their power to tax citizens (*see infra* Part V, Chapter 2, § 1).

*332.* Should the Federation violate its mandate to respect the cantonal autonomy (Article 47 of the Constitution), the Cantons can take recourse to the Federal Court. The possibility of recourse is however limited by Article 190 of the Constitution.

*333.* Nevertheless, the Federation restricts, and in other cases supports, cantonal autonomy. Firstly the restrictions, and then the support function, (Federal Guarantees) of the Confederation will be regarded.

### *B. The Federal Restrictions on Cantonal Autonomy*

#### 1. Approval of the Cantonal Constitution

*334.* According to the Federal Constitution, the adoption and revision of cantonal constitutions must be approved by the Confederation. The Confederation then shall grant the approval if the cantonal constitution is not contrary to federal law (Article 51(2) of the Constitution). The federal approval is a prerequisite for the validity of the cantonal constitutional provisions. However the Confederation does not have the means to prevent the Cantons from including not approved provisions in the cantonal publication of the Constitution. The official cantonal publication of the Constitution of the Canton of Jura for example, includes a provision that declares the aim to reunite a part of the geographical region, which is currently part of the Canton of Berne, with the Canton of Jura. This provision was not approved by the Confederation because of its opposition to the federal guarantee of the territory of the Cantons (*see infra* Part III, Chapter 2, § 1, III.) and the solidarity principle. The *official federal publication* of the constitution of the Canton of Jura omits this disputed provision.

*335.* Despite the Jura example, the Confederation is very reluctant to deny the approval of constitutional provisions. For instance, Federal Parliament approved a constitutional provision that mandated a Canton to take all possible measures to prevent the establishment of a nuclear power plant on the cantonal territory, even though this provision can be regarded as opposed to the principle of comity (*see supra* Part III, Chapter 1, § 3, II.).[1]

1. *See* Jaag Tobias, 'Die Rechtsstellung der Kantone in der Bundesverfassung', in Thürer *et al.*, § 30, 481; Forster Peter, 'Eigenständigkeit der Kantone, Vorrang und Einhaltung des Bundesrechts und Bundesgarantien', in: Fleiner *et al.*, 136–140; St. Galler Kommentar, Ruch Alexander ad Article 51, 626–628; Tschannen, § 18.

2. Federal Restrictions Concerning the Cantonal Organization

*336.* The Federal Constitution, the federal statutory law and the Federal Court established a series of restrictions concerning cantonal organization, based on their interpretation of federal and international law. The list given below is not all-inclusive.

*337.* (1) *Written Constitution.* According to Article 51(1) of the Constitution, the Cantons must adopt a cantonal constitution. In accordance with this provision, all the Cantons have adopted *written constitutions.*

*338.* (2) *Democratic Constitution.* The Federal Constitution sets minimum standards for the content of cantonal constitutions. According to Article 51(1) of the Constitution, the cantonal constitution must be *democratic.* It is from this provision that the requirement of cantonal *separation of powers* is deducted.[1]

1. *See* Auer/Malinverni/Hottelier, 61; Tschannen, § 18.

*339.* (3) *Constitutional Referendum.* The canton must hold a popular vote in order to *adopt or amend* its cantonal constitution.

*340.* (4) *Constitutional Initiative.* The Federal Constitution mandates the Cantons to foresee a *constitutional initiative.* A majority of the People of the Cantons can demand that a proposal for the amendment of the Constitution is submitted to the People in a cantonal vote. However, all Cantons have established a lower requisite number of signatures for the constitutional initiative than the one established in the Federal Constitution (*see supra* Part II, Chapter 2, § 3, II.).

*341.* (5) *Cantonal Elections and Voting.* Under Article 39(2) of the Constitution, the Cantons are restricted in defining their *electorate.* The Federal Constitution proscribes that all Swiss domiciled in the canton have the same political rights. Therefore the Cantons cannot give special political rights to their citizens who live outside of the canton, and they cannot exclude Swiss citizens who do not have cantonal citizenship (for citizenship *see infra* Part IV, Chapter 1). Based on the non-discrimination principle established in Article 8 of the Constitution (or Article 4 of the Constitution of 1874), the Federal Court deducted several restrictions for the cantonal organization. Several cases concerned cantonal elections and voting. In *Theresa Rohner* (Decision of the Federal Court 116 Ia 359) the Court held that the Cantons must allow women the right to vote and hold public office. Further, in the *Quota* case (Decision of the Federal Court, 123 I 152), the Court decided that allowing women a quota in relation to their share in the cantonal population in the cantonal parliament, government and the courts is in violation of the non-discrimination principle.

*342.* (6) *Cantonal Authorities.* In several cases based on the European Convention on Human Rights, the Federal Court established criteria for the establishment of the right to an independent judge and to independent courts (Decisions of the

Federal Court, 123 I 87, 121 II 53).[1] The Cantons must also establish independent judicial authorities for all administrative law matters that can be brought to the Federal Court based on an Administrative Law Action (Article 98(a) of the Federal Judicial Act).

1. Further examples in Auer/Malinverni/Hottelier, Vol. I, 62–63.

*343.* The federal level can define which or what kind of cantonal authorities shall implement federal law, and in some cases, federal law even proscribes the creation of new institutions. For instance, the Cantons have the duty to establish cantonal laboratories for food control purposes. In other cases federal law mandates that the Cantons establish judicial authorities, e.g., the authority for the surveillance of tutelage.[1]

1. *See* Auer/Malinverni/Hottelier, 60–63; Häfelin & Haller, 291–295; Jaag Tobias, 'Die Rechtsstellung der Kantone in der Bundesverfassung', in Thürer *et al.*, § 30, 479.

### 3. Federal Restrictions Concerning Cantonal Activities

*344.* Cantonal activities, including legislative activities, must not be opposed to federal law and shall be based on the principle of comity (*see supra* Part II, Chapter 1, § 3, II.).

In order to assure that federal law is not violated, the Confederation must take the necessary measures to ensure the implementation of federal law, cantonal constitutions, and intercantonal treaties (Articles 186(4) and 173(1)(e) of the Constitution. Two different types of federal control can be distinguished: preventive control and repressive control.

*345.* The duty to submit the cantonal constitutions for approval is one case of a *preventive control.* Formerly, under the Constitution of 1874, cantonal treaties also required approval of the Confederation. Today, cantonal treaties need only the approval of Federal Parliament when the Federal Council or another canton protests against the treaty (*see infra* Part V, Chapter 1, § 2). Cantonal statutes and regulations will only be submitted to preventive control when a federal act explicitly foresees such approval procedure. For instance, the Federal Civil Code requires that the Cantons must have their introductory legislation approved.

*346.* *Repressive control* can consist of:

(1) the revocation of a cantonal act – this is mainly problematic when the cantonal act has already entered into force, normally such control is limited to a legality control unless federal statutes foresee a more far-reaching control;
(2) the curbing of subsidies – there must however be a nexus between the violation of a cantonal duty and the subsidy in question;
(3) the execution by substitution – in this case federal authorities act instead of the Cantons to fulfil the cantonal duty, and as *ultima ratio*;
(4) the military federal executive measure – under which the Federation can use military means to force the Cantons to fulfil their duties.

In contrast to the federal intervention (*see infra* C. 1.) which aims to support cantonal authorities, the military federal executive measure is directed against cantonal authorities who do not fulfil their duties. So far, this has never been applied.[1]

1. *See* Auer/Malinverni/Hottelier, 63–64; Jaag Tobias, 'Die Rechtsstellung der Kantone in der Bundesverfassung', in Thürer *et al.*, § 30, 485–487; Ruch Alexander, 'Äussere und innere Sicherheit', in: Thürer *et al.*, § 56, 900.

## III. Federal Guarantee

347 On the other hand, the Confederation does not only restrict the cantonal authority but also supports the Cantons to uphold their autonomy. The Confederation guarantees the cantonal constitutional order, as well as the existence and territory of the Cantons.

### *A. Guarantee of the Cantonal Constitutional Order*

*348.* According to Article 52(1) of the Constitution, the Confederation shall protect the constitutional order of the Cantons. While primary responsibility for ensuring constitutional order lies with the Cantons (Article 57 of the Constitution), the Confederation and the other Cantons are called to support the concerned canton if it cannot ensure its own constitutional order (*principle of comity*). This duty of support is based on Article 44(1) and (2) of the Constitution, which states that the Confederation and the Cantons shall support each other in the fulfilment of their tasks.

*349.* A *federal intervention* is foreseen when the inner order of a canton is disturbed or threatened and cannot be protected by the canton alone or with the help of other Cantons (Article 52(2) of the Constitution). The Confederation will only intervene when the general support to the canton is not sufficient to reestablish the constitutional order and when the disturbance of the constitutional order does not emanate from a cantonal institution or agency. The measures to be taken for reestablishment of the constitutional order are decided by the respective federal agency – in most cases, the Federal Council. In several cases the Confederation has delegated a commissioner to the concerned canton to act as representative of the Federal Council and to issue orders towards the cantonal executive and legislature. As *ultima ratio*, the Confederation can intervene with military force. There have been ten such military interventions since 1848, with the last one taking place in Geneva in 1932. In that case, leftists had tried to disturb a meeting of rightwing extremists. When the situation got out of hand, the Canton of Geneva requested the support of the Federal Council, which sent military troops. Federal Parliament can decide who covers the costs for the intervention.[1]

1. *See* e.g., Häfelin & Haller, 295–298; Jaag Tobias, 'Die Rechtsstellung der Kantone in der Bundesverfassung', in Thürer *et al.*, § 30, 481–482; Forster Peter, 'Eigenständigkeit der Kantone, Vorrang und Einhaltung des Bundesrechts und Bundesgarantien', in: Fleiner *et al.*, 136–140; Rhinow, Verfassungsrecht, § 10; Tschannen, § 18.

*350.* As an alternative to federal intervention, the Federal Military Act of 3 February 1995 (SR 510.10) foresees the possibility that the Confederation can provide the concerned canton with troops that act under the direction of the canton. Troops may only be sent when there is a serious threat to the cantonal order, and the decision to send troops must be taken by Federal Parliament. If there is an absolute immediate threat and Federal Parliament is not in session, the Federal Council has authority to put troops of a limited number and for a limited time at the disposal of the canton. For any extension of the mandate, Federal Parliament must be convened. Through this measure, the canton can continue to act independently while relying on additional military forces.[1]

1. *See* Häfelin & Haller, 298.

### *B. Guarantee of the Existence and Territory of the Cantons*

*351.* The territory of the Cantons is neither defined in the Constitution nor in other legal documents. At the time of the formation of the federation in 1848 the cantonal territory was not disputed, and only some areas that had been subject to disputes and agreements had later been defined in treaties or in court opinions.

*352.* The Confederation has the duty to protect the existence and territory of the Cantons (Article 53(1) of the Constitution). Changes in the number of Cantons or the redistribution of territory are only permissible in accordance with the constitutional procedure of Article 53(2) and (3) of the Constitution.[1]

1. *See* e.g., St. Galler Kommentar, Ruch Alexander ad Article 53, 641–648; Jaag Tobias, 'Die Rechtsstellung der Kantone in der Bundesverfassung', in Thürer *et al.*, § 30, 475–477; Forster Peter, 'Eigenständigkeit der Kantone, Vorrang und Einhaltung des Bundesrechts und Bundesgarantien', in: Fleiner *et al.*, 140–142; Rhinow, Verfassungsrecht, § 10; Ruch Alexander, 'Äussere und innere Sicherheit', in: Thürer *et al.*, § 56, 899–900.

*353.* The former Constitutions of 1848 and 1874 did not foresee a procedure for territorial modifications. The rules introduced in Article 53 were developed on a case-by-case basis. The most important example for a territorial modification was the creation of the Canton of Jura in 1978.[1]

1. For the Jura case, *see* Linder, Swiss Democracy, 25–27, 65–68; Basta Fleiner, Lidija R., 'Minority and Legitimacy of a Federal State: An Outsider Perception of the Swiss Model', in: Basta Fleiner & Fleiner, 90–94.

*354.* The now established procedure for territorial changes includes as its main element the consent of the concerned populations. Article 53 distinguishes three different cases of modifications that concern the existence and territory of the Cantons:

*355.* (1) The modification can concern the total number of Cantons, or it can change their status (Article 53(2) of the Constitution). The number of Cantons can be increased – e.g., through the creation of a new canton as in the case of the creation of the Canton of Jura – or the number can be decreased – e.g., through the merger of two Cantons. The status of the Cantons can be changed – e.g., by elevating a half canton to the status of ordinary canton. In these cases the modification must be based of the consent of the populations concerned, of the Cantons concerned, and of the People and the Cantons. This procedure requires a cascade of popular votes on the district and/or communal level, on the cantonal level, and on the federal level so as to create the highest possible legitimacy for the new boundaries. The creation of a new canton needs the consent of:

(1) the population inhabiting it;
(2) the population inhabiting the canton that the territory formerly belonged to;
(3) the Swiss population; and
(4) a majority of cantonal populations.

Changes in the number and the status of the Cantons must fulfil the requirements of a Constitutional revision because the Constitutional text must be amended (Article 1 with the enumeration of the Cantons, in the case of a change of status additionally Articles 142 and 150(2) of the Constitution). Switzerland is one of the very few countries that have an established procedure for such internal secession.

*356.* (2) The modification can concern the cantonal territory without changing the number of Cantons or their status – e.g., through the change of the municipality of one canton to another canton, as was the case with the municipality of Vellerat, which left the Canton of Berne to join the Canton of Jura (Article 53(3) of the Constitution). According to the established procedure, such modifications must be based on the consent of the population concerned and of the Cantons concerned. At the federal level, the assent of Federal Parliament in the form of a federal decree (not submitted to a popular referendum) suffices.

*357.* Before the introduction of Article 53(3) of the Constitution, territorial changes were also submitted to the approval of the People and the Cantons based on the argument that even though no explicit change of the Federal Constitution was necessary, the procedure for the amendment of the Constitution should be applied because of the federal guarantee of cantonal territory and the possible effect on the internal power balance in Switzerland. The framers of Article 53 of the new Constitution decided on a lower standard in order to avoid popular votes on the federal level that in most cases directly affect only a small number of inhabitants.

*358.* (3) Finally, the modification can concern small boundary settlements. Such border settlements can be made by treaty between the Cantons concerned.

## IV. Intercantonal Treaties and Cooperation

*359.* The tasks the Cantons are supposed to fulfil have become more and more complex and interconnected. The complexity and interconnectedness of tasks creates on the one hand a pressure towards the unification of cantonal law and, on the other hand, a pressure towards an enhancement of cooperation between Cantons. In order to prevent the transferral of powers to the federal level, the Cantons try to reach the necessary unification of law and cooperation through *intercantonal treaties.*

*360.* According to Article 48(1) of the Constitution, the Cantons may conclude intercantonal treaties (called *concordats*). Such concordats may not be opposed to the law, including the distribution of powers between the Federation and the Cantons, the interests of the Confederation, and the rights of other Cantons. The Confederation must be notified of such treaties (Article 48(3) of the Constitution).[1]

1. *See* e.g., Auer/Malinverni/Hottelier, Vol. I, 547–560; Häfelin & Haller, 357–366; Hänni Peter, 'Verträge zwischen den Kantonen und zwischen dem Bund und den Kantonen', in: Thürer *et al.*, § 28, 443–455; St. Galler Kommentar, Knapp Blaise ad Article 48, 596–601; Rhinow, Verfassungsrecht, 149 *et seq.*

*361.* Intercantonal treaties can regulate subject matters, such as administrative agreements or a unification of legislation, and can create common institutions. Political intercantonal treaties are prohibited because they violate the principle of comity laid down in Article 44(2) of the Constitution. Concordats can be concluded between two or more Cantons, and the Confederation can be party to the treaty and/or can participate in the common institutions (Article 48(2) of the Constitution). This provision is of relevance in areas where the federal level and the Cantons have parallel powers. For instance, the Confederation is party to the concordat on the equivalence of scientific degrees. Based on this concordat, the criteria for the equivalence of high school diplomas were unified.[1] The concordat may not transfer cantonal powers to the federal level, and the Confederation may only get involved in areas where the federal constitution foresees a federal power.

1. *See* Häfelin & Haller, 359.

*362.* Intercantonal institutions are mainly introduced for implementation purposes. In some cases the concordat delegates to these institutions the power to issue regulations. Due to the legality principle, these regulations may only concern issues of minor importance.

*363.* Intercantonal treaties allow for flexible cooperation between Cantons and the Confederation. The cooperation for schooling can be a different from one for environmental protection or land planning. Frey suggests a system of functional overlapping of competing jurisdictions (FOCJ).[1] According the FOCJ system more competition shall be introduced and the possibility of free choice enhanced by providing that different overlapping sub-units offer services to the People. This can create a system that is difficult for citizens to understand. For politicians and the civil servants, the multiple forms of cooperation create the necessity of a high level of coordination. The main challenge for these kinds of cooperation is to assure democratic control of intercantonal bodies.

1. Frey Bruno S., Ein *neuer Föderalismus für Europa: Die Idee der FOCJ (Functional, Overlapping, Competing Jurisdictions)*, Tübingen 1997.

*364.* The Cantons regulate the procedure for joining intercantonal treaties. The Canton of Grisons demands a mandatory referendum for all intercantonal treaties, while in many other Cantons the cantonal parliament can decide on the adhesion without the possibility of a referendum (e.g., Obwalden, Zug, Schaffhausen, Appenzell Inner Rhodes, St. Gallen, Fribourg, Ticino, and Geneva). All other Cantons require a mandatory referendum for the more important intercantonal treaties, particularly those that include the unification of law.[1]

1. *See* e.g., Auer/Malinverni/Hottelier, Vol. I, 551–552.

*365.* The number of concordats is rising steadily. Important concordats, especially those that are open to all the Cantons, are published in the Official Federal Register (for example the concordat on the coordination of education (SR 411.9)). However, many lesser concordats are not necessarily included in the cantonal official registers, making them difficult to access.

*366.* Many Cantons rely today on very close intercantonal cooperation affecting nearly all areas of cantonal powers. Quantitatively, it seems only a small step to go from close cooperation to the merger of Cantons. According to one proposal, the Cantons of Geneva and Vaud would merge. Other proposals plan the merger of the small Cantons in the heart of Switzerland, and some are even more radical and demand a completely new territorial division to create six to nine new Cantons. These proposals are based primarily on an efficiency rationale and underestimate the legitimacy component.

## § 2. Organization of the Cantons

### I. Right to Self-Organization

*367.* Within the limitations established by federal law, the Cantons have the right to self-organization (for the federal limitations, *see supra* §1, II., B.). This allows the Cantons to develop their institutions in accordance with their traditions and to preserve their specificities. The organization of the Cantons is established in the cantonal constitutions. The cantonal constitutions differ decisively from each other mainly depending on the date of their adoption. The older constitutions often include only rudimentary provisions and seem relatively unsystematic. The newer Constitutions – those adopted in the last forty years – are normally very systematic and include a Bill of Rights, along with provisions concerning the organization of the Cantons.

*368.* The Cantons can decide on the organization of their territory (*see supra* General Introduction, Chapter 3; *infra* Part III, Chapter 3), on the setup of institutions, and how those institutions operate. They can limit their own cantonal powers or they can delegate part of their powers to districts or municipalities. While the actual organization of the Cantons shows several similarities between the Cantons, and between the Cantons and the Confederation, there are nevertheless important nuances in cantonal organization.[1]

1. *See, inter alia*, Rhinow, Verfassungsrecht, 135 *et seq*.

## II. Forms of Cantonal Organization

### *A. Cantonal People*

*369.* The possibilities of the Cantons to determine to whom they want to confer political rights are limited (*see supra* Part III, Chapter 2, § 1 II., B.).[1] The Cantons have the option to give non-Swiss persons the right to vote, elect and be elected, and to deprive citizens of their political rights. Presently, the Cantons of Jura and Neuchâtel are the only Canton that accord the right to vote, elect and be elected to non-Swiss persons. All persons who are domiciled in the Canton for a certain period of time can participate in elections and voting at the cantonal level. The Cantons of Appenzell Outer Rhodes and Vaud allow political rights for foreigners at the municipal level. Finally, the Canton of Appenzell Outer Rhodes delegates the right to include foreigners into the polity of the municipalities. In some Cantons there have been cases in which the political rights are curbed, for example, in the Canton of Jura persons who receive social assistance from the canton are deprived of their political rights at the cantonal level.

1. *See* e.g., Auer/Malinverni/Hottelier, Vol. I, 66–68.

*370.* The cantonal polity is more powerful than the federal polity. For instance, in the Cantons, the citizens elect the members of the cantonal parliament, the cantonal government, and in some cases the civil servants and the teachers. Further, the Cantons provide a more direct means of democracy than the Confederation (*see supra* Part II, Chapter 2, § 3 and § 4).

*371.* In most Cantons, elections are decided by secret ballot. However, two Cantons, the Canton of Appenzell Inner Rhodes and the Canton of Glarus, are still governed by an assembly of the People (*Landsgemeinde*), which is derived from the 13th century. This institution includes all citizens that inhabit the canton and it convenes normally once a year. The *Landsgemeinde* elects the cantonal government (Appenzell Inner Rhodes), the members of the higher courts, and higher civil servants. In addition, the *Landsgemeinde* has constitution-making, legislative as well as certain executive powers. The voting takes place by raising the hand, and the votes are estimated, not counted.

*372.* The Cantons of Nidwalden, Appenzell Outer Rhodes, and Obwalden respectively abolished their *Landsgemeinde* in 1996, 1997, and 1998.

### *B. Cantonal Parliament*

*373.* All Cantons have a parliament.[1] These parliaments are composed of one Chamber and they normally meet in regular sessions. Similar to Federal Parliament, the cantonal parliaments are based on the militia system. Members of parliament are not full-time parliamentarians – they are expected to continue working in their profession.

The number of members of parliament differs in each canton. The Canton of Obwalden has the smallest parliament with fifty-five representatives. The Canton of Berne has the largest parliament with two hundred members. All Cantons, except for the Cantons of Ticino and Grisons, elect their representatives based on the proportional system. The Cantons of Ticino and of Grisons, on the other hand, apply the majoritarian system. Finally, the Cantons of Lucerne, Uri, Obwalden, Nidwalden, and Appenzell Inner Rhodes require elected citizens to accept their election to the parliament (*Amtszwang*).

1. On the cantonal parliaments, *see* e.g., Auer/Malinverni/Hottelier, Vol. I, 68–71; Germann Raimund E., 'Die Kantone: Gleichheit und Disparität', in: Klöti *et al.*, 398–401; Nuspliger Kurt, 'Grundzüge der Behördenstruktur im Verfassungsrecht der Kantone', in: Thürer *et al.*, § 69, 1087–1090.

*374.* The cantonal parliaments' principal task is legislation. However, due to the more important role of direct democracy at the cantonal level, the powers of the cantonal parliaments are more limited than those of Federal Parliament. According to Article 43 of the Federal Constitution, the Cantons can decide within their powers what tasks they want to fulfil. In other words, the Cantons are not obliged to assume the powers they have. Some Cantons self-restrict their right to assume tasks. For example, the Constitutions of the Cantons of Aargau and Basle-Land, which foresee that the assumption of new tasks needs a basis in the cantonal constitution. If the Canton wishes to assume new tasks, it must first amend the cantonal constitution so as to introduce the necessary constitutional basis. These provisions are designed to prevent an over-regulation of private life, as well as to prevent over-intrusiveness by the State.

*375.* In addition to being involved in the legislative process, the cantonal parliaments determine cantonal taxes, vote on the budget, approve accounts, and decide on spending. Here again the powers are limited by the means of direct democracy, especially by the financial referendum (*see supra* Part II, Chapter 2, § 4, III.).

*376.* In a majority of the Cantons, the parliament elects the members of the higher courts. Most other functions are elected directly by the People.

*377.* The working of the Cantons differs decisively depending on their history, size and demography. The urban Cantons – Basle-City, Zurich, Vaud, and Geneva – mainly have modern parliaments that are comparable to Federal Parliament.

### *C. Cantonal Government*

*378.* All Cantons have a cantonal government,[1] which, like the Federal Council *see supra* Part II, Chapter 4), are councils composed of five or seven members. In contrast to the Federal Council, the cantonal governments are not elected by parliament but directly by the People. In most Cantons, the election of the government is based on the majority principle, although the Cantons of Zug and Ticino elect their government members according to the proportional system. Three Cantons require a minimum age for the members of cantonal government (twenty-five in the Cantons of Fribourg and Schwyz, twenty-seven in the Canton of Geneva). Some smaller Cantons have a government based on the militia system, but the more populous Cantons have governments composed of full-time members.

1. On cantonal governments, *see* e.g., Auer/Malinverni/Hottelier, 71–72; Germann Raimund E., 'Die Kantone: Gleichheit und Disparität', in: Klöti *et al.*, 405–408; Nuspliger Kurt, 'Grundzüge der Behördenstruktur im Verfassungsrecht der Kantone', in: Thürer *et al.*, § 69, 1091–1094.

*379.* Just as with election to the cantonal parliament, the Cantons of Lucerne, Uri, Schwyz, Obwalden and Appenzell Inner Rhodes require citizens to serve in the cantonal government if elected (*Amtszwang*).

*380.* The function of cantonal governments is to represent the Cantons as well as direct and control the cantonal administrations. Cantonal governments have collective decision-making structures and every member of government also directs one department of the cantonal administration. Finally, the president of the government is elected either the People (Canton of Uri), the *Landsgemeinde* (Appenzell Inner Rhodes and Glarus), by the cantonal parliament (German-speaking Cantons), or by the government itself (French-, Italian- and Romansh-speaking Cantons). With the exception of these three to five parties, all are represented in the cantonal government. Only the government of the Canton of Appenzell Inner Rhodes is a one-party council.

## *D. Cantonal Courts*

*381.* The Cantons have an important autonomy with respect to the court system,[1] which differs significantly not only among Cantons, but also between the different administrative, civil, criminal, and specialized courts within the canton. (For more information, *see supra* Part II, Chapter 5).

1. *See* e.g., Auer/Malinverni/Hottelier, 72–75; Nuspliger Kurt, 'Grundzüge der Behördenstruktur im Verfassungsrecht der Kantone', in: Thürer *et al.*, § 69, 1094–1097.

# Chapter 3. The Municipalities

## § 1. The Position of the Municipalities in the Confederation

*382.* The municipalities form the grassroots level of the Swiss federal system, and are territorially defined legal entities with a special public law status. They are often depicted as the cradle of Swiss democracy.[1]

1. On municipalities in Switzerland, *see* e.g., Auer/Malinverni/Hottelier, Vol. I, 77–104; Braaker Christa, 'Die Gemeindeautonomie', in: Fleiner *et al.*, 225–246; Geser Hans, 'Die Gemeinden in der Schweiz', in: Klöti *et al.*; 421–468; Geser Hans *et al.*, *Die Schweizer Gemeinden im Kräftefeld des gesellschaftlichen und politisch-administrativen Wandels*, Zurich 1996; Ladner Andreas *et al.*, *Gemeindereformen zwischen Handlungsfähigkeit und Legitimation, Ein Forschungsprojekt des Schweizerischen Nationalfonds im Rahmen des Schwerpunktprogramms 'Zukunft Schweiz'*, Berne 2000; Rhinow, Verfassungsrecht, 109 *et seq.*; Steiner Reto, *New Public Management in the Swiss Municipalities*, Berne 2000; Steiner Reto, *Kooperationen und Fusionen der Gemeinden in der Schweiz, Konzeptionelle Grundlagen und Ergebnisse aus einer empirischen Studie*, Berne 1999; Tschannen, § 17.

*383.* From a historical point of view, most municipalities are older than the Cantons or the Federation, and form the basis of the democratic system. Most Swiss citizens have strong emotional links to their municipality of origin. Constitutionally speaking, however, the Cantons are the constituting entities of the state (Article 3 of the Constitution). As part of cantonal autonomy they can determine their territorial organization, create and dissolve municipalities and can confer or revoke municipal autonomy. Most Cantons, however, accord their municipalities a high degree of autonomy that corresponds to their historical and emotional importance. The municipalities thus continue to play a decisive role in politics.

### I. Types of Municipalities

#### *A. Political Municipality*

*384.* The Swiss system knows different types of municipalities.[1] The most important one being the *political municipality*, which is formed by all the inhabitants of the municipality. A decisive element for membership is the domicile (*see infra* Part IV, Chapter IV, § 3 on domicile and residence).

1. On the different types of municipalities, *see* e.g., Auer/Malinverni/Hottelier, Vol. I, 80–81; Geser Hans, 'Die Gemeinden der Schweiz', in: Klöti *et al.*, 422–425; Seiler Hansjörg, 'Gemeinden im schweizerischen Staatsrecht', in Thürer *et al.*, § 31, 494.

*B. Citizens and Bourgeois Municipality*

*385.* The political municipality can be distinguished from the *citizens or bourgeois municipality*, which only includes citizens of the municipality (*see infra* Part IV, Chapter 1, § 1) or descendants of one of the old families of the municipality. The *citizens or the bourgeois municipality* does not exist in all the Cantons. The French-speaking Cantons of Geneva, Vaud and Neuchâtel have only political municipalities. The Constitution of the Canton of Appenzell Outer Rhodes of 1995 provides for the dissolution of its citizens municipalities within five years from the coming into force of the Constitution.

*386.* The *citizens or bourgeois municipalities* are remnants of aristocratic or oligarchic institutions. Democracy in Switzerland before 1798 (the year of the French invasion) was not all-encompassing, but rather limited to certain families. The preservation of the *citizens and the bourgeois municipality* was a concession in order to convince the former ruling families to accept inclusive suffrage thus, through this concession, the citizens and bourgeois could maintain part of their privileges. Today, the role of the *citizens or the bourgeois municipality* is decreasing. In some cases they can decide on municipal citizenship and administer their own patrimony and cultural heritage (e.g., forests, buildings, vineyards).

*387.* In the dualistic system, the *citizens and the bourgeois municipalities* have their own institutions (Fribourg, Glarus, Schwyz, Zurich), whereas in the so-called mixed system, they are represented by the institutions of the political municipality. However, in cases that concern matters of the *citizens and the bourgeois municipality*, only those members of the political municipality who are also members of the *citizens and the bourgeois municipality* have the right to vote.

*C. Specialized Municipalities – Agglomeration*

*388.* The specialized municipalities have powers in only one defined subject matter while the *political municipalities* have general powers. Not all Cantons have specialized municipalities. It is mainly the German-speaking Cantons that rely on specialized municipalities in addition to the *political* and *citizens or the bourgeois municipality*. There are more than 4,000 specialized municipalities in Switzerland.[1]

1. On specialized municipalities, *see* e.g., Geser Hans, 'Die Gemeinden in der Schweiz', in Klöti *et al.*, 422–425.

*389.* An important case of the specialized municipality is the *school municipality*, which does not necessarily have to correspond territorially with the political municipality, but can include a smaller or a larger territory. As indicated by its name, the school municipality fulfils functions in the area of schooling.

*390.* Some Cantons foresee specialized *municipalities for the poor* that have the task to support the needy members of the municipality.

*391.* The status of *ecclesiastic municipality* is conferred by some Cantons to the parishes of the main religious denominations (*see infra* Part V, Chapter 3 on state and religion). Their territory and members do not necessarily coincide with the ones of the political municipalities. Only adherents of the religion are included. The Cantons request a relatively democratic organization of the ecclesiastic municipalities. Therefore, as a side effect, the main religious groups (Catholic and Protestant) rely on a relatively democratic form of organization.

*392.* In order to take the special situation of cities and the surrounding municipalities into account, several Cantons created legislation on *agglomerations*, which are designed as legal entities and are conferred certain powers. Bernard Dafflon calls the agglomeration a 'fusion sélective', a selective merger.[1] In other words, they can be described as a new form of specialized municipality. They are territorially based legal entities with a special public law status and with selective powers.

1. Dafflon Bernard, 'Structure communales: qu'est-ce qui distingue la collaboration intercommunale, l'agglomération et la fusion?', *Journée d'étude: Réformes et Politiques communales*, Berne, 5 November 2002.

## II. Municipal Autonomy

### *A. Provisions in the Federal Constitution*

*393.* The Federal Constitution dedicates one provision to the municipalities, mainly dealing with municipal or local autonomy. The Constitution, however, does not establish municipal autonomy, although in accordance with the distribution of powers in the Federal Constitution (*see supra* Part III, Chapter 1, § 2, II.), it guarantees municipal autonomy to the extent that the Cantons confer autonomy to the municipalities (Article 50(1) of the Constitution). In other words, the Confederation respects the cantonal right to self-organization and leaves it to Cantons to define the municipal autonomy. Only in cases where the Cantons illegally violate the municipal autonomy will the Confederation protect municipal autonomy.[1]

1. *See* e.g., St. Galler Kommentar, Kägi-Diener Regula ad Article 50, 613–616.

*394.* Federal law, however, sets the maximum scope of municipal autonomy. The Cantons cannot attribute more autonomy than they have themselves under the Federal Constitution.

*395.* Next to the guarantee of municipal autonomy, the Confederation is called to take the possible consequences of its activities for the municipalities into account. In particular it shall pay attention to the special situations of the cities, agglomerations, and mountainous regions (Article 50(1) and (2) of the Constitution).[1]

1. *See* e.g., St. Galler Kommentar, Kägi-Diener Regula ad Article 50, 616–619.

*B. Cantonal Provisions*

*396.* Due to the cantonal powers, there are twenty-six different regimes of municipal autonomy. While all Cantons and half Cantons accord municipal autonomy, the form of the cantonal attribution of local autonomy and the scope of accorded autonomy differ decisively. The following is a general outline of the cantonal provisions.

1. Form of the Attribution of Local Autonomy

*397.* Local autonomy is either based on the cantonal constitution, on cantonal statute(s), or – as in most cases – on a combination of both. If the status of their municipalities is defined by statutory law, the municipality's autonomy is far less protected than when status is determined by the cantonal constitution. When status is determined by statute, the Cantons can change the status of the municipalities with the normal legislating procedure. In cases of constitutional guarantees, however, a constitutional revision is necessary. According to the Federal Court, even the abolition of a municipality or the forced merger of municipalities in accordance with cantonal law is not opposed to the guarantee of municipal autonomy in the Federal Constitution (Decision of the Federal Court *Comune et patriziato di Fusio*, 104 Ia 387).

2. Scope of Attributed Autonomy

*398.* By relying on simplification, it can be said that the more important the municipalities have been in the history of the canton the more powers they are attributed. For instance, in the French-speaking Cantons the municipalities are less embedded in the cantonal history than in most German-speaking Cantons. Therefore, the Canton of Geneva is, for example, much more centralized than the Cantons of Berne, Thurgau or Schaffhausen. Culturally diverse Cantons like the Canton of Grisons tend to accord more autonomy than homogeneous ones. In some Cantons – e.g., the Cantons of Aargau and Glarus – the municipalities have even residual powers.

*399.* In most cases the municipalities have the right to self-administration and legislative and administrative powers in areas that directly concern the local level or that are especially culturally sensitive, such as municipal citizenship, primary education, schooling, municipal police and municipal infrastructure. In addition, all municipalities have the right to raise their own taxes (*see infra* Part V, Chapter 2, § 1, III.). However, judicial powers are in most cases very limited, although in some cases, federal law delegates powers not globally to the Cantons but directly to the municipalities. An example is the area of zoning, in which the Cantons are mandated to make general plans that then serve as a basis for the municipal zoning plans.[1]

1. *See* e.g., Auer/Malinverni/Hottelier, Vol. I, 82, 89–98; Seiler Hansjörg, 'Gemeinden im schweizerischen Staatsrecht', in Thürer *et al.*, § 31, 499–503.

### C. Cantonal Support and Control

*400.* The Cantons have extensive control and support powers over the municipalities. Measures aim to guarantee that the municipal order functions well.[1] Here three different kinds of measures shall be regarded: supportive, preventive, and repressive measures. The controlling instruments and measures that Cantons apply to the municipalities are more extensive and more frequently used than those applied from the federal level towards the cantonal level. Generally, control mechanisms are stricter when the municipalities execute federal or cantonal law than when they act within their own powers.

1. *See* e.g., Auer/Malinverni/Hottelier, Vol. I, 82–83.

#### 1. Supportive Measures

*401.* Supportive measures aim at strengthening the municipal order. There are multiple examples for supportive measures, which can be financial, e.g., through the mechanisms of financial subsidies and grants as well as financial equalization; they can be operational by providing the preconditions, framework and infrastructure so that the municipal institutions functions well, e.g., through information and counselling or the creation of a legal framework for voluntary intermunicipal co-operation; or they can be educational, e.g., through the provision of training programs. Because many municipalities are faced with a lack of well-trained personnel for the cantonal administration, the Cantons normally provide voluntary or mandatory training programs for the empowerment of the municipal civil servants. Judicial measures can be included in the category of supportive measures as well. The Cantons can accord remedies against the infringement of municipal autonomy, therefore, the system of remedies differs from canton to canton.

#### 2. Preventive Measures

*402.* Preventive measures shall prevent that the municipality neglects the fulfilment of its tasks. The least intrusive case of preventive measures would be the oversight of municipal activities. These oversight programs can include control in the form of reporting, information, and inspection, and they can be combined with the (mandatory) self-control and self-evaluation done directly by the municipality. Preventive measures – like the requirement of approbation of legislation and decrees, requirements concerning planification and budgets, or the setting of minimal standards for the management of the municipality and for its services – curb municipal autonomy.

#### 3. Repressive Measures

*403.* Repressive measures are applied when the municipality does not satisfactorily fulfil its tasks. In cases when municipalities execute cantonal law, the cantonal control can include a control of appropriateness. When municipal powers are concerned, the canton is limited to a control of legality. These repressive measures can include legal actions, revocation of municipal acts, financial subsidies and contributions, execution by substitution, disciplinary measures, forced cooperation between municipalities to assure better services, or tutelage. Tutelage is the *ultima ratio* of repressive measures because it results in cantonal authorities acting in place of municipal authorities. This tutelage will be restricted in time and will only be applied when the municipality is temporarily not able to fulfil its tasks. For instance, at one time the municipality of Leukerbad was bankrupt and no longer able to establish a balanced budget on its own. Therefore, the Canton of Valais put it under tutelage. In most such cases, the canton will not put the municipality under tutelage for all subject matters, but rather act for the municipality to fulfil one task, as was in 1995, when the municipality of the City of Berne was not able to pass a budget in accordance with the financial powers of the city, the canton forced the city to adopt higher taxes. That same year the Canton of Zurich forced a new zoning law on the municipality of the City of Zurich because the one passed by the City of Zurich had triggered hundreds of complaints.[1]

1. *See* Geser Hans, 'Die Gemeinden in der Schweiz', in: Klöti *et al.*, 432–33.

### D. *Judicial Protection of Municipal Autonomy by the Federal Court*

*404.* Based on Article 50 of the Constitution, which guarantees the autonomy of municipalities within the limits fixed by cantonal law, the federal court provides a remedy against the violation of municipal autonomy. This remedy can be invoked by all forms of municipalities (i.e., political municipalities, special municipalities, etc., *see supra* A.).[1]

1. For judicial protection, *see* e.g., Auer/Malinverni/Hottelier, Vol. I, 98–104; Seiler Hansjörg, 'Gemeinden im schweizerischen Staatsrecht', in: Thürer *et al.*, § 31, 502–503; Tschannen, § 17 III.

*405.* According to the Federal Court, municipalities are autonomous in areas where they have a *relatively important decision making power*. In other words, the municipalities must have the right to make a choice between different self-defined options based on their own responsibilities (Decision of the Federal Court, *Municipality of Ritzingen*, 101 Ia 259). Municipalities can therefore even be deemed autonomous when they implement cantonal or federal law as long as they have a relatively important decision making power.

*406.* Additionally, the municipalities are competent to interpret their own regulations. The canton cannot arbitrarily impose a specific reading to a municipal legal act (Decision of the Federal Court, *Municipality of Lausanne,* 108 Ia 74), rather, the Cantons are bound by the legality principle. All cantonal involvement in municipal affairs that is not based on cantonal powers is in violation of municipal autonomy. For example, the cantonal authorities may not review the appropriateness of municipal action when the cantonal law only requires a legality control (Decision of the Federal Court, *Political Municipality of Obfelden*, 114 Ia 364).

*407.* In case of violation of the municipal autonomy, federal law allows for a Public Law Action to remedy the violation of municipal autonomy (*see supra* Part IV, Chapter 2, § 4, III. and Article 189(1)(e) of the Constitution).

*408.* The guarantee of municipal autonomy is a constitutional right of the municipalities (*see infra* Part IV, Chapter 2, § 1, C.), so standing is normally limited to municipalities. Individuals can claim the violation of municipal autonomy only in combination with other grievances, not as an independent cause of action. The scrutiny of the Federal Court is normally limited to the arbitrary and capricious test, unless the violation of federal or cantonal constitutional law is invoked. In such cases, the Court has free scrutiny.

For discussion of the Public Law Action and the expected reforms, *see supra* Part IV, Chapter 2, § 4, III. and IV.

## III. Intermunicipal Cooperation and Mergers of Municipalities

*409.* The municipalities have had increasing difficulty fulfilling the tasks they are accorded. Generally, small, financially weak municipalities have insufficient capacities to respond to the challenges of a globalised world. In order to prevent a centralization of tasks they are no longer able to fulfil, the municipalities can either rely on cooperation or on mergers with other municipalities.[1]

1. *See* e.g., Auer/Malinverni/Hottelier, Vol. I, 84; Geser Hans, 'Die Gemeinden in der Schweiz', in: Klöti *et al.*, 460–463; Seiler Hansjörg, 'Gemeinden im schweizerischen Staatsrecht', in: Thürer *et al.*, § 31, 503–504.

*410.* Cooperation provides the flexible interplay between different governments without changing the distribution of powers or the territorial organization.

### A. *Intermunicipal Cooperation*

*411.* In most cases, cooperation is limited to municipalities of one canton. There are however also cases of transborder cooperation. Two-thirds of the Swiss municipalities have intensified their intermunicipal cooperation within the last five years, aiming primarily to improve quality of services.

*412.* Cooperation requires that the municipalities are legally and factually able to cooperate. The Cantons provide the legal framework for cooperation, either by allowing and promoting voluntary cooperation or even by mandating cooperation. For instance, the *Cantonal Act on Municipalities* of the Canton of Berne establishes a three-step procedure to 'convince' the municipalities to optimize their services through cooperation:

(1) First, the Canton created a legal framework favouring voluntary cooperation;
(2) Second, when the municipalities do not cooperate even though a cooperation would be economical, the Canton can revoke subsidies and grants as incentives for cooperation; and

(3) Finally, when the municipalities are still not willing to cooperate on a voluntary basis, the Cantonal Act allows the possibility to force cooperation.[1]

1. Steps two and three of the procedure have never been applied, yet.

*413.* Most municipalities concluded multiple cooperations with neighbouring municipalities. Cooperation can be based on either, constitutionally or legally institutionalized cooperation, or on contractual cooperation. For example, contractual cooperation can include stock corporations (for tasks that need important financial means) or leasing contracts, such as those implemented in the Canton of Ticino, where some municipalities concluded police leasing contracts with the City of Chiasso so as to avoid having to establish its own police force. Most of the larger cities that provide infrastructure, which is used by surrounding municipalities, attempt to make agreements to have the profiting municipalities cover part of the costs.[1] These cases are being more and more regulated in special legislation on agglomerations (*see supra* Part III, Chapter 3, § 1, I.).

1. For different types of cooperation, *see* e.g., Schenkel Walter & Serdült Uwe, in Klöti, 471–482; Geser Hans, 'Die Gemeinden in der Schweiz', in: Klöti *et al.*, 460–463.

### *B. Merger of Municipalities*

*414.* Most discussion on mergers of municipalities is essentially a debate on the optimal size of local government. The merger of two municipalities can guarantee a more efficient and effective government by cutting costs and establishing joint administrations. As a result, decisions can be made in a more organized, centralized, and supposedly more efficient way, thus allowing development and infrastructure policies to be introduced with less externalities. Additionally, it can be argued that mergers promote democracy because, even though the influence of each individual citizen will be reduced nominally, the actual influence could increase due to the higher importance and the better financial position of the larger municipality. The creation of larger units may lead to less input from each individual, but perhaps – at least for some time – it could assure the more effective influence of the municipality. Larger units may, however, seem less accessible to the citizens and the incentive to be politically active might decrease.

*415.* The merger of municipalities, however, does not necessarily guarantee the needed flexibility and can provoke a legitimacy crisis, particularly where identity arguments are involved.

*416.* Discussions about mergers have been taking place all over Europe. However, only in Northern Europe – that is, in Denmark, Sweden and Norway – have more decisive territorial reforms taken place. In these countries the reforms have been conducted in order to create municipalities with enough resources to carry out social programs. Statistics indicate that in Switzerland there is only a limited willingness to merge from the side of municipalities.[1] Serious discussions about the merger of municipalities have taken place mainly in the Cantons of Thurgau,

Fribourg, Ticino, and Grisons. Some Cantons allow the possibility to force the merger of municipalities (e.g., Ticino) while other Cantons try to give financial incentives for mergers. For instance, the Canton of Fribourg actively promotes the merger of communes by offering financial but it also plans to allow the forcing of mergers in the draft of a new.[2]

1. *See* Geser Hans, 'Die Gemeinden in der Schweiz', in: Klöti *et al.*, 426.
2. *See* e.g. Seiler Hansjörg, 'Gemeinden im schweizerischen Staatsrecht', in: Thürer *et al.*, § 31, 504; Steiner *Reto, Kooperationen und Fusionen der Gemeinden in der Schweiz, Konzeptionelle Grundlagen und Ergebnisse aus einer empirischen Studie*, Berne 1999.

## § 2. Organization of the Municipalities

### I. Right to Self-Organization

*417.* To a large extent, the form of organization in each municipality is regulated by cantonal law. The municipal right to self-organization is therefore very limited. Municipalities cannot decide on their form of government to the extent that the Cantons can define their own form of cantonal organization. Some Cantons accord municipalities a limited autonomy to define their body politic, e.g., with respect to the participation of foreigners. Other Cantons give municipalities the option to introduce a municipal parliament while yet other Cantons allow municipalities to adopt an electoral system of their choice for the municipal parliament.

### II. Form of Municipal Organization

#### *A. In General: Bipartite and Tripartite Organization*

*418.* Municipal organization is to a large extent regulated by cantonal law. All municipalities have at least two institutions: the electorate (the People) and the municipal government (*bipartite or ordinary municipal organization*) and some Cantons even have a municipal parliament (*tripartite or extraordinary municipal organization*). The highest authority lies with the municipal People.[1]

1. *See* Auer/Malinverni/Hottelier, Vol. I, 84–86; Geser Hans, 'Die Gemeinden in der Schweiz', in: Klöti *et al.*, 444–446; Seiler Hansjörg, 'Gemeinden im schweizerischen Staatsrecht', in: Thürer *et al.*, § 31, 498–499.

*419.* Approximately five out of six Swiss municipalities are organized based on the bipartite organization, with only the People and the government as municipal institutions. All Cantons, except for the Cantons of Geneva and Neuchâtel, have the ordinary municipal organization. In some Cantons (Uri, Schwyz, Obwalden, Nidwalden, Glarus, and Appenzell Inner Rhodes) the bipartite organization is mandatory for all municipalities. All other Cantons designate bipartite organization for the smaller municipalities.

*420.* About one out of six municipalities is organized based on the tripartite organization. Although only a relative small number of municipalities rely on this form of organization, about half of the Swiss population lives in these municipalities. In the Cantons of Neuchâtel and Geneva all municipalities are organized in the form of the tripartite form of organization, while in most other Cantons the tripartite form of organization is reserved for the more populous ones. Some Cantons give larger municipalities the choice between the bipartite and the tripartite form of organization.

*421.* The municipalities have hardly any judicial functions. Courts are normally situated at the district level and some Cantons accord the municipalities the right to introduce Justices of Peace (*see supra* Part I, Chapter 5, § 2, III.).

*422.* Finally, many municipalities have introduced the so-called *Amtszwang*, mandating that persons who are elected to office must accept the office.

### *B. Municipal People*

*423.* The municipal People are the highest authority of a municipality.[1]

1. *See* e.g., Auer/Malinverni/Hottelier, Vol. I, 86–88; Seiler Hansjörg, 'Gemeinden im schweizerischen Staatsrecht', in: Thürer *et al.*, § 31, 497.

*424.* The canton is not completely free to define the body politic of the canton or municipality, because restrictions based on federal law that apply to the canton also apply to the municipalities (for these restrictions, *see supra* Part III, Chapter 2, II.). Normally the definition of the body politic at the municipality level corresponds with the one at the cantonal level. However, the canton can leave some autonomy in this respect to the municipalities. For instance, the Canton of Appenzell Outer Rhodes accords the municipalities the right to give foreigners political rights at a municipal level upon demand and after ten years of residency in Switzerland, with a minimum of five years in the Canton. In the Canton of Thurgau, foreigners have a consultative vote at the municipal level, whereas in other Cantons (e.g., the Canton of Solothurn), foreigners can participate in the decision making of ecclesiastic municipalities.

*425.* In cases of bipartite organization (*supra* 1.), the People vote on all municipal legislation as well as on certain administrative acts. In cases of tripartite organization (*supra* 1.), where mandatory or facultative referenda are foreseen, the People can sign and vote on initiatives and referenda as well as elect the members of municipal government. Only in the Canton of Neuchâtel are the members of municipal government elected by the municipal Parliament. Further, in municipalities with parliaments, the People additionally elect their parliamentary representatives.

*426.* In municipalities with a tripartite organization, the People mainly vote by secret ballot whereas those municipalities with a bipartite organization normally take decisions in the municipal assembly – which is comparable with the *Landsgemeinde* (*see supra* Part III, Chapter 2, §2, II.). The municipal assembly is made up of all the inhabitants of the municipality with political rights, and votes are taken by a showing of hand. Some municipalities used vote by secret ballot for more important decisions or when demanded. In municipalities with a bipartite organization the influence of political parties is much smaller than in those with a tripartite organization.

### *C. Municipal Parliament*

*427.* About one-sixth of Swiss municipalities – including all those in the Cantons of Geneva and Neuchâtel – have a parliament. In the Canton of Vaud, municipalities with more than eight hundred inhabitants rely on a parliament. In the German-speaking Cantons, the urban centres are generally accorded parliaments. Bigger municipalities some times have the choice between the tripartite or the bipartite form of organization.[1]

1. On municipal parliament, *see* e.g., Auer/Malinverni/Hottelier, Vol. I, 88; Geser Hans, 'Die Gemeinden in der Schweiz', in: Klöti *et al.*, 444–446.

*428.* The parliament is always elected by the municipal People and in most Cantons the municipality can decide on the mode of election. Most municipal parliaments are elected based on proportional representation.

*429.* Municipal parliaments have the ordinary functions of a parliament. They legislate, supervise the municipal administration and executive and adopt the budget, the accounts as well as the zoning plans and in some cases the parliamentarians elect or nominate civil servants. Ultimately, the powers of municipal parliaments are, however, limited by direct democracy.

### *D. Municipal Government*

*430.* Similar to the government at cantonal and federal levels, municipal government is normally composed of a five- to fifteen-member council. The People elect the municipal government in all Cantons, except in the Canton of Neuchâtel. The municipal government prepares legislative drafts and can issue regulations. The council is normally headed by a president who exercises his function on a full-time basis, while the other members of government are frequently on a part-time basis. In contrast to the situation at federal and cantonal levels, in most municipalities the president is not *primus inter pares*, but has additional powers and responsibilities.[1]

1. On municipal government, *see* e.g., Auer/Malinverni/Hottelier, Vol. I, 89; Geser Hans, 'Die Gemeinden in der Schweiz', in: Klöti *et al.*, 446–452.

# Part IV. Citizenship and the Administration of Justice

## Chapter 1. Rules Concerning Citizenship and Relevance of Citizenship

### § 1. Rules Concerning Swiss Citizenship

#### I. In General

*A. Citizenship and Nationality*

*431.* Citizenship and nationality are often used as synonyms. Citizenship, however, is a status – or more precisely, the legal link between a person and the state. It is often understood as including political rights. Nationality, on the other hand, denominates belonging to a nation. Whenever the nation incorporates all citizens, citizenship and nationality are identical. However, when the definition of nationhood does not rely on citizenship but rather on other criteria, such as ethnicity, then nationality and citizenship diverge. The United States and France are examples of nation-states where citizenship coincides with nationality, while for instance Germany and Croatia are examples of nation-states where anyone can be a citizen but not a national, a national but not a citizen, both, or neither. While citizenship can be defined by relying on legal criteria, nationality normally evades objective definition.[1]

1. *See* e.g., Brubaker Rogers, *Citizenship and Nationhood in France and Germany*, Harvard University Press, Cambridge, 1992.

*432.* In Switzerland, it is vividly debated whether there is a Swiss nation, and therefore whether the Swiss nationality exists. Those who suspect a Swiss nation, define it based on shared political values such as federalism, direct democracy and neutrality, and/or on belonging to one of the Cantons. Often the Swiss nation is depicted as a *Willensnation* – a nation based on the will of the People to belong to the state and the nation. On the other hand, those who argue that a Swiss nation does not exist claim that the cultural diversity of the Swiss population – and moreover, the Swiss respect for that given diversity – eliminates the possibility of nationhood.

*433.* The individual definition of 'a nation' normally influences the criteria required in order to establish citizenship. Nation-states that rely on an ethnic understanding of the nation tend to apply foremost the *ius sanguinis* principle, according to which citizenship is accorded based on descent. Nation-states that define their nation as the totality of its citizens are more likely to apply at least some forms of the *ius soli* principle, under which one's residency or birth in the territory are decisive for the attribution of citizenship.

*434.* Nation-states relying on ethnic concepts are normally very restrictive in their naturalization policies. The request will be granted only when the citizenship candidate can prove that he or she is completely assimilated and loyal foremost to the country from which he or she is requesting citizenship. Nation-states relying on civil concepts are normally more willing to naturalize and either presuppose integration and/or demand only the acceptance of some (mainly political) values.

*435.* Switzerland predominately applies the *ius sanguinis* principle and is rather restrictive in its naturalization policy. Integration is one of the main criteria for naturalization. The citizenship policy, however, is not derived from a concept of Swiss ethnicity, but rather from the notion that in order to belong to the Swiss state the person must share and identify with the political values and institutions to such an extent as only descent or integration and assimilation can guarantee. Essentially, Switzerland has *turned its politics into a quasi-ethnicity.*

### *B. Three Level Citizenship*

*436.* The three-level federal system in Switzerland has an important influence on citizenship law in Switzerland. This influence is not only visible in the distribution of powers, which still leaves considerable power to the Cantons, but even more in the phenomenon of a *three level citizenship.* Every Swiss citizen has at least three citizenships. He or she is citizen of Switzerland, of a canton, and of a municipality. Although these three citizenships are distinguishable, they also form a unity and federal and cantonal citizenship cannot be obtained without municipal citizenship. Cantonal citizenship derives from municipal citizenship, and cantonal and municipal citizenship are a necessity for federal citizenship. Thus, according to Article 37(1) of the Constitution, every person in possession of a citizenship of a municipality and of the Canton to which they belong has Swiss citizenship. This three-level citizenship – constructed from the bottom up – stresses the importance of bottom up democratization and the idea of federalized democracy.[1] Cantonal and municipal citizenship do not depend on a person's place of residence – as in the United States for state citizenship – but are ascribed through descent, adoption or marriage, or are attributed through naturalization. Double or multiple citizenship on all three levels is permitted.

1. *See* e.g., Auer/Malinverni/Hottelier, Vol. I, 127–128; St. Galler Kommentar, Hafner Felix & Buser Denise ad Article 37, 502–504; Häfelin & Haller, 370; Schaffhauser René, 'Bürgerrechte', in: Thürer *et al.*, § 19, 318–319; Rhinow, Verfassungsrecht, 49 *et seq.*; Tschannen, § 13 II.

## II. Obtaining Swiss Citizenship

### *A. Constitutional Provision*

*437.* The Constitution contents itself with the determination of the *distribution of powers* and does not set special principles or substantive requirements for obtaining Swiss citizenship except that the Confederation is mandated to facilitate naturalization for stateless children.

*438.* According to the Swiss Federal Constitution of 1999, it is the federal level, which establishes the rules concerning the obtaining and reinstating of Swiss citizenship through status like birth, marriage and adoption. Additionally, the federal level sets minimum requirements for naturalizations by the Canton, grants naturalization permits, and regulates the loss of Swiss citizenship. It shall facilitate the naturalization of stateless children (Article 38 of the Constitution).[1]

1. *See* Rhinow, Verfassungsrecht, 53 *et seq.*; St. Galler Kommentar, Hafner Felix & Buser Denise ad Article 38, 506–509; Tschannen, § 13 II.

### *B. Other Legal Sources*

*439.* The most important federal source next to the Constitution is the *Federal Statute on the Obtaining and Loss of Swiss Citizenship of 29 September 1952* (SR 141.0, cited as Federal Citizenship Act). In addition, the case law of the *Federal Court* has gained high importance, and the *Cantons* have their own legislation concerning naturalization that also must be consulted.

*440.* Presently, several *revisions* in the area of citizenship law are under discussion. These mainly concern helping second or third generation immigrants obtain citizenship. In 1992 the Federal Council had already suggested a revision of the Constitution to facilitate the naturalization of young foreigners who grew up in Switzerland, but the proposal was rejected in a 1994 referendum. Even though it was accepted by a majority of the Swiss People, it did not obtain the majority in the cantonal votes. Again, in 2004, the People and the Cantons rejected clearly the facilitated naturalization of foreigners living in Switzerland for the second and third generation.

### *C. Swiss Citizenship Based on Status*

*441.* Normally citizenship is acquired by birth. In principle, Switzerland accords citizenship based on the *ius sanguinis* principle. Children of Swiss parents will receive Swiss citizenship whether born in Switzerland or in another country. Therefore, citizenship is accorded based on descent, rather than the place of birth. As a rule, children of a married couple, of which at least one of the spouses is Swiss, automatically receives Swiss citizenship. However, under the old law, if a woman who previously had obtained Swiss citizenship automatically through marriage to a Swiss person remarries to a foreigner, the child of this latter marriage receives Swiss citizenship only when it otherwise would not obtain citizenship by birth or would be stateless before coming of age.

*442.* A child who is born to a Swiss woman who is not married to the father receives Swiss citizenship. A child who is still a minor, born to a woman who is not Swiss but whose father is, will automatically receive Swiss citizenship when the parents of the child marry as if they had been married at the time of the child's birth. The child born to an unmarried couple where only the father has Swiss citizenship, can demand facilitated naturalization to obtain Swiss citizenship.

*443.* The *adoption* of a minor child will lead to the ascription of Swiss citizenship as if the child had been born to the person or persons who adopted it.

*444.* Formerly, a woman obtained citizenship automatically when she married a Swiss citizen or a Swiss woman would automatically lose citizenship when she married a foreigner, if she had gained Swiss citizenship because of her marriage to a Swiss man. Divorce did not influence citizenship.

*445.* Today, *marriage* has no direct influence on citizenship, but it gives access to a facilitated naturalization for spouses of Swiss citizens, male and female. The spouse can obtain Swiss citizenship after three years of marriage when he or she has lived a total of five years in Switzerland and resided there at least the year prior to naturalization (Article 27 of the Federal Citizenship Act). When the couple does not live in Switzerland, the spouse can receive Swiss citizenship after six years of marriage when he or she has connections to Switzerland (Article 28 of the Federal Citizenship Act). Marriage and divorce do not lead to the loss of citizenship.[1]

1. *See* e.g., Auer/Malinverni/Hottelier, Vol. I, 128–130; Häfelin & Haller, 374–376; Schaffhauser René, 'Bürgerrechte', in: Thürer *et al.*, § 19, 324; Tschannen, § 13 II 2.

### *D. The Ordinary Naturalization*

*446.* The federal level has only limited competencies concerning ordinary naturalization. The Confederation issues a naturalization authorization, which forms the prerequisite for a naturalization demand on cantonal and municipal levels. Apart from this authorization, the Confederation can only set minimum requirements for naturalization. The Cantons have the right to complement the requirements and, within the principles established by the Confederation, can regulate the details of naturalization.

*447.* The procedure for naturalization is therefore always divided into *two parts*:

(1) a federal one; and
(2) a cantonal/municipal one.

*448.* (1) First the foreigner must obtain a *federal naturalization authorization* (Article 12 of the Federal Citizenship Act). In order to receive this authorization, the foreigner must show:

(a) his or her aptitude; and
(b) that he or she has resided in Switzerland the requisite number of years.

(a) 'Aptitude' is understood to mean that the foreigner is integrated into Switzerland and that he or she is accustomed to the Swiss traditions and Swiss way of life (Article 14 of the Federal Citizenship Act).

(b) Normally twelve years of residence are required to qualify for a naturalization permit. The time that was spent in Switzerland between the age of ten and twenty counts double (Article 15 of the Federal Citizenship Act). According to a new proposal, the required time of residency would be reduced from twelve to eight years. However, polls suggest that this revision is not backed by a majority of the Swiss citizens.

*449.* Once issued, the authorization is valid only in one Canton and expires after a period of three years, unless prolonged (Article 13 of the Federal Citizenship Act). The authorization does not accord a right to naturalization but it is a prerequisite for deposing a naturalization demand in the canton and municipality.

*450.* When the authorization is refused, the foreigner or the canton can appeal to the Federal Ministry of Justice and Police (Article 51 of the Federal Citizenship Act). The decision of the Federal Ministry is final.

*451.* (2) The *Canton* establishes (a) the criteria, and (b) the procedure for obtaining cantonal and municipal citizenship. Both foreigners and Swiss citizens who have the citizenship of a different canton can demand naturalization. Cantons can establish different criteria for naturalizing Swiss and foreigners.

(a) Criteria for foreigners normally include a minimum time of residency in the canton, a degree of integration, respect and identification with the Swiss traditions and Swiss way of life, the character of the foreigner as well as a tax for naturalization. There has been a proposal to outlaw taxes for naturalization that are higher than the actual costs of naturalization, although polls indicate this proposal does not find the support of the Swiss population. Criteria for the naturalization of Swiss citizens in a canton are normally less strict and in many instances it will give a right to naturalization if the criteria are fulfilled.
(b) The procedure normally includes cantonal and municipal authorities. In most instances, both those authorities must give the assent to naturalization. However, the municipal procedure is disputed. Some municipalities rely on direct democracy for naturalization. In these municipalities it is the People who vote on the demand of each individual candidate. As a result, naturalization on the municipal level is normally the most difficult to obtain.[1]

1. In a landmark case in Autumn 2003 the Federal Court decided that procedures that demand a popular vote for naturalization are not permissible by arguing that the foreigner who is refused

naturalization has the right to receive an explanation why naturalization was denied (Article 29 of the Constitution). Popular votes could not provide such an explanation. How far reaching this decision will be is not yet clear. *See, inter alia*, Auer Andreas & Von Arx Nicolas, 'Direkte Demokratie ohne Grenzen? Ein Diskussionsbeitrag zur Frage der Verfassungsmässigkeit von Einbürgerungsbeschlüssen durch das Volk', in: AJP/PJA 2000, 923 *et seq.*; Hangarnter Yvo, 'Grundsätzliche Fragen des Einbürgerungsrechts', in: AJP/PJA 2001, 949 *et seq.*; Kiener Regula, 'Rechtsstaatliche Anforderungen an Einbürgerungsverfahren', in: *Recht* 2000, 213 *et seq.*

*452.* The candidates for naturalization normally do not have any possibility for appeal against the cantonal and municipal decision unless the Canton has provided a right to appeal or gives a right to naturalization – e.g., the Cantons of Zurich and Zug for persons born in Switzerland, and the Canton of Basle after a certain time of residency.[1,2]

1. *See* e.g., Auer/Malinverni/Hottelier, Vol. I, 130–134; Häfelin & Haller, 376–378; Schaffhauser René, Bürgerrechte, in: Thürer *et al.*, § 19, 324–326; Rhinow, Verfassungsrecht, 54 *et seq.*; Tschannen, § 13 II 5.
2. According to Fleiner, Switzerland is a 'four-fifth democracy' (*see infra* Part IV, Chapter 4, § 1). In view of the results of the popular vote of 26 September 2004, which rejected proposals to make naturalization easier for second and third generation immigrants, it is high time to fundamentally re-think the ordinary procedure for obtaining citizenship. According to Tschannen, § 13 II 6, who denominates the procedure as a 'federal anachronism', it is not rare that municipalities set the requirements for obtaining citizenship so high that even most Swiss citizens would not pass the naturalization procedure if they had to do so. He argues, *inter alia*, that the concept of obtaining citizenship as an act of *political discretion* may violate a set of fundamental liberties (e.g., the right to privacy in Article 13 of the Constitution), the non-discrimination clause in Article 8(2) of the Constitution, the arbitrary and capricious clause in Article 9 of the Constitution, and several due process clauses. *See* also the Decisions of the Federal Court concerning the procedure of certain municipalities (not) to grant Swiss citizenship *by secret ballot* (1P.1/2003 and 1P.228/2002) that violated the due process clause in Article 29 of the Constitution. Tschannen, *opt. cit.*, proposes a federal act including clear-cut and exhaustive criteria for obtaining Swiss citizenship and abolish the concept of obtaining citizenship as an act of *political discretion*. We would add provisions concerning adequate legal remedies as well.

### *E. Facilitated Naturalization and Reattribution of Swiss Citizenship*

*453.* The *facilitated naturalization* is regulated exclusively by federal law. Therefore, the Cantons must not establish additional criteria and the procedure is established and conducted by federal authorities. According to Article 32 of the Citizenship Act, it is the Federal Ministry of Justice and Police that decides on naturalization after consultation with the canton. Apart from a simple fee, the facilitated naturalization is free of charge. A negative decision can be appealed before the Federal Court.

*454.* The Federal Citizenship Act allows four groups of persons to benefit from facilitated naturalization:

(1) the spouse of a Swiss citizen living in Switzerland (Article 27 of the Federal Citizenship Act) and/or living abroad (Article 28 of the Federal Citizenship Act);

(2) persons who based on good faith believed that they were Swiss citizens (Article 29 of the Federal Citizenship Act);
(3) persons who could have obtained Swiss citizenship based on an international treaty but who excusably neglected to apply for it (Article 30 of the Citizenship Act); and
(4) the minor child of a Swiss father who is not married to the mother (Article 31 of the Federal Citizenship Act).

*455.* There is a proposal to facilitate naturalization of second generation immigrants and to attribute Swiss citizenship automatically to third generation immigrants. According to polls, a clear majority of Swiss citizens seemed to be in favour of these revisions. However, on September 2004, the People and the Cantons clearly rejected both proposals. *See* note 452.

*456.* Persons who lost their Swiss citizenship through marriage according to old law or who gave up their citizenship can be *reattributed* citizenship upon their demand when the person has close links with Switzerland, and when he or she is regarded as meriting Swiss citizenship and does not pose a threat to the internal and external security of Switzerland (Article 18 of the Citizenship Act).[1]

1. *See* e.g., Auer/Malinverni/Hottelier, Vol. I, 134–136; Häfelin & Haller, 378–380; Schaffhauser René, Bürgerrechte, in: Thürer *et al.*, § 19, 325–326; Tschannen, § 13 II 3.

## III. Losing Swiss Citizenship

*457.* Swiss citizenship can be lost based on the intervention of Swiss authorities and based on the request of the citizen to give up Swiss citizenship.

*458.* There are three cases in Swiss law in which Swiss citizenship is lost *ex officio*:

(1) when the link of parentage to the person who transferred Swiss citizenship is annulled (Article 8 of the Federal Citizenship Act);
(2) when a Swiss child is adopted by foreigners and receives the foreign citizenship (Article 8a of the Federal Citizenship Act); and
(3) at the age of twenty-two when a Swiss was born and has always lived outside of Switzerland, when he or she has another citizenship and was never registered with a Swiss authority outside of Switzerland or did not declare that he or she wants to maintain Swiss citizenship (Article 10 of the Citizenship Act).

*459.* The *Swiss authorities can intervene to annul citizenship* when citizenship was attained through false declarations or the misrepresentation of essential facts (Article 41 of the Citizenship Act). Swiss authorities can also annul citizenship, when the person has double citizenship, if the person's conduct seriously jeopardizes the interests and the reputation of Switzerland.

*460.* Additionally, all Swiss citizens living abroad who have a dual citizenship can request to be dismissed from their Swiss citizenship (Article 42 of the Federal Citizenship Act).[1]

1. *See* e.g., Auer/Malinverni/Hottelier, Vol. I, 136–137; Häfelin & Haller, 380–381; Rhinow, Verfassungsrecht, 56 *et seq.*; Schaffhauser René, 'Bürgerrechte', in: Thürer *et al.*, § 19, 326–327.

## § 2. Relevance of Swiss Citizenship

*See also* discussion *infra* Part IV, Chapter 4 on foreigners.

*461.* Swiss citizenship status establishes special rights and duties. Political rights on the federal level, which are only accorded to citizens, include the right to participate actively and passively in elections, to organize and take part in initiatives, and to demand and vote in referenda. On the cantonal and municipal levels, foreigners can receive political rights.

*462.* Swiss citizens have the right to a Swiss passport, an identification card, and to an act of origin. They further have the right to live in Switzerland, to choose freely their place of residence in Switzerland, and to leave Switzerland. Swiss citizens benefit from diplomatic protection outside of Switzerland. Also, Swiss citizens must not be expelled from Swiss territory and can only be extradited to foreign authorities when he or she gives his or her consent.

*463.* Citizenship also establishes duties and restrictions for the citizen. Swiss citizens have a general duty to be loyal to Switzerland. Men must do military service or alternative service. When they cannot do either, they must pay a tax (Article 59 of the Constitution). Swiss citizens are prohibited to serve in the army of a foreign country. This is mainly problematic for persons with double citizenship. Some international treaties allow exceptions so as to dispense persons from Swiss military and allow foreign military service and vice versa. For instance, it is permitted to serve in the army of the Vatican. Additionally, Swiss citizens have a duty to assist at elections for collecting and for counting votes and, in some Cantons they must serve jury duty when so requested. Also, in some Cantons and municipalities Swiss citizens must accept political office when elected (*supra* Part III, Chapter 2 and Chapter 3).[1]

1. *See* e.g., Auer/Malinverni/Hottelier, Vol. I, 137–140; Häfelin & Haller, 370–372; Schaffhauser René, 'Bürgerrechte', in: Thürer *et al.*, § 19, 327–330.

# Chapter 2. Fundamental Rights and Freedoms

## § 1. General

### I. The Concept of Fundamental Rights and Freedoms in the Swiss Constitution

#### A. *Human Rights and Fundamental Rights and Freedoms*

*464.* Fundamental rights and liberties are commonly defined as a set of norms embodied in the constitution or in international human rights treaties protecting the individual or a group from undue governmental intrusion. The general concept of fundamental rights and liberties draws a distinction between *human rights* (*Menschenrechte*) and *fundamental rights and freedoms* (*Grundrechte*). Based upon the theory of natural law, *human rights* are pre-constitutional, inalienable, indivisible, and belong to every individual as such, independent of the existence of a state. Alternatively, *fundamental rights and freedoms* (*Grundrechte*) are guaranteed by the state in the form of a Bill of Rights and are sometimes directly linked to the status of citizenship, e.g., political rights.[1]

1. *See* Robert Alexy, Theorie der Grundrechte, 3rd ed., Frankfurt a.M. 1996; Auer/Malinverni/Hottelier, Vol. II, ch. 1 (esp. 14–15), 71 *et seq.*; Häfelin & Haller, § 6 (with further references); Jörg Paul Müller, *Elemente einer schweizerischen Grundrechtstheorie*, Berne 1982, 1–42; Id., 'Allgemeine Bemerkungen zu den Grundrechten', in: Thürer *et al.*, § 39; Rhinow, 97–99; Rhinow, Verfassungsrecht, 165 *et seq.*; Tschannen, § 7 I.

#### B. *Forms of Fundamental Rights*

*465.* The Bill of Rights of the Swiss Constitution contains different forms of fundamental freedoms and rights:

*466.* *First*, the protection from undue intrusion of the State in essential spheres of human existence falls within the penumbra of *fundamental freedoms or fundamental liberties* (*Freiheitsrechte*). Based upon the idea of a *status negativus*, the Constitution imposes upon government and its bodies an *obligation* to *tolerate* the constitutionally protected spheres of human existence and to *refrain* from undue interference.[1]

1. *See* Auer/Malinverni/Hottelier, Vol. II, 6–8, 71 *et seq.*; Häfelin & Haller, 69; Rhinow, 98–99; Rhinow, Verfassungsrecht, 170 *et seq.*; Tschannen, § 7 II.

*467.* *Second*, the equal protection clause in Article 8, as well as additional guarantees deriving from the Rechtsstaat principle (e.g., Articles 9 and 29(2) of the Constitution), are structurally different from fundamental freedoms (*Freiheitsrechte*) insofar as they confer to the individual a *right* to be treated equally before the law as well as the means to *enforce* this right before court.[1]

1. *See* Auer/Malinverni/Hottelier, Vol. II, 8–10; Häfelin & Haller, 69–70; Rhinow, 98; Rhinow, Verfassungsrecht, 170 *et seq.*

*468.* *Third*, the so-called *social fundamental rights* (*Sozialgrundrechte*) confer to the individual a directly enforceable right to be supported by the state in certain situations or under certain conditions, such as the right to aid in distress (Article 12 of the Constitution) and the right to primary education (Article 19 of the Constitution). There is a certain reluctance to expand the set of social fundamental rights (e.g., right to housing rejected in 1970; the right to education rejected in 1973). The social goals in Article 41 of the Constitution differ from social fundamental rights insofar as no direct subjective right to services by the state may be derived from social goals (Article 41(4) of the Constitution).[1]

1. *See* Auer/Malinverni/Hottelier, Vol. II, 10–12; Häfelin & Haller, 70; Rhinow, 98–99; Rhinow, Verfassungsrecht, 170 *et seq.*

*469.* *Fourth*, as opposed to fundamental rights, some constitutional scholars have proposed the category of *fundamental obligations* (*Grundpflichten*), such as the obligation of every Swiss male to render military service.[1]

1. *See* Kley Andreas, *Grundpflichten Privater im schweizerischen Verfassungsrecht*, St. Gallen 1989; Rhinow, 102–103 (with further examples).

## *C. The Concept of Constitutionally Guaranteed Rights*

*470.* In practice, from an important procedural perspective, the Swiss concept of fundamental rights and freedoms is based upon the idea of *constitutionally guaranteed rights* (*verfassungsmässige Rechte*). According to Article 189(1)(a) of the Constitution, the Federal Court has jurisdiction over complaints about the violation of constitutional rights (*supra* § 4). The case law of the Federal Court determines which fundamental rights and liberties fall within the penumbra of constitutionally guaranteed rights.[1]

1. *See* Auer/Malinverni/Hottelier, Vol. II, 15; Häfelin & Haller, 71; Kälin, Staatsrechtliche Beschwerde, 5–6; Rhinow, Verfassungsrecht, 171.

*471.* The concept of constitutionally guaranteed rights is important not only with respect to protecting fundamental rights and liberties enumerated in the Articles 7 through 36, but also with respect to protecting other fundamental rights and liberties *outside* Chapter 1, Title 2 – e.g., the non-discrimination clause of Swiss citizens in another canton in Article 37(2) of the Constitution, the principle of legality in taxation matters, and the prohibition of intercantonal double taxation in Article 127 of the Constitution.[1]

1. *See* Häfelin & Haller, 581; Rhinow, 99.

### *D. The Importance of the European Convention on Human Rights*

*472.* In November 1974, the Swiss Confederation ratified the European Convention on Human Rights of 1950. Based upon the concept of *monism*, the provisions of the Convention (with the exception of Article 13) are given the same status as are national fundamental rights and liberties and are therefore *directly applicable* before the courts and public officials of the Cantons and the Confederation.[1]

1. *See* Villiger Mark E., 'EMRK und UNO-Menschenrechtspakte', in: Thürer *et al.*, § 40; Auer/Malinverni/Hottelier, Vol. II, 45–48; Häfelin & Haller, 74–75; Rhinow, Verfassungsrecht, 176 *et seq.*

*473.* However, being a (theoretically) revocable convention of international public law, the Swiss Legislature decided to incorporate the provisions of the Conventions into the new Constitution. Under the Constitution of 1874, the Federal Court pointed out that the provisions of the Convention had the same procedural status as the fundamental rights and freedoms of the Constitution. Hence, the new catalogue of fundamental rights and liberties reflects how important the impact of the European Convention is upon Swiss constitutional law and the Bill of Rights.[1]

| | European Convention on Human Rights | Swiss Constitution of 1999 |
|---|---|---|
| Right to Live | Article 2 | Article 10(1) |
| Prohibition of Torture | Article 3 | Articles 10(3) and 25(3) |
| Prohibition of Slavery and Forced Labour | Article 4 | Article 10(2) |
| Right to Liberty and Security | Article 5 | Articles 10(2) and 31 |
| Right to a Fair Trial | Article 6 | Articles 29, 30 and 32 |
| No Punishment without Law | Article 7 | Article 8(1) [and 5(1)] |
| Right to Respect for Private and Family Life | Article 8 | Article 13 |
| Freedom of Thought, Conscience and Religion | Article 9 | Article 15 |
| Freedom of Expression | Article 10 | Articles 16, 17, 20 and 21 |
| Freedom of Assembly and Association | Article 11 | Articles 22, 23 and 28 |
| Right to Marry | Article 12 | Article 14 |
| Prohibition of Discrimination | Article 14 | Article 8(2) |

1. The schema is inspired by Häfelin & Haller, 76; Häfliger Arthur & Schürmann Frank, *Die Europäische Menschenrechtskonvention und die Schweiz*, 2nd ed., Berne 1999; Villiger Mark E., *Handbuch der Europäischen Menschenrechtskonvention* (EMRK), 2nd ed., Zurich 1999.

## II. The System of Fundamental Rights and Freedoms in the Swiss Constitution

### *A. Textual Fundamental Rights and Freedoms in the Constitution of 1874*

*474.* The Bill of Rights of the Constitution of 1874 contained a very limited set of textual fundamental rights and liberties, such as the equal protection clause, the right to economic freedom, freedom of domicile, freedom of religion and philosophy and the free exercise thereof, freedom of marriage, freedom of the press, freedom of association, and the right to petition. In its early case law, the Federal Court granted protection only to *textual* fundamental rights and liberties. Moreover, protection was granted only if the cantonal constitution of the plaintiff contained an explicit textual basis for further protection beyond that provided by the Constitution of 1874.[1]

1. *See* Auer/Malinverni/Hottelier, Vol. II, 34–35; Häfelin & Haller, 71–73.

### *B. The Recognition of Non-Textual Fundamental Rights and Freedoms*

*475.* In 1959, the Federal Court developed a new formula for the recognition of *non-textual* fundamental liberties. A non-textual fundamental right can only be assumed if it constitutes a *precondition* for the exercise of the textual fundamental rights and liberties of the Constitution. The recognition of a non-textual fundamental right must be *essential to the democratic order of the Confederation and to the Rechtsstaat principle*. Furthermore, the recognition of a non-textual fundamental right must reflect an already *widely shared constitutional practice in the Cantons* and its recognition must be *generally accepted.*[1]

1. *See* Rossinelli Michel, *Les libertés non écrites*, Lausanne 1987; Auer/Malinverni/Hottelier, Vol. II, 35–37 (with further references and case law); Häfelin & Haller, 73; Misic Alexander, 'Der Grundrechtskatalog', in: Fleiner *et al.*, 74–75.

*476.* Based upon this formula, the Federal Court recognized the following non-textual rights: personal freedom and the right to live, the liberty of language, freedom of speech and opinion, freedom of assembly, and the right to aid in distress. Before 1969, the right to property and the takings clause were part of the set of non-textual fundamental rights and liberties.

*477.* The Bill of Rights of the Constitution of 1999 enumerates both the textual and the non-textual fundamental rights and liberties of the Constitution of 1874. However, Chapter 1 of the Constitution is *not exhaustive*. According to the concept of open codification, the Federal Court may recognize further fundamental rights and freedoms.[1] Note that there is still a non-textual fundamental right in the new Constitution: in the field of taxation and other fiscal impositions, the Federal Court has accorded to the principle of legality ('*nulla poena sine lege*') the status of an independent constitutionally guaranteed right (as a derivative of Article 4 of the Constitution of 1874).

1. *See* Rhinow, 100.

### *C. Fundamental Rights and Freedoms in the New Constitution: An Overview*

*478.* The Swiss Constitution contains a transparent catalogue of all currently recognized fundamental rights and liberties, illustrating their *evolution* since 1874 in Switzerland.

#### 1. Human Dignity and the Equal Protection Clause

*479.* The first chapter of Title 2 opens with the human dignity clause as a philosophical and normative foundation of all fundamental rights and liberties,[1] followed by the equal protection clause in Article 8 of the Constitution (*infra*, § 2, II.), and the protection against arbitrariness and the principle of good faith in Article 9 of the Constitution.[2] Note that it was the intention of the framers of the new Constitution (and *inter alia*: the People) to confer to the protection against arbitrariness provision the status of an *independent* constitutionally guaranteed right. However, in practice, the Federal Court did not contest the independent character of the right as such, but nevertheless *reaffirmed* that Article 9 of the Constitution does not constitute a direct and sufficient legal basis for actions against arbitrariness as long as a legally protected interest cannot be deduced from other substantive or procedural provisions (Decision of the Federal Court 126 I 81).[3]

1. *See* Mastronardi Philippe, 'Menschenwürde als materielle "Grundnorm" des Rechtsstaates?', in: Thürer *et al.*, § 14; Müller Jörg Paul, Grundrechte, 1–5; Rhinow, Verfassungsrecht, 29 *et seq.*
2. *See* Häfelin & Haller, 233–234, for the threefold content of the principle of good faith: (1) protection of confidence, (2) prohibition of abuse of rights (*see also* Article 17 of the European Convention on Human Rights), and (3) the prohibition of *actus contrarius*; Rhinow, Verfassungsrecht, 316 *et seq.*
3. *See, inter alia*, Auer/Malinverni/Hottelier, Vol. II, 529–546; Häfelin & Haller, 229 *et seq.*; Misic Alexander, Der Grundrechtskatalog, in: Fleiner *et al.*, 81–84; Müller Jörg Paul, Grundrechte, 467–492; Rhinow, Verfassungsrecht, 315–316; St. Galler Kommentar, Rohner Christoph ad Article 9, 126 *et seq.* (with further references).

## 2. Fundamental Liberties

*480.* Furthermore, the Constitution contains a catalogue of *fundamental liberties*, such as:

- The *constitutional protection of privacy and personhood*, which ensures the right to live and the guarantee of personal freedom in Article 10 of the Constitution, the protection of children and adolescent persons in Article 11 of the Constitution, the right to privacy in Article 13 of the Constitution, and the right to marriage and to a family in Article 14 of the Constitution (*infra*, Part IV, Chapter 2, § 2, II.).
- The *freedom of religion and expression* in Article 15 of the Constitution, which guarantees the right of free choice of religion or philosophical convictions and to practice them alone or in community with others (Article 15(2) of the Constitution), the right to join or to belong to a religious community, to follow religious teachings (Article 15(3) of the Constitution), and the prohibition to be forced to join or belong to a religious community, to participate in a religious act, or to follow religious teachings (Article 15(4) of the Constitution).[1] The relationship between State and Church is discussed *infra* in Part V, Chapter 3.
- The *constitutional protection of communication and expression*, which includes: the freedom of opinion and information in Article 16 of the Constitution, the freedom of the media in Article 17 of the Constitution, and the freedom of language in Article 18 of the Constitution (for the language provisions on the Federal level, cf. *infra* Part IV, Chapter 3, § 2).
- The *freedom of science and of art* in Articles 20 and 21 of the Constitution, which have been newly introduced and are inspired by Article 15(3) of the UN-Pact I, Article 19(2) of the UN-Pact II, and Article 5(3) of the German Basic Law. Their scope of application is still subject to evolving Federal Court case law. The freedom of science guarantees scientific research and teaching, whereas

the freedom of art guarantees protection for the artist, the presentation of her art and the piece of art as such. The Swiss concept of the freedom of art is less extensive than the interpretation given by the United States Supreme Court to the First Amendment.[2]

- The *freedom of assembly* in Article 22 of the Constitution, which grants the right to organize assemblies, to participate or refrain from taking part in them. The *freedom of association* in Article 23 of the Constitution allows every person to form associations, to join, belong to or participate in their activities. However, no person can be forced either to join or belong to them.[3]
- The *freedom of domicile* in Article 24 of the Constitution, which grants every Swiss citizen the right to establish her domicile anywhere in the country as well as the right to leave and return to Switzerland.[4]
- The *protection against expulsion and extradition of Swiss citizens*, as well as the *protection of refugees* against removal by force and extradition to a state in which they are persecuted or threatened by torture, or other means of cruel and inhumane treatment or punishment, are guaranteed in Article 25 of the Constitution.[5]
- The *property clause* in Article 26 of the Constitution guarantees the right to property. According to the *takings clause* in Article 26(2) of the Constitution, every expropriation and all restrictions of ownership equivalent to expropriation shall be fully compensated (*infra*, Part IV, Chapter 2, § 2, VI.).
- The *economic freedom clause* in Article 27 of the Constitution, which is a unique provision insofar as no other national constitution expressly guarantees economic freedom in general, the freedom to choose one's profession, and to enjoy free access to and free exercise of private economic activity in particular (*infra*, Part IV, Chapter 2, § 2, VII.).
- The *freedom to unionize* in Article 28 of the Constitution, which grants workers, employers, and their organizations to form, join or remain out of unions and the right to unionize for the defence of their interest. Whenever possible, conflicts shall be resolved through negotiation and mediation. Strike and lockout are only permitted when they are not contrary to obligations to keep labour peace intact or to resort to conciliation. Some categories of persons, such as public officers, prisoners or members of the Army, may be exempt from striking.[6]

1. *See* Auer/Malinverni/Hottelier, Vol. II, 205–248; Häfelin & Haller, 121–130; St. Galler Kommentar, Cavelti Urs J. ad Article 15, 222 *et seq.* (with further references); Hafner Felix, 'Glaubens- und Gewissensfreiheit', in: Thürer *et al.*, § 44; Hufen Friedhelm, 'Aktuelle Probleme der Religionsfreiheit im schweizerisch-deutschen Rechtsvergleich', in: Festschrift Fleiner, 343 *et seq.*; Maurer Hartmut, 'Gott in der Verfassung', in: Festschrift Fleiner, 395 *et seq.*; Mieth & Pahud de Mortanges (eds.), *Recht, Ethik, Religion. Der Spannungsbogen für aktuelle Fragen, historische Vorgaben und bleibende Probleme*, Lucerne 2002; Pahud de Mortanges René (ed.), *Le droit des religions dans la nouvelle Constitution fédérale*, Fribourg 2001; Rhinow, Verfassungsrecht, 237 *et seq.*
2. *See* Glaus Bruno & Studer Peter, Kunstrecht, Zurich 2003; Müller Jörg Paul, Grundrechte, 301–322; St. Galler Kommentar, Meyer Christoph/Hafner Felix ad Article 20, 282 *et seq.* (with further references); St. Galler Kommentar, Meyer Christoph/Hafner Felix ad Article 21, 288 *et seq.* (with further references); Schwander Verena, *Das Grundrecht der Wissenschaftsfreiheit im Spannungsfeld rechtlicher und gesellschaftlicher Entwicklungen*, Berne 2002.
3. *See* Decision of the Federal Court 127 I 164 (demonstrations on public ground are subject to authorization; the balancing test between divergent interests must be based upon objective criteria); Manfrini Pierre Louis, 'La liberté de réunion et d'association', in: Thürer *et al.*, § 46

(with further references). *See* Decision of the Federal Court 129 I 113 (discriminatory behavior of the State as an employer towards a labor union); Garrone Pierre, 'La liberté syndicale', in: Thürer *et al.*, § 50.

4. *See* St. Galler Kommentar, Cavelti Ulrich ad Article 24, 310 *et seq.* (with further references); Zufferey Jean-Baptiste, 'La liberté d'établissement', in: Thürer *et al.*, § 47.
5. *See* Auer/Malinverni/Hottelier, Vol. II, 553–560; St. Galler Kommentar, Breitenmoser Stephan ad Article 25, 315 *et seq.* (with further references); Kälin Walter, *Grundriss des Asylverfahrens*, Basle etc. 1990; Rhinow, Verfassungsrecht, 280 *et seq.*; *See also* Decisions of the Federal Court 123 II 511, 521 (extradition is only lawful if assurance is given that the death penalty will neither be pronounced nor executed) and 129 II 100 (extradition lawful even though detention conditions are less mild than in Switzerland).
6. *See* St. Galler Kommentar, Klaus A. Vallender ad Article 28, 382 *et seq.* (with further references); Rhinow, Verfassungsrecht, 273 *et seq.*

## 3. Social Fundamental Rights

*481.* Within the catalogue of fundamental liberties, a special category of fundamental rights has been introduced: the so-called *social fundamental rights*, such as the right to aid in distress (Article 12 of the Constitution), and the right to free primary education (Article 19 of the Constitution).[1] The Federal Court has held that in case of limitations of social fundamental rights Article 36 of the Constitution is applicable *per analogiam*: a restriction requires a sufficient legal basis, the preponderance of a public or private interest, and must be proportionate to the goal achieved (Decision of the Federal Court 129 I 12; *see infra* Part IV, Chapter II, § 3). The situation of distress presupposes must be the result of the incapacity of the addressee to earn her own living; Article 12 of the Constitution does not apply if the distress arose from petitioner's refusal to take appropriate employment (Decision of the Federal Court 2P.147/2002 of 4 March 2003).

1. *See* Meyer-Blaser Ulrich & Gächter Thomas, 'Der Sozialstaatsgedanke', in: Thürer *et al.*, § 34; Auer/Malinverni/Hottelier, Vol. II, 10–12; Häfelin & Haller, 70; Plotke Herbert, Schweizerisches Schulrecht, 2nd ed., Berne 2003; Rhinow, 98–99; Amstutz Kathrin, Das Grundrecht af Existenzsicherung, Berne 2002. *See* Decision of the Federal Court 129 I 12 concerning excluded elementary school students.

## 4. Due Process Provisions

*482.* Several d*ue process provisions*, such as fundamental guarantees for fair procedures before civil and criminal courts and public officers, follow the catalogue of fundamental liberties (Articles 29–32 of the Constitution; *infra*, Part IV, Chapter 2, § 2, V.).

## 5. Right to Petition and Political Rights

*483.* The *right to petition* allows every person to address petitions to authorities without suffering prejudice, and authorities must take notice of the petition (Article 33 of the Constitution).[1] Article 34 of the Constitution guarantees *political rights* in general and the protection of the free formation of opinion by citizens in particular, such as the unaltered expression of their will (Decision of the Federal Court 124 I 55, 57).[2]

1. *See* Hotz Reinhold, 'Petitionsfreiheit', in: Thürer *et al.*, § 52; St. Galler Kommentar, Steinmann Gerold ad Article 33, 462 *et seq.* (with further references).
2. *See* Tschannen, § 51 and § 52; Zen-Ruffinen Piermarco, 'L'expression fidèle et sure de la volonté du corps electoral', in: Thürer *et al.*, § 21; St. Galler Kommentar, Steinmann Gerold ad Article 34, 468 *et seq.* (with further references).

### 6. The Realization and Limitation of Fundamental Freedoms

*484.* The Swiss Bill of Rights closes with two important provisions concerning the *realization of fundamental rights in the entire legal system.* According to this provision (Article 35 of the Constitution), everyone exercising state functions must respect the fundamental rights and contribute to their realization.[1] The Federal Court has stressed that fundamental rights and liberties always bind the State, even if acting on a private law basis (Decision of the Federal Court 126 I 250, 254). Private individuals or corporations fulfilling delegated public functions or private holders of legal monopolies or concessions are bound by fundamental rights and liberties (Decision of the Federal Court 127 I 84, 90). Finally, Article 36 of the Constitution sets up the constitutional framework for the *limitation of fundamental rights and liberties* (*infra*, Part IV, Chapter 2, § 3).

1. *See* for a thorough analysis Tschannen, § 7 V. *See also* St. Galler Kommentar, Schweizer Rainer J. ad Article 35, 478 *et seq.* (with further references); Müller Jörg Paul, *Elemente einer schweizeirschen Grundrechtstheorie*, Berne 1982, 45 *et seq.*; Rhinow, Verfassungsrecht, 190 *et seq.*

## § 2. The Particular Rights and Freedoms of the Constitutions

## I. Equal Protection and Non-Discrimination Clause

### *A. The Importance of the Equal Protection Clause under the Constitution of 1874*

*485.* When Switzerland became a federal state, Article 4 of the Constitution of 1848 declared all Swiss citizens to be treated equally before the law. However, the provision gained its real importance in terms of *justiciability* with the creation of the Federal Court under the Constitution of 1874.

*486.* In 1876, the Federal Court stated that the equal protection clause does not grant *absolute* equality. As a result, the Federal Court introduced the concept of *relative* equality in 1880 stating that, under the Constitution of 1874, 'equal treatment shall be only required under the condition of equality of all relevant factual conditions' (Decision of the Federal Court, *Jäggi*, 6, 174.) This case was a milestone in Swiss constitutional law and Article 4 of the Constitution of 1874 became the focal point for the highly creative case law of the Federal Court.[1]

1. *See* Weber-Dürler Beatrice, 'Rechtsgleichheit', in: Thürer *et al.*, § 41, 658–659; Rhinow, Verfassungsrecht, § 18.

### *B. The Evolution of the Equal Protection Clause in Article 8 of the Constitution*

*487.* Article 8 contains the general equal protection clause as well as the special protection clause. The general equal protection clause corresponds to Article 4 of the Constitution of 1874. Additionally a non-discrimination clause has been newly introduced in the Bill of Rights.

#### 1. The General Equal Protection Clause

*488.* The general equal protection clause in Article 8(1) of the Constitution is a fully justiciable legal norm applicable to all human beings and legal persons (e.g., corporations, associations). It binds all branches of government.[1]

##### a. The Equal Protection Clause in the Process of Law-Making and Rule-Making

*489.* In the process of *law-making and rule-making on all levels of the Confederation* (federal, cantonal and municipal), a statute (or a rule) violates the general equal protection clause if:

(1) the legislation draws distinctions *without a reasonable or objective cause and justification*; or
(2) the legislation ignores *significant* factual differences.[2]

Based on this two-tier test, the Federal Court affirmed the unconstitutionality of a cantonal taxation scheme imposing higher taxes on married couples than unmarried couples (Decision of the Federal Court, *Hegetschweiler*, 110 Ia 15 *et seq.*). The Court, however, did not declare the provision void.

1. *See* Auer/Malinverni/Hottelier, Vol. II, 482–506; Häfelin & Haller, 214 *et seq.*; Müller Jörg Paul, Grundrechte, 396 *et seq.*; St. Galler Kommentar, Schweizer Rainer J. ad Article 8, 101 *et seq.*; Rhinow, Verfassungsrecht, 289 *et seq.*
2. *See* Auer/Malinverni/Hottelier, Vol. II, 483–497; Müller Jörg Paul, Grundrechte, 396 *et seq.*; Häfelin & Haller, 215–217; Weber-Dürler, 'Rechtsgleichheit', in: Thürer *et al.*, § 41, 661; Schweizer, *opt. cit.*, 106–107.

*490.* Regarding the question whether a provision of a cantonal statute constitutes a violation of the general equal protection clause, the Federal Court leaves to the cantonal legislature considerable discretionary powers with the exception of the provision in respect to equality between men and women in Article 8(3) of the Constitution. There are two main reasons for the Federal Court's reluctance to become too involved:

*491.* *First*, the Swiss concept of federalism demands that federal authorities do not interfere with the competencies of the Cantons as long as the Cantons do not *manifestly* violate Article 8(1) of the Constitution. The general equal protection clause leaves the Cantons wide discretionary powers, and their decisions must be tolerated by the federal branches of government.

*492.* *Second*, the democratic principle and the principle of separation of powers demands that the concreteness of the general equal protection clause in the process of law- and rule-making is primarily a task to be fulfilled by the democratically legitimized legislature, and not by the Federal Court.

*493.* Contrary to fundamental liberties, limitations of the equal protection clause are not subject to the justification of Article 36 of the Constitution (*infra*, Part IV, Chapter 2, § 3).

b. The Equal Protection Clause in the Process of Law Application and Adjudication

*494.* In the process of *law application and adjudication*, the general protection clause prescribes that the law must be applied equally in all cases. The general protection clause is violated in cases where the agency treats two similar factual situations differently without objective grounds (Decision of the Federal Court, *M.*, 125 I 161, 163).

*495.* However, the Federal Court held in *Association de l'Ecole Française* that cantonal laws and regulations, even with the same or similar wording of the norm, can be applied differently in different Cantons (Decision of the Federal Court, *Association de l'Ecole Française*, 91 I 480, 491).

*496.* Furthermore, the unlawful application of a norm does not confer to other addressees of the norm the right to be treated unequally as well.[1] In these cases, the *principle of legality* supersedes Article 8(1) of the Constitution. However, the Court has indicated that Article 8(1) of the Constitution may prevail in those rare and exceptional cases where:

(1) an agency constantly derogates from the applicable norm; and
(2) an agency indicates that, from now on and in the future, it will not adjudicate in conformity with the law. In this case, the Court has affirmed the right to be treated unequally as well (Decision of the Federal Court, *Tax on Securities*, 122 II 446 *et seq.*).

1. *See* Waldmann Bernhard, *Das Diskriminierungsverbot von Art. 8 Abs. 2 BV als besonderer Gleichheitssatz: unter besonderer Berücksichtigung der völkerrechtlichen Diskriminierungsverbote einerseits und der Rechtslage in den USA, in Deutschland, Frankreich sowie im europäischen Gemeinschaftsrecht andererseits*, Berne 2003; Müller Jörg Paul, Grundrechte, 407–410; Häfelin & Haller, 219; Schweizer, *opt. cit.*, 108 (with further cases); Rhinow, Verfassungsrecht, 299 *et seq.*

2. The Special Equal Protection Clauses

a. Non-Discrimination Clause

*497.* The non-discrimination clause in Article 8(2) of the Constitution prohibits discrimination that is de facto or on its face grounded on *origin, race, sex, age, language, social position, lifestyle, religious, philosophical and political convictions, or corporal or mental disabilities.*[1] It is the first explicit use of the term 'discrimination' in a federal constitution worldwide. The enumeration in Article 8(2) of the Constitution is exemplary and not exhaustive.

1. *See* Auer/Malinverni/Hottelier, Vol. II, 506–513; Müller Jörg Paul, Grundrechte, 410–455.

*498.* However, it is uncertain whether the Federal Court will treat this provision independently or in connection with the general protection clause (Article 8(1) of the Constitution). There is no consensus among Swiss constitutional scholars.

- According to the theory of 'blind' equal protection, the state is not entitled to draw *any* legal distinction based upon the grounds listed in Article 8(2) of the Constitution. Thus, the non-discrimination clause grants *symmetrical* protection for everyone.[1]
- The theory of specific equal protection is grounded in the idea that the non-discrimination clause was introduced into the Bill of Rights to grant protection to specific groups that have suffered or are still suffering from discrimination. According to this theory, the state is entitled to draw legal distinctions as long as they are *objectively justified.* Said distinction must be *effectively in favour of the protected group.* Consequently, the non-discrimination clause grants *asymmetrical* protection for the protected group only, whereas individuals not within the penumbra of Article 8(2) of the Constitution can only invoke the general equal protection clause.[2]

1. *See* Müller Jörg Paul, Grundrechte, 412–414 (with references to German doctrine and U.S. Supreme Court case law, pointing out that Article 8(2) is susceptible to a more differentiated interpretation); Rhinow, 141 *et seq.* (claiming that Article 8(2) seems to favor the theory of blind equal protection).
2. *See* Müller Jörg Paul, Grundrechte, 414–417; Rhinow, 142.

b. Equality between Men and Women

*499.* According to Article 8(3) of the Constitution, 'men and women have equal rights.' This provision constitutes a *lex specialis* to the principle of relative equality. Article 8(3) demands a nearly *absolute* equal treatment before the law. As a rule, gender cannot be grounds for unequal treatment by the State, which, according to a formula of the Federal Court, only allowed in those rare cases where 'biological or functional differences' exclude *per se* and absolutely an equal treatment (Decision of the Federal Court, *Sils-Domleschg*, 123 I 56, 58).[1]

1. *See* Auer/Malinverni/Hottelier, Vol. II, 514–518; St. Galler Kommentar, Bigler-Eggenberger Margrith ad Article 8, 117 *et seq.* (with further references); Kägi-Diener Regula, 'Grundrechte im Föderalismus: Welche Chancen für Frauen?', in: Festschrift Fleiner, 71 *et seq.*; Müller Jörg

Paul, Grundrechte, 455–461; Müller Jörg Paul, 'Die Diskriminierungsverbote nach Art. 8 Abs. 2 der neuen Bundesverfassung', in: Zimmerli (ed.), 103 *et seq.*; Rhinow, Verfassungsrecht, 307 *et seq.*; Weber-Dürler, Rechtsgleichheit, in: Thürer *et al.*, § 41, 670–671.

*500.* Furthermore, Article 8(3) of the Constitution mandates that the legislature shall ensure *equality in law and in fact*, particularly in family, education, and work. In 1995, Parliament enacted an important federal act in order to promote equality between men and women (Equality Promotion Act, SR 155). The statute envisions the effective promotion of factual equality between men and women not only within the government, but also in the private sector, e.g., labour and employment law. In order to fight discrimination effectively, the statute contains several procedural provisions for arbitration proceedings, class actions, and the facilitation of the burden of proof.[1]

1. *See* Auer/Malinverni/Hottelier, Vol. II, 518–524; Bigler-Eggenberger, *opt. cit.*, 120–121; Weber-Dürler, 'Rechtsgleichheit', in: Thürer *et al.*, § 41, 671–673.

*501.* *Quotas* are another controversial issue in the promotion of equality between men and women.[1] The Federal Court had to deal with this question in two famous cases addressing quotas. In the *Solothurn* case, the Court had to decide the constitutionality of a cantonal initiative according to which the number of representatives in all branches of the cantonal government had to correspond to the proportion of the female population in the canton of Solothurn. The Court seemed to exclude the admissibility of quotas (Decision of the Federal Court, *Solothurn*, 123 I 165, 170). In the opinion of the Court, quotas do not seem adequate to ensure *equality in fact* between men and women. Furthermore, the *Solothurn* scheme constituted an undue restriction of political rights (Article 34 of the Constitution). However, in the following *Uri* case, the Court distinguished that a scheme to *promote equality within an agency* is not per se unconstitutional (Decision of the Federal Court, *Uri*, 125 I 21, 29 *et seq.*).

1. *See* Müller Jörg Paul, Grundrechte, 463–464; Weber-Dürler, 'Rechtsgleichheit', in: Thürer *et al.*, § 41, 672–673.

*502.* Finally, Article 8(3) of the Constitution demands equal pay for work of equal value.[1] It is one of the rare provisions of the Bill of Rights conferring to addressees a direct right to sue *private* employers for the violation of a fundamental right or freedom (*indirekte Drittwirkung*).

1. *See* Auer/Malinverni/Hottelier, Vol. II, 524–527; Bigler-Eggenberger, *opt. cit.*, 121–123; Müller Jörg Paul, Grundrechte, 464–466.

### 3. Elimination of Disadvantages Affecting Disabled Persons

*503.* Article 8(4) of the Constitution encourages the legislature to provide for measures to eliminate disadvantages affecting disabled persons.[1] Federal Government recently proposed a preference rule in cases of equal qualification for disabled People applying for jobs in Federal agencies. Furthermore, the right to sufficient education shall be ensured for children with seeing and hearing disabilities. However, on 18 May 2003, the People voted in a referendum against a proposed disability act. On 1 January 2004, the Federal Disabilities Act (SR 151.3) entered into force. Its aim is to eliminate discrimination against people with disabilities mainly in the field of construction law (access to public buildings), public transport, and employment law.

1. *See* Bigler-Eggenberger, *opt. cit.*, 124–125; Weber-Dürler, 'Rechtsgleichheit', in: Thürer *et al.*, § 41, 674; Rhinow, 146; Rhinow, Verfassungsrecht, 310 *et seq.*; Previtali Adriano, 'Quelques réflextions sur l'évolution du statut des personnes handicapées', in AJP/PJA 2002, 1297 *et seq.*

## II. Constitutional Protection of Personal Freedom and Privacy

### *A. The Evolution of the Concept of Personal Freedom*

*504.* The Bill of Rights of the Constitution codifies the elements of the concept of personal freedom, as developed by the Federal Court and influenced by international treaties, namely Articles 2–5 of the European Convention on Human Rights and by Articles 6–11 of the UN-Pact II. Furthermore, Switzerland has ratified Protocol No. 6 to the European Convention on Human Rights concerning the abolition of the death penalty (SR 0.101.06).[1]

1. *See* Auer/Malinverni/Hottelier, Vol. II, 133–190; Häfelin & Haller, 104–117; Müller Jörg Paul, Grundrechte, 7–79; Rhinow, Verfassungsrecht, 209 *et seq.*; St. Galler Kommentar, Schweizer Rainer J. ad Article 10, 148 *et seq.* (with further references).

*505.* The Constitutions of 1848 and 1874 did not grant a general protection of personal freedom, which was primarily protected by cantonal constitutional law. However, in 1963, the Federal Court recognized *personal freedom as a non-textual fundamental liberty* of the Constitution of 1874.

*506.* In its case law, the Federal Court held that *corporal integrity* (Decision of the Federal Court 89 I 92, 98), the *autonomy of the person* (Decision of the Federal Court 90 I 29 *et seq.*, 34 *et seq.*) and *mental integrity* form the core of the concept of personal freedom.

*507.* The Court pointed out that the Swiss concept of personal freedom does not correspond with the general concept of personal liberty (*allgemeine Handlungsfreiheit*) in Article 2 of the German Basic Law. However, under the influence of the European Convention on Human Rights and the case law of the European Court on Human Rights (Articles 5 and 8), the originally narrow concept of personal freedom has been continually extended. In recent cases, the Court also has had to deal with issues not expressly protected by the Convention, e.g., organ transplantation and medical assistance to procreation.[1]

1. Schweizer Rainer J., *Verfassungs- und völkerrechtliche Vorgaben für den Umgang mit Embryonen, Föten sowie Zellen und Geweben*, Zurich 2002.

*B. The Elements of Personal Freedom*

*508.* The Bill of Rights contains the following elements of personal freedom:

- The right to life and the prohibition of the death penalty (Article 10(1) of the Constitution).
- Prohibition of torture and any cruel, inhumane and degrading treatment or punishment (Article 10(3) of the Constitution).
- The right to corporal and mental integrity, and to freedom of movement (Article 10(2) of the Constitution).
- Prohibition of deprivation of liberty except in the cases and in the forms provided by statute; habeas corpus clause in the meaning of Article 5 European Convention on Human Rights (and Article 31 of the Constitution).
- Protection of the use of human reproductive and genetic material (Article 119(2) of the Constitution).
- Protection of the integrity of children and young people and the encouragement to their development (Article 11(1) of the Constitution).
- Right to aid in distress (Article 12 of the Constitution).

*509.* The question of whether the human dignity clause may serve as a *subsidiary fundamental right* (*Auffangrundrecht*) in those cases not covered by the concept of personal freedom is still controversial.

*C. The Right to Privacy*

*510.* The right to secrecy of mail and telecommunication constituted the only express fundamental right under the Constitution of 1874, whereas the general right to privacy formed an *element of the non-textual fundamental right to personal freedom*. In substance, Article 13 of the Constitution corresponds with Article 8 of the European Convention on Human Rights and contains the following elements:

- Protection of privacy.
- Respect for the home (Article 13(1) of the Constitution).
- Respect for private, non-verbal communication (Article 13(1) of the Constitution).
- Protection against abuse of personal data (Article 13(2) of the Constitution). *See also* Decision of the Federal Court 126 I 7.

## III. Rights of Communication and Expression

*511.* The Constitution of 1874 expressly protected freedom of the press, and in 1965, the Federal Court recognized the liberty of opinion as a *non-textual fundamental right of the Constitution* (Decision of the Federal Court, *Sphinx-Film AG case*, 87 I 117; Decision of the Federal Court, *Association de l'Ecole française case*, 91 I 485).[1]

1. *See* Auer/Malinverni/Hottelier, Vol. II, 249–305; Müller Jörg Paul, Grundrechte, 181–394; Barrelet Denis, 'Les libertés de la communication', in: Thürer *et al.*, § 45; Häfelin & Haller, 131–147; Kley Andreas, 'Die Medien im neuen Verfassungsrecht', in: Zimmerli (ed.), 183 *et seq.*; Rhinow, Verfassungsrecht, 251 *et seq.*; St. Galler Kommentar, Kley Andreas & Tophinke Ester ad Article 16, 238 *et seq.* (with further references); St. Galler Kommentar, Burkert Herbert ad Article 17, 255 *et seq.* (with further references).

*512.* Contrary to the general clause in Article 10 of the European Convention on Human Rights, the Swiss Bill of Rights contains an enumeration of the elements protected by the fundamental right to communication and expression:

- The *freedom of opinion*, guaranteed in Article 16(1) of the Constitution, constitutes, as set out by the European Court for Human Rights, 'the prerequisite of a democratic society and the free expression of every individual.' (Decision of the European Court for Human Rights, *Handyside*, 7 December 1976, Ser. A, Nr. 24, § 49). Article 16(2) of the Constitution states that all persons shall have the right to freely form, express and disseminate their opinions.
- The *freedom of information* – derived from the freedom of opinion – is guaranteed in Article 16(1) of the Constitution. Article 16(3) provides that all persons shall have the right to freely receive information, to gather it from generally accessible sources, and to disseminate it.
- The *freedom of the media* (press, radio, television, and other forms of public telecasting of production and information) is guaranteed in Article 17 of the Constitution.
- Article 21 of the Constitution guarantees the *freedom of art*. While 'freedom of film' is not expressly listed in Article 17 of the Constitution, it is attached to the freedom of art.
- The rights of communication and expression also include the freedom of scientific research and teaching (Article 20 of the Constitution). The freedom of assembly in Article 22 ascribes every person the right to organize assemblies, to participate in or to avoid them. The freedom of association in Article 23 of the Constitution guarantees every person the right to form associations, to join and belong to them, as well as to participate in their activities.
- In its political implications, the guarantee of political rights protects the free formation of opinion by the citizen, and the unaltered expression of their will.

## IV. Procedural Due Process

*513.* The main principles of procedural due process have been developed by the Federal Court under Article 4 of the Constitution of 1874. However, these principles were not considered as non-textual fundamental rights, but rather as *derivatives* of the *Rechtsstaat* principle and of Article 4 of the Constitution of 1874. Their primary function was to form a minimal procedural safeguard against incomplete or lacunary cantonal procedures.

*514.* The Bill of Rights details most principles of procedural due process recognized by the Federal Court in Articles 29–32 of the Constitution. Again, in their form and substance, the due process provisions of the Constitution reflect the strong influence of the European Convention on Human Rights.

*515.* As a result of the reform of the Judiciary in 2000, the People voted for the introduction of Article 29(a) into the Bill of Rights. In the event of a legal controversy, regardless of the nature of the controversy (i.e., litigation with two or multiple parties, process of adjudication in administrative matters), the provision grants every person *access* to a judicial authority. Article 29(a) of the Constitution has not yet entered into force of law.[1]

1. *See* Rhinow, Verfassungsrecht, 457 *et seq.* and § 30; St. Galler Kommentar, Kley Andreas ad Article 29(a), 413 *et seq.* (with further references).

## *A. General Procedural Guarantees (Article 29 of the Constitution)*

### 1. Prohibition of Denial of Justice

*516.* According to Article 29(1), every person has the right *in legal or administrative proceedings* to be treated equally and have their case conducted fairly. Any governmental authority that is unable to handle a case equally and fairly commits a *denial of justice.*[1] The same applies to actions presented before an authority lacking jurisdiction or actions that do not satisfy formal requirements. In these cases, the authority must explain its motives for not handling the case. A denial of justice may also be found in cases where the agency has indeed started an investigation, but without the requisite intensity (e.g., performing fact-finding). A special manifestation of the prohibition of denial of justice is the *prohibition of excessive formalism.* The Court held that excessive formalism is present in proceedings where, without any objective justification, rigorous formal requirements or excessive hardship are imposed upon plaintiff (Decision of the Federal Court, *Bonaduz*, 112 Ia 305, 308).

1. *See* Müller Jörg Paul, Grundrechte, 495–509; Häfelin & Haller, 236–237; Michel Hottelier, 'Les garanties de procédure', in: Thürer *et al.*, § 51, 810; St. Galler Kommentar, Hotz Reinhold ad Article 29, 396–403 (with further references); Rhinow, Verfassungsrecht, 481.

### 2. Judgment within Reasonable Time

*517.* Article 29(1) of the Constitution, in accordance with Article 6(1) of the European Convention on Human Rights, demands *a case to be judged within reasonable time.*[1] The European Court for Human Rights deemed three essential criteria for determining the reasonableness of time: the complexity of the case, the behaviour of the authority, and the party involved (*Van Pelt* v. *France*, 23 May 2000, § 35; *Leterme* v. *France*, 29 April 1998). The Federal Court stated in a recent case that the reasonable time requirement is violated if a case is pendent for thirty-three months and could have been judged already after six months of pendency (Decision of the Federal Court, 125 V 373, 375).

1. *See* Hottelier Michel, 'Les garanties de procédure', in: Thürer *et al.*, § 51, 810–811.

## 3. Right to be Heard

*518.* Article 29(2) of the Constitution contains the right to be heard *in all legal proceedings*. The authorities are obliged to inform individuals about the preparation of an administrative order limiting their rights or imposing new obligations upon them. This shall give the party concerned the chance to argue the case before a competent authority, to ask for new relevant evidence, and to be informed of arguments, findings of relevant facts and evidence given to the authority by third parties or by civil servants.[1]

1. *See* Auer/Malinverni/Hottelier, Vol. II, 607–621; Häfelin & Haller, 237–238; Müller Jörg Paul, Grundrechte, 509–542; St. Galler Kommentar, Hotz Reinhold ad Article 29, 404–409 (with further references); Rhinow, Verfassungsrecht, 482.

*519.* While the addressee of an administrative order has the right to be heard by the administration, this does not mean the addressee has the right to a formal hearing in the Common Law sense. It is up to cantonal legislation to determine the precise content of the right to be heard.

*520.* Article 29(2) represents only a minimal standard. The Federal Court does only apply the *arbitrary and capricious test*. However, in cases where cantonal legislation goes below the minimal standard, the case can be brought directly before the Federal Court, which examines the case fully.

*521.* The right to be heard constitutes the backbone of the Swiss concept of procedural due process. Its violation – as a rule – renders the administrative order *null and void* (so-called *formal nature* of the right to be heard) unless the violated party could have presented her case before a higher instance disposing of the same powers as the lower instance (so-called *healing effect* of a violation of the right to be heard).[1]

1. *See* for a critical account of the formal nature of the right to be heard and the healing effect in certain cases of its violation Seiler Hansjörg, 'Abschied von der formellen Natur des rechtlichen Gehörs', in: SJZ 2004, 377 *et seq.*

## 4. Right to Free Legal Assistance and Representation

*522.* The right to free legal assistance and representation includes the right to financial assistance and the right to representation.[1] Article 29(3) of the Constitution contains the fundamental right to *free legal assistance* before an administrative authority or before a court. Two conditions must be fulfilled:

(1) the person must lack the necessary financial means; and
(2) the case must appear to be with some chance of success. Under these circumstances, plaintiff will be exempt from paying any fee until she disposes of sufficient financial means to refund the costs. This provision constitutes a minimal standard that must be concretized by cantonal legislation.

1. *See* Auer/Malinverni/Hottelier, Vol. II, 697–718; Häfelin & Haller, 238–239; Müller Jörg Paul, Grundrechte, 542–553; St. Galler Kommentar, Hotz Reinhold, ad Article 29, 409–412 (with further references); Rhinow, Verfassungsrecht, 483.

*523.* The right to *free representation* is available if conditions (1) and (2) above are fulfilled, and the case satisfies a third factor as well: legal representation is necessary to protect the person's rights (Article 29(3), 3d phrase). Again, this provision constitutes a minimal standard that must be concretized by cantonal legislation.

### *B. Procedural Due Process in Judicial Proceedings*

*524.* Article 30 contains the most important *principles for judicial proceedings* developed under the Constitution of 1874, the European Convention on Human Rights, and the UN-Pact II.[1]

1. *See* Auer/Malinverni/Hottelier, Vol. II, 573–590; Häfelin & Haller, 240–243; Müller Jörg Paul, Grundrechte, 569–592; St. Galler Kommentar, Hotz Reinhold ad Article 30, 427–435 (with further references); Rhinow, Verfassungsrecht, 484 *et seq.*

#### 1. Right to an Independent and Impartial Court Established by Law

*525.* According to Article 30(1) of the Constitution, in judicial proceedings, every person has the right to be judged by a court *established by law*, which has *jurisdiction*, and is *independent* and *impartial* (*supra* Part II, Chapter 5, § 1). *Exceptional tribunals* acting outside the constitutional framework are prohibited. However, *specialized tribunals* granted with special jurisdiction (e.g., in taxation law or landlord and tenant law) are admissible.

#### 2. Right to be Heard before the Court at the Defendant's Domicile

*526.* For civil actions, Article 30(2) of the Constitution grants the person against whom a civil action is brought the right to have the case heard before the *court at the defendant's domicile*. However, federal and cantonal legislation and international treaties may provide for another jurisdiction. Examples of such treaties and acts are the Federal Bankruptcy Act of 1889 (SR 281.1), the Lugano Convention on Jurisdiction and the Enforcement of Civil and Commercial Matters of 1988 (SR 0.275.11), and the Federal Civil Jurisdiction Act of 2000 (SR 272).

3. Right to a Public Hearing before a Court

*527.* Finally, Article 30(3) of the Constitution provides that court hearings shall be public, and the judgment shall be publicly proclaimed. The Constitution of 1874 did not contain a similar provision. Deliberations on cases involving the judges of the Federal Court are also open to the public, unless the case is decided by circulation.

*528.* Even though the influence of Article 6, § 1 of the European Convention on Human Rights is paramount, Article 30(3) of the Constitution is broader in its scope of application. The provision applies to all judicial proceedings and is not restricted to 'civil rights and obligations' and 'criminal charges' (Article 6, § 1 of the European Convention on Human Rights).

*C. Habeas Corpus*

*529.* According to the principle of Habeas Corpus, no person may be deprived of liberty except in cases and in the forms provided by statute (Article 31(1) of the Constitution). In case of a deprivation of personal liberty and deprivation of the freedom of movement, under the meaning of Article 10(2) of the Constitution, the party concerned disposes of several Habeas Corpus rights provided by Article 31 of the Constitution, which are in accordance with Article 5 of the European Convention on Human Rights and Article 9 of the UN-Pact II.[1]

1. *See* Häfelin & Haller, 243–244; Hottelier Michel, 'Les garanties de procédure', in: Thürer *et al.*, § 51, 818–820; St. Galler Kommentar, Vest Hans ad Article 31, 436–448 (with further references).

1. Right to be Informed Immediately in Case of Deprivation of Liberty

*530.* Mainly as a concretization of the right to be heard, Article 31 contains the right of the party concerned to be *informed immediately*. The party must be informed in a *language* she understands and of the *reasons* of the detention (Article 31(2) of the Constitution). Furthermore, all persons deprived of their liberty must be informed of their rights, e.g., the right to judicial review of the legality of the detention, the right to remain silent, or the right to have their close relatives informed. However, the right to immediate legal council does not fall within the penumbra of Article 31(2) of the Constitution.

2. Preventive Detention

*531.* According to Article 31(3) of the Constitution, in cases of *preventive detention*, every person shall have the right to be brought before an impartial and independent judge without delay. The judgment must be delivered within a reasonable time.

3. Judicial Review of the Legality of the Detention

*532.* Finally, Article 31(4) of the Constitution guarantees every person deprived of her liberty without trial access to a judge at any time. The Federal Court judged that a waiting period of one month to present a case before court is in accordance with Article 5, § 4 of the European Convention on Human Rights. However, the Federal Court has regarded the period of forty-one days to deliver a judgment as excessive, possibly subject to tort claims (Article 5, § 5 of the European Convention on Human Rights).

## *D. Due Process in Criminal Procedures*

*533.* Article 32 contains three important guarantees in criminal procedures, which were developed by the Federal Court under Article 4 of the Constitution of 1874. These guarantees are:

(1) The right to be presumed innocent;
(2) the right to be informed of the accusation; and
(3) the right to be reviewed by a superior court. The Constitution does not mention the principle of *double jeopardy* enacted in the 7th Protocol of the European Convention on Human Rights and Article 14, § 6 of the UN-Pact II.

Nor does the Constitution mention the *right to be recompensated in cases of illegal detention or error in court* as provided by Article 5 § 5 of the European Convention on Human Rights and Article 9 § 4 of the UN-Pact II.[1]

1. *See* Auer/Malinverni/Hottelier, Vol. II, 621–667; Häfelin & Haller, 240–243; Müller Jörg Paul, Grundrechte, 554–569; St. Galler Kommentar, Vest Hans ad Article 32, 449–461 (with further references).

1. Presumption of Innocence

*534.* In accordance with Article 6, § 2 of the European Convention on Human Rights and Article 14, § 2 of the UN-Pact II, every person shall be *presumed innocent* until the person is subject to a condemnation having the force of law (Article 32(1) of the Constitution).

2. Right to Be Informed of the Accusation

*535.* Under Article 32(2) of the Constitution, every accused person has the right to be informed of any accusations as soon as possible and in full detail. Furthermore, the person must have the right to exercise rights of defence – e.g., the right to sufficient time to prepare a case, the right to defence by legal council or by the defendant, the right to cross-examination, and eventually the right to free assistance of an interpreter.

3. Right to Review by a Superior Court

*536.* Finally, according to Article 32(3) of the Constitution, every condemned person has the *right to have the judgment reviewed by a superior court.* The provision does not apply to cases where the Federal Court sits as court of sole instance (*supra*, Part II, Chapter 5, § 2, IV., B.).

## V. Right to Property

### *A. The Evolution of the Right to Property*

*537.* The Constitutions of 1848 and 1874 did not contain express provisions of the right to property. This task was left mainly to the cantonal legislature. In its earlier case law, however, the Federal Court developed the basic legal framework for the protection of property. Finally, in 1960, the Court recognized the right to property as a *non-textual fundamental right of the Confederation* (Decision of the Federal Court, *Zurzach*, 11 May 1960, not published). In 1969, the right to property was – together with the framework legislation in the field of planning and construction law – anchored into the Constitution of 1874 (Article 22ter) in accordance with the jurisprudence of the Federal Court.

*538.* The right to property was also introduced without any changes in Article 26 of the Constitution of 1999. Additionally, all cantonal constitutions protect property. The Swiss Confederation signed the First Additional Protocol of the European Convention on Human Rights, which protects in its Article 1 the right to property.

### *B. The Double Nature of the Right to Property*

*539.* The right to property is twofold. *First*, it protects the individual's ownership interest in land, tangibles, servitudes, patents, and rights in the present given situation (*Bestandesgarantie*). *Second*, Article 26 of the Constitution guarantees the right to property as an essential and inviolable feature of the Swiss legal order (*Institutsgarantie*).

*540.* According to Federal Court case law, a legislative act would violate the essence or the core of Article 26 if the act ignored the basic rights deriving from the right to property – e.g., the right to use or to dispose of property – or if it was aimed at extinguishing the right to property. As such, the Federal Court held that a taxation scheme that is *confiscatory* in nature and not limited in time violates the substance of the right to property.[1]

1. *See* Auer/Malinverni/Hottelier, Vol. II, 363–385; Häfelin & Haller, 173–176; Hänni Peter, *Planungs-, Bau- und besonderes Umweltschutzrecht unter Berücksichtigung des Raumplanungs- und Umweltschtzrechts des Bundes*, 4th ed., Stämpfli, Berne 2002; Müller Jörg Paul, Grundrechte, 569–592; Rhinow, Verfassungsrecht, 283 *et seq.*; Riva Enrico & Müller-Tschumi Thomas,

'Eigentumsgarantie', in: Thürer *et al.*, § 48; St. Galler Kommentar, Vallender Klaus A. ad Article 26, 328–343, 350–352 (with further references).

### *C. The Takings Clause*

*541.* The double nature of the right to property is extended by the constitutional *guarantee of full compensation* in the takings clause (Article 26(2) of the Constitution). Given a limitation of the right to property is *lawful* because it fulfils the requirements set out in Article 36 (*infra*, Part IV, Chapter 2, § 3), Article 26(2) provides that expropriation and restrictions of ownership equivalent to expropriation shall be fully compensated.

- *A taking* in the meaning of Article 26(2) of the Constitution (*formal expropriation*) always involves a *transfer of the title of ownership* from the individual to the State.
- In cases of *restrictions of ownership equivalent to a taking* (*material expropriation*), the individual *keeps* the title of ownership but, *as a matter of fact*, the State's restriction partially or totally deprives the landowner of her ability to use or dispose of her property.

The distinction between restriction to ownership equivalent to a taking, which is subject to full compensation (Article 26(2) of the Constitution), and restrictions to property not subject to compensation is delicate.[1] In the *Barret* case (Decision of the Federal Court, 91 I 329, 338 *et seq.*), however, the Federal Court relied on several criteria, such as the intensity of the restriction, the equal distribution of the charges, the harm caused by the restriction, and the probability of a diminished value of the restricted use of property.

1. *See* Hänni Peter, *Planungs-, Bau- und besonderes Umweltschutzrecht unter Berücksichtigung des Raumplanungs- und Umweltschtzrechts des Bundes*, 4th ed., Stämpfli, Berne 2002; Riva Enrico/Müller-Tschumi Thomas, 'Eigentumsgarantie', in: Thürer *et al.*, § 48, 773–775; Auer/Malinverni/Hottelier, Vol. II, 386–397; Häfelin & Haller, 176–178; Müller Jörg Paul, Grundrechte, 605–631; St. Galler Kommentar, Vallender Klaus A. ad Article 26, 343–350 (with further references).

## VI. Economic Freedom

### *A. The Concept of Economic Liberty*

*542.* In a comparative constitutional law perspective, *the general guarantee of economic freedom* in Article 27 of the Swiss Constitution is unique. Other constitutions only grant certain aspects of economic freedom, e.g., the contracts clause in the American Constitution (Article I, Section 10, § 1). The Swiss Constitution contains a threefold concept of economic liberty. *First*, the Constitution recognizes economic liberty as a *fundamental liberty* of every person (Article 27 of the Constitution). *Second*, economic freedom fulfils an *institutional function* insofar as Article 94 of the Constitution contains the basic principles for an economy based upon free competition. *Third*, according to Article 95(2) of the Constitution, the Confederation shall strive to create a unified Swiss economic area and guarantee that persons having a university degree or a federal or cantonal education certificate or an education certificate recognized by a canton may exercise their profession throughout Switzerland; hence, economic freedom fulfils a *federal function.*[1]

1. *See* Auer/Malinverni/Hottelier, Vol. II, 307–321; Häfelin & Haller, 180–181; Müller Jörg Paul, Grundrechte, 637–643; Rhinow, 299–306, 307 *et seq.*; Rhinow, Verfassungsrecht, 493 *et seq.*; St. Galler Kommentar, Vallender Klaus A. ad Article 27, 354–356 (with further references).

### *B. The Protection of Individual Economic Liberty*

*543.* The Federal Court has always pointed out that within the legal framework, economic freedom protects *every remunerative activity in the private sector*. According to the Federal Court, a public notary cannot invoke the protection of economic freedom insofar as his activity is a governmental act (Decision of the Federal Court 109 Ia 107 *et seq.*). In its early case law, the Federal Court granted economic freedom only to independent contractors. Since 1958, *independent and non-independent economic activities* fall under the protection of economic freedom.

*544.* The beneficiaries of economic freedom are *physical persons* (Swiss citizens and aliens) and *legal persons* (corporations, associations).

*545.* Article 27(2) of the Constitution contains three aspects of economic freedom: *First, the freedom to choose one's profession*, which prohibits the state from regulating education according to its will and needs, but does not guarantee *per se* a right to access to any public education.

*546.* *Second*, the freedom to enjoy *free access to private economic activity* prohibits the state from taking measures to hinder, totally or partially, the individual's access to the market on the territory of the Swiss Confederation (Decision of the Federal Court 100 Ia 169, 175).

*547.* *Third*, within the boundaries of the law, the freedom of free exercise of private economic activity allows the individual to choose freely the *means* for the exercising of the activity, the form of *organization* and employment policy of the enterprise or corporation, and one's own *domicile*. Furthermore, within the boundaries of antitrust regulations, the concept of economic freedom includes the right to *free advertisement*, the *choice* of contract partners, and choice on the *content* of contracts.[1]

1. *See* Auer/Malinverni/Hottelier, Vol. II, 329–341; Biaggini Giovanni, 'Wirtschaftsfreiheit', in: Thürer *et al.*, § 49, 781–785; Häfelin & Haller, 183–189; Müller Jörg Paul, Grundrechte, 644–655; Rhinow, 308–309; St. Galler Kommentar, Vallender Klaus A. ad Article 27, 356–368.

### *C. Restrictions of Economic Freedom*

*548.* Concerning the restriction of economic freedom, a general rule and specific rules can be distinguished.[1]

1. *See* Auer/Malinverni/Hottelier, Vol. II, 341–361; Biaggini Giovanni, 'Wirtschaftsfreiheit', in: Thürer *et al.*, § 49, 785–789; Häfelin & Haller, 189–201; Müller Jörg Paul, Grundrechte, 656–673; Rhinow, 310–316; Rhinow, Verfassungsrecht, 511 *et seq.*; St. Galler Kommentar, Vallender Klaus A. ad Article 27, 368–378.

### 1. Restrictions of Economic Freedom in General

*549.* Restrictions of economic freedom follow the general rule of Article 36 of the Constitution. They require a legal basis, must be justified by public interest, and must be proportionate to the goal pursued. Furthermore, the essence of economic liberty must remain untouched (*infra*, Part IV, Chapter 2, § 3).

### 2. The Methodology of the Restriction of Economic Freedom

*550.* According to Article 94(1) of the Constitution, the principle of economic freedom shall be respected by the Confederation and the Cantons. Swiss constitutional scholars have developed a methodology to distinguish between two categories of restrictions of the principle of economic freedom:

*551. First*, restrictions *in conformity with the principle of economic freedom*; they must correspond to the requirements of Article 36 of the Constitution.

*552. Second*, restrictions *in derogation of the principle of economic freedom* (Article 94(4) of the Constitution).

#### a. Restrictions *in Conformity* with the Principle of Economic Freedom

*553.* Federal and cantonal statutory laws and regulations – e.g., environmental regulations and licenses – may affect or distort competition and constitute *measures against competition* in the meaning of Article 94(4) of the Constitution (which requires a *constitutional basis* for derogations from the principle of economic freedom).

*554.* However, according to the theory of *police goods* (*Polizeigüter*), those federal and cantonal statutory laws and regulations are considered to be in conformity with the principle of economic freedom if they are protecting *peace, order, security, public health, morality, and good faith in business relations*. The concept of police goods has been continually extended and now also includes restrictions of the principle of economic freedom for *social policy reasons*.

*555.* According to Article 95(1) of the Constitution, the Confederation may legislate on the exercise of private economic activity. The Cantons are free to regulate private economic activities for *police goods reasons* in conformity with the principle of economic freedom as long as the Confederation has not legislated. The Federal Labour Law (SR 822.11) has considerably diminished the competencies of the Cantons to regulate for *social policy reasons*.

*556.* *The principle of equal treatment of direct competitors* follows from the principle of economic freedom, requiring that measures undertaken by the state be neutral in effect. The Federal Court has held that measures undertaken by the state are unconstitutional if *competition between direct competitors is distorted in effect*. Direct competitors are the members of the same branch of business offering the same products to the same group of consumers in order to satisfy the demand of that group of consumers (125 I 431, 436). As a consequence, the equal treatment requirement in the equal protection clause (Article 8 of the Constitution) is much narrower than the equal protection requirement of the economic freedom provision.

b. Restrictions *in Derogation* of the Principle of Economic Freedom

*557.* *Restrictions in derogation* of the principle of economic freedom, in particular measures against competition, shall be allowed *only if foreseen by the Federal Constitution or based on cantonal monopolies* (Article 94(4) of the Constitution):

- Therefore, with the exception of core areas of economic freedom, the *federal level* may impose derogation from the principle of economic freedom in foreign trade (Article 101 (2, *in fine*) of the Constitution), through the insurance of the supply of essential goods and services (Article 102(2) of the Constitution), in structural policy (Article 103, *in fine*, of the Constitution), in agriculture (Article 104(2) of the Constitution), and tacitly in the areas of transportation, electricity and film.
- For the *Cantons*, derogations from the principle of economic freedom are extremely limited, e.g., in the food and beverage industry subject to license until 2009 (*see* Transitory Provision No. 7 to Article 103 of the Constitution).
- According to Article 94(4) of the Constitution, derogations by the Cantons may only be based in *historical* cantonal monopolies – e.g., in the field of mining, hunting, fishing, and commerce with salt. A recent case of the Federal Court indicates, however, that the introduction of *new* cantonal monopolies is in conformity with the Constitution (Decision of the Federal Court 128 I 3, 10).

## § 3. Limitations of Fundamental Rights and Freedoms

### I. General

*558.* The exercise of fundamental rights and liberties can be subject to constitutional limitations. According to Article 36 of the Constitution, which codifies the case law of the Federal Court, four conditions must be met in order to limit the scope of a fundamental right or liberty:

(1) there must be a *legal basis* or a clear and present danger (Article 36(1) of the Constitution);
(2) the limitation must be for the *public interest* or for the protection of fundamental rights of others (Article 36(2) of the Constitution);
(3) the limitation must meet the standard of *proportionality* of means and ends (Article 36(3) of the Constitution); and
(4) there can be *no violation of the essence* of the fundamental right at stake (Article 36(4) of the Constitution).[1]

1. *See* Auer/Malinverni/Hottelier, Vol. II, 65 *et seq.*; Häfelin & Haller, 93 *et seq.*; Müller Jörg Paul, Grundrechtstheorie, 103 *et seq.*; Rhinow, 153–157; St. Galler Kommentar, Schweizer Rainer J. ad Article 36, 490 *et seq.* (with further references); Tschannen, § 7 VII and VIII; Rhinow, Verfassungsrecht, § 13; Weber-Dürler Beatrice, Der Grundrechtseingriff, in: Zimmerli (ed.), 131 *et seq.*

*559.* According to dominant Swiss doctrine, Article 36 does not apply to the human dignity clause, the equal protection clause, the due process provision, and certain other fundamental rights and liberties (esp. political fundamental rights).[1] Nevertheless, in a recent case (Decision of the Federal Court 126 I 26, 28 *et seq.*), the Federal Court also applied Article 36 to the due process clause in Article 31(4) of the Constitution. Furthermore, the Federal Court has held that in case of limitations of social fundamental rights Article 36 of the Constitution is applicable *per analogiam* (Decision of the Federal Court 129 I 12).

1. *See, inter alia,* Auer/Malinverni/Hottelier, Vol. II, 65 and 82; Häfelin /Haller, 94; Rhinow, 154; *see* for convincing criticism of the Court's approach: Tschannen, § 7 VIII 94–98.

## II. The Essence of Fundamental Rights is Inviolable

*560.* According to Article 36(4) of the Constitution, the essence or the core (*Kerngehalt*) of fundamental rights and liberties is inviolable. The concept of a *Kerngehalt* of fundamental rights and liberties is relatively new to Swiss constitutional law and is mainly influenced by Article 19(2) of the German Basic Law.[1] Depending on the fundamental right in question, the *Kerngehalt* describes a sphere of constitutional protection, which cannot be limited under any circumstances by the State. The normative substance of the *Kerngehalt* cannot be described in general or abstract terms.[2] The case law on the takings clause and on the right to personal freedom illustrates that the Federal Court has given preference to a pragmatic approach, which does not allow clear-cut conclusions.

1. *See* Müller, Grundrechtstheorie, 141; St. Galler Kommentar, Schweizer Rainer J. ad Article 36, 499; Tschannen, § 7 VIII. 5.
2. *See* Schefer Markus, *Die Kerngehalte von Grundrechten*, Berne 2001; Wiederkehr René, *Die Kerngehaltsgarantie am Beispiel kantonaler Grundrechte*, Berne 2000.

*561.* In accordance with Article 15(2) of the European Convention on Human Rights, the Bill of Rights of the Swiss Constitution contains guarantees, which are *per se* inviolable. Hence, Article 36 does not apply to certain fundamental rights and freedoms, such as the prohibition of capital punishment in Article 10(1) of the Constitution and the prohibition of torture in Article 10(3) of the Constitution.

### *A. Any Limitation Requires a Legal Basis*

*562.* According to Article 36(1) of the Constitution, any limitation of a fundamental right requires a legal basis.[1] According to the doctrine of the requirement of a legal basis, the limitation must be – from a nomotechnical perspective – described in general and abstract terms. Furthermore, the rule must be sufficiently precise to permit the addressee of the rule to foresee the consequences of her actions to a certain degree of certainty and previsibility (Decision of the Federal Court 117 Ia 472, 480).

1. *See* Häfelin & Haller, 95–97; Müller Jörg Paul, Grundrechtstheorie, 104–118; St. Galler Kommentar, Schweizer Rainer J. ad Article 36, 494–496; Rhinow, Verfassungsrecht, 202 *et seq.*; Tschannen, § 7 VIII. 2.

*563.* Grave limitations must be *expressly* foreseen by *statute* (Article 36(1) of the Constitution), whereas minor limitations can be foreseen by *administrative regulation.* The underlying idea of the doctrine of the requirement of the adequate legal form is that governmental interference into constitutionally protected spheres of the individual must be democratically legitimized.[1]

1. *See* Häfelin & Haller, 95–96; Müller, Grundrechtstheorie, 107–108.

*564.* It is obvious that not all threats and dangers to security and to public order can be foreseen by statute. Therefore, in case of a clear and present danger (Article 36(1) of the Constitution), the general police power clause (*polizeiliche Generalklausel*) can temporarily replace the requirement of an express legal basis. The Federal Court has already affirmed the constitutionality of the general police clause under the Constitution of 1874 (reaffirmed in Decision of the Federal Court 126 I 112, 117).

### *B. Any Limitation must be Justified by Public Interest*

*565.* Any limitation of a fundamental right must be justified by public interest, or serve for the protection of the fundamental rights of others (Article 36(2) of the Constitution).[1] There can be no abstract and clear-cut formula of what public interests are – they can diverge from place to place and change during the course of time. According to the Federal Court, one important area of the public interests penumbra are *police interests*, which may impose limitations of fundamental rights for the protection of 'public order, peace, security, health, morality and good faith in business relations' (Decision of the Federal Court 91 I 457, 460).

1. *See* Häfelin & Haller, 97–99; Müller Jörg Paul, Grundrechtstheorie, 124–132; St. Galler Kommentar, Schweizer Rainer J. ad Article 36, 497–498; Tanquerel Thierry, 'Le juge comme arbitre de l'intérêt public', in: Mélanges Perrin, Geneva 2002, 221 *et seq.*; Rhinow, Verfassungsrecht,

204 *et seq.*; Tschannen, § 7 VIII. 3.; Wyss Martin Phillip, *Öffentliches Interessen – Interessen der Öffentichkeit?, Das öffentliche Interesse im schweizerischen Staats- und Verwaltungsrecht*, Stämpfli, Berne 2001.

*566.* The notion of public interest also includes other areas, such as the protection of the environment (Article 74 of the Constitution) and zoning (Article 75 of the Constitution). Also, conflicts between a fundamental right or liberty and the fulfilment of a regulatory task often occur in the area of free speech in a public forum or in property law cases (e.g., conflicts between the owner of land and the regulatory interest to maintain or create affordable housing).

*567.* The case law of the Federal Courts indicates a preference for a balancing test of the fundamental values at stake (*Güterabwägung*), comparable to the substantial relationship test of the American Supreme Court (*Nebbia* v. *New York*, 291 U.S. 502, 54 S.Ct. 505 (1934)).[1]

1. *See* Müller, Grundrechtstheorie, 124.

### *C. Any Limitation must be Proportionate to the Goals Pursued*

*568.* According to Article 36(3) of the Constitution, any limitation of fundamental rights must be proportionate to the goals pursued. The underlying idea of the doctrine of proportionality is that a limitation of a fundamental right and liberty should not go further than is required by the public interest or for the protection of fundamental rights of others in the meaning of Article 36(2) of the Constitution.

*569.* The threefold proportionality test of the Federal Court requires:

(1) that the regulatory measure is *adequate* to attain the goal pursued by public interest;
(2) that a regulatory measure be suppressed if *milder means to attain the goal pursued are available*; and
(3) that the public interest is *necessary to prevail over the private interest.*[1]

1. *See* Häfelin & Haller, 99–100; Moor Pierre, 'Systématique et illustration du principe de la proportionnalité', in: Mélanges Fromont, Strasbourg 2001, 319 *et seq.*; Müller Jörg Paul, Grundrechtstheorie, 132–141; Rhinow, 156; Rhinow, Verfassungsrecht, 205 *et seq.*; St. Galler Kommentar, Schweizer Rainer J. ad Article 36, 498–499; Tschannen, § 7 VIII. 4.

### *D. Limitations based upon a Special Status of a Category of Persons*

*570.* Basically, every individual is a beneficiary of fundamental rights and freedoms. However, in case of a special relationship (*Sonderstatusverhältnis*) between a certain category of persons and the state, these freedoms may be subject to restrictions. Mainly, the addressees of the limitations are public officers, soldiers and other members of the Army, students, and prisoners. In order to be constitutional, the limitation must be expressly foreseen by statute, justified by the public interest, and meet the proportionality standard (*see* e.g., Decision of the Federal Court 98 Ib 301, 305). Thus, for example, the liberty of opinion of public officers may be restricted by their duty of loyalty.[1]

1. *See* Hänni Peter, *Die Treuepflicht im öffentlichen Dienstrecht*, Fribourg 1982; Müller Markus, *Das besondere Rechtsverhältnis*, Berne 2003; Rhinow, Verfassungsrecht, 204; Tschannen, § 7 VIII. 5.

## § 4. The Protection of Fundamental Rights and Freedoms

### I. No Swiss Constitutional Court

*571.* According to Article 189(1)(a) of the Constitution, the Federal Court has jurisdiction over complaints against the violation of *constitutionally guaranteed rights* (*supra*, Part IV, Chapter 2, § 1, I., C.). Contrary to the Supreme Court of the United States or the German *Bundesverfassungsgericht*, there is no special Constitutional Court (Verfassungsgericht) in Switzerland.

*572.* Switzerland is one of a number of countries that had already introduced constitutional review in the nineteenth century. This constitutional review, however, was limited to the review of cantonal statutes by the Federal Court. The Constitution of 1848 provided a very limited possibility for the citizens to sue their Cantons before the Federal Court and to defend their constitutional rights against violations by cantonal authorities.

*573.* Although there have been many initiatives in Swiss history to introduce the possibility of constitutional review of federal statutes, Federal Parliament has ultimately rejected all those proposals. The majority of the Swiss citizens are still too much committed to the idea of Rousseau and his *volonté générale*, which is the notion that bills and statutes are not only written law but also the very implementation of justice, and they cannot be nullified by a court. In their view, the legislature is the highest representative of the nation and therefore proclaims the *volonté générale*, which cannot be questioned for any constitutional reasons (for some exceptions, *see infra* para. 576 *et seq.*).

*574.* As all statutes passed by Federal Parliament are subject to an optional referendum (Article 141 of the Constitution), they are considered to be ratified either silently by the People when they do not invoke the right of referendum, or explicitly because they have been approved in a referendum by the majority of the People. Accordingly, there is no judicial body that would have the legitimacy to put into question what has been tacitly or explicitly ratified by the sovereign.

*575.* This argument has proved, even today, to be more convincing to the public against the traditional Common Law argument that men should be governed by law and not by men. As a consequence, the Cantons have no judicial channel to defend their autonomy against infringements by the federal legislature. Thus, constitutional review has remained a one-way road, providing protection against cantonal violations but not against violations by the federal legislature.[1]

1. *See inter alia*, Kälin Walter, 'Verfassungsgerichtsbarkeit', in: Thürer *et al.*, § 74 (with further references); Rhinow, Verfassungsrecht, 460 *et seq.*

## II. Protection of Fundamental Rights and Freedoms: The Remedies under the Current System

*576.* According to the Judicial Act of 1943, there are several remedies against violations of *federal law*. Since Federal Court case law has expressly attached to federal constitutional law the status of 'federal law' in the meaning of the Judicial Act of 1943, review of the constitutionality of governmental acts can be obtained through several actions:

- According to Article 84 of the Judicial Act of 1943, a *Public Law Action* (staatsrechtliche Beschwerde) can be brought before the Federal Court against *cantonal laws and orders* for violation of federal (constitutional) law.
  In practice, the Public Law Action is the most important remedy against violations of fundamental rights and liberties. In 1999, 2265 of the 5597 cases brought before the Federal Court were Public Law Actions. The heavy caseload of Public Law Actions is one of the main reasons for judiciary reform.
- According to Article 97 of the Judicial Act of 1943, an *Administrative Court Action* (Verwaltungsgerichtsbeschwerde) can be brought before the Federal Court against *federal administrative orders* for violation of federal (constitutional) law (*infra*, Part IV, Chapter 5, § 4, II.).

*577.* The general judiciary reform aims at simplifying the complicated system of review of constitutionality (*supra*, General Introduction, § 2, IV., C.).

## III. The Public Law Action (Staatsrechtliche Beschwerde)

*578.* According to Article 84(1)(a) of the Judicial Act (SR 173.110), a Public Law Action can be brought before the Federal Court if a *cantonal statute* or *cantonal administrative order or decision* violates constitutionally protected rights. Additionally, the case must be ripe and plaintiff must have standing to sue before the Federal Court. The Federal Court will hear the case only if these requirements are met, subject to special procedural restrictions.[1]

1. *See* Häfelin & Haller, 569 *et seq.* (with further references); Kälin Walter, *Das Verfahren der staatsrechtlichen Beschwerde*, 2nd ed., Berne 1994.

### *A. The Limitation of the Public Law Action to Cantonal Acts and Orders*

*579.* Initially, owing to the few competencies of the Confederation in the 19th century, the main function of the Public Law Action was the judicial control of constitutionality of cantonal statutes and decisions. This is the reason why federal statutes and decisions can never be the *direct* object of a Public Law Action – with the exception of *incidental* review of legality of a federal act upon which a cantonal act or decision is based.

*580.* According to Article 84(1)(a) of the Judicial Act, a Public Law Action can be brought before the Federal Court if *cantonal statutes* or *cantonal decisions and administrative orders* violate constitutionally protected rights. The distinction between (1) cantonal statute and (2) cantonal decisions or administrative orders is procedurally crucial to the *mode of control* by the Federal Court.

- Cantonal statutes are subject to the *abstract control of norms* (*abstrakte Normenkontrolle*). Within thirty days of publication of a cantonal statute, plaintiff can invoke the remedy of the Public Law Action before Federal Court for the violation of constitutional guaranteed rights (*supra*, Part IV, Chapter 2, § 1, I., C.). The Federal Court will grant *virtual standing* only if plaintiff can make plausible that she could be (with a minimum of probability) a future addressee of the provision declared unconstitutional by her. If the Court reviews a cantonal statute in the abstract mode, the statute will only be declared unconstitutional if an interpretation in conformity with the Constitution is hardly imaginable. The abstract control of constitutionality of the Federal Court includes all possible reasons and constellations (and is not only limited to the special fact pattern of the case presented to the Court).[1]
- Cantonal decisions and cantonal administrative orders are subject to the *control of the individual act* (*konkrete Normenkontrolle*). A plaintiff can invoke within thirty days after publication of the individual act either:
  (1) challenging the constitutionality of the cantonal decision or administrative order as such, without the claim that the cantonal statute upon which the decision or order are based upon are unconstitutional as well (*control of the individual act without preliminary control of the norm*); or
  (2) arguing that the cantonal decision or administrative order are unconstitutional because they derive from a substantively unconstitutional cantonal statute (*control of the individual act with preliminary control of the norm*). In the second case, the Court will preliminarily review the constitutionality of the cantonal statute, but without the possibility of going beyond the particular circumstances of the case. If the cantonal statute is found unconstitutional, the decision or the administrative order will be declared null and void (but not the underlying cantonal statute).[2]
- According to Article 190 of the Constitution, federal statutes and international law bind the Federal Court and the other authorities applying the law. Since the provision does not mention regulations issued by the Federal Council, the Federal Court may primarily control their constitutionality and legality. Preliminary control is the only possibility to review regulations of the Federal Council or of other Federal authorities. *Another direct and independent remedy*, such as the Public Law Action or the Administrative Court Action, *is excluded.*

1. *See* Kälin, 132.
2. *See* Kälin, 133–134.

*581.* The Federal Court may fully review the constitutionality of regulations of the Federal Council based upon a constitutional delegation (independent regulations of the Federal Council). However, the Court *gives particular weight to the political leeway* granted to the Federal Council by the constitutional delegation.[1]

1. *See* Häfelin & Haller, 619–620.

*582.* Regulations of the Federal Council based upon a delegation in a Federal statute or decree (dependent regulations) are only subject to a limited review. The Federal Court examines whether the Federal Council has respected the boundaries of the conceded delegation. In a recent case, the Court held that it would review the constitutionality of the dependent regulation of the Federal Council if the statute contains a clause authorizing the Federal Council to derogate from the Constitution.

*583.* However, the Court will not intervene if the delegation clause of the Federal statute grants to the Federal Court broad discretionary powers in order to regulate the matter in a regulatory form. The Federal Court may not replace the discretionary powers of the Federal Council with its own, it may only examine whether the regulation is in manifest conflict with the delegated powers conferred to the Federal Council, or whether the regulation is unconstitutional or illegal on other grounds (Decision of the Federal Court, *World Wild Life Switzerland*, 126 II 283, 290).[1]

| **Abstract Control** | **Individual Control** |
|---|---|
| Cantonal statutes | Cantonal decisions and administrative orders |
| 30 days after publication of the cantonal statute | 30 days after the issuance of the decision/order |
| Virtual standing | Actual standing |
| Standard: interpretation in conformity to the Constitution hardly imaginable. | Standard: concrete violation of the Constitution |

1. The schema is inspired by Kälin, 134; *see also* Häfelin & Haller, 619–620.

### *B. Violation of Constitutional Rights of the Individual*

*584.* According to Articles 84 and 85 of the Judicial Act, only a limited set of norms can be the object of a Public Law Action, e.g., the violation of constitutional rights of the individual, the violation of international treaties, the violation of federal provisions concerning jurisdiction of agencies, the violation of the political right of the citizen in respect to cantonal elections and voting, and the violation of provisions of the Federal Act on International Private Law regarding arbitration.

*585.* The concept of *constitutionally guaranteed rights of the individual* has already been discussed above (*supra*, Part IV, Chapter 2, § 1, I., C.). According to this concept, not only the provisions of Title 2, Chapter 1, fall within the penumbra of constitutional rights of the individual, but also norms *outside* the Bill of Rights, the provisions of the European Convention on Human Rights, and – eventually – new non-textual fundamental rights and freedoms of the Constitution.

*586.* It also includes fundamental rights and liberties of *cantonal constitutional law*, which grant further protection to that of the Federal Constitution. However, with the introduction of the Bill of Rights in the new Constitution, the importance of cantonal constitutional fundamental rights and freedoms has diminished considerably. One important body of cantonal constitutional law still lies in the area of *political rights.*

*587.* Finally, some provisions deriving from the *Rechtsstaat* principle and the federal principle fall within the penumbra of constitutional rights of the individual, such as the principle of separation of powers, the supremacy clause in Article 49(1) of the Constitution, the prohibition of intercantonal double taxation (Article 127(3) of the Constitution).

1. Ripeness

*588.* According to Article 86 of the Judicial Act, a case must be ripe to be heard before the Federal Court. All cantonal remedies must be exhausted (*relative ripeness*) – with the exception in the area of intercantonal double taxation and the sequestration of the patrimony of foreign governments.

*589.* Furthermore, the public law action is only admitted in the absence of another federal law remedy (*absolute ripeness*), such as the Administrative Court Action (*infra*, Part IV, Chapter 5, § 4).

2. Standing

*590.* According to Article 88 of the Judicial Act, the Public Law Action available under three conditions:

(1) claimants must be private and legal persons;
(2) the addressee of an administrative order or a judgment must have a *personal interest* in the case (or a *virtual interest* if the statute has not entered into force yet); and
(3) the act of government must constitute a *violation of legal (and not merely factual) interests*. Further, the case law of the Federal Court requires that the

plaintiff is still suffering from a prejudice of the violation at the moment of the judgment or is relieved of the prejudice when the Court decides in favour of plaintiff (*actual interest in legal protection*).[1]

1. *See* Kälin, 223 *et seq.*

### 3. Procedural Requirements

#### a. Provisions must be Expressly Invoked by Plaintiff

*591.* In practice, Public Law Action is a very rigid remedy. According to Article 90(1) of the Judicial Act, *the Federal Court's power of review is limited to the provisions invoked by plaintiff.* The Court will not examine other provisions not invoked by plaintiff and here lies one of the main differences from other legal remedies, such as the Administrative Court Action (*infra*, Part IV, Chapter 5, § 4), where the Court's power of review is not limited to the provisions invoked by plaintiff. Theoretically, an Administrative Court Action plaintiff does not have to invoke anything, but only needs to make a claim – e.g., a violation of federal law as such. In contrast, in her deposition, a Public Law Action plaintiff does not only have to set out which provision was violated by the cantonal act of government, but she must also *conclusively and in detail demonstrate to what extent that provision in question has been violated.* This rigid practice of the Federal Court has been widely criticized.[1]

1. *See, inter alia*, Kälin, 364 *et seq.*; Kölz & Häner, 40.

#### b. The Levels of Scrutiny of the Federal Court

*592.* If the Public Law Action constitutes an available remedy, the Federal Court examines the violation of fundamental rights and liberties on two different levels of scrutiny: the *free scrutiny test*, and the *arbitrary and capricious test.* Federal Court case law is very detailed and not always transparent.[1]

1. *See* Kälin, 197 *et seq.*

*593.* In principle, the Federal Court reviews under the free scrutiny test *the interpretation and application* of the provisions of the Federal Constitution and of the constitutions of the Cantons. Free scrutiny will be applied to review the violation of constitutional rights of the individual (*supra,* Part IV, Chapter 2, § 1, I., C.), the application of the provisions of the European Convention on Human Rights, and of the UN-Pact II.

*594.* In principle, the Federal Court applies *the arbitrary and capricious test* to review the interpretation and application of statutory provisions, the process of investigation in administrative and judicial proceedings, as well as the application of discretion. Except in cases of a manifest violation of fundamental rights and liberties, the Court will not squash the cantonal statute or decision. Instead the Court will advise the Canton to amend the legislation.

## IV. Judiciary Reform

*595.* The complicated system of judicial remedies is soon to be replaced through a thorough judiciary reform. In 2000, the People voted for the introduction of three new acts: the Federal Court Act, the Federal Criminal Court Act, and the Federal Administrative Court Act.

*596.* The new Federal Court Act will facilitate the complicated system of remedies insofar as there will be three main remedies: the civil law action, the criminal law action, and the action in public law matters (*Einheitsbeschwerde in öffentlich-rechtlichen Angelegenheiten*). The latter remedy in particular will considerably facilitate the difficult distinction between the Public Law Action and the Administrative Court Action (*see infra* Part IV, Chapter 5, § 4, II., B.).

# Chapter 3. Constitutional Problems of Minorities

## § 1. What is a Minority and What is a Problem?

*597.* In order to discuss constitutional problems of minorities, as a first step it has to be defined what group constitutes a minority and what kind of constitutional status is deemed problematic.

### I. Definition of the Term Minority

*598.* If the meaning of minority is to be interpreted from its linguistic origin, then a minority is a group that does not form a majority, or more precisely, a group that includes less than half of all the people. Under this definition, a minority is distinguished based on the numerical importance of the group. A numerical minority can in fact dominate the country, and sometimes the numerical majority might form the vulnerable part of the population. However, minority status is not solely meant to express the numerical relevance of a group, as it normally also includes the assumption that there is some kind of difference that distinguishes the minority from the majority. Furthermore this difference leads to inequality and tends to render the group and its members vulnerable. Therefore, inequality and/or vulnerability seem to be the better criteria for the distinction of minorities.

### II. Minorities and the Constitution

*599.* A group will be especially vulnerable when the differences are based on fixed criteria like race or on criteria that cannot easily be adopted or relinquished, such as ethnicity, religion or culture. Inequality can be expressed in open or hidden, legal or social negative discrimination. In general there is probably a consensus that legal negative discrimination of minorities is problematic and that the constitution should prevent such discrimination. More disputed is the issue of social discrimination. Has the state the right or even the duty to intervene in order to alleviate social discrimination? Can the state use affirmative action or even positive discrimination in order to favour minorities?

*600.* The adequate status and the relevancy within the state and its constitution of minority ethnicity, minority religion, minority culture, and minority language in comparison to the status of the majority ethnicity, majority religion, majority culture, and majority language are of further dispute. Is it discrimination when the minority language does not have the same official status as the majority language?

*601.* Inequality can as well be instituted through an unequal status on the state building level. For instance, a group will feel disfavoured when it is excluded from the constituent power because the state is defined as the state of and for the majority group. This unequal status is even more problematic when the state has as one of its aims to maintain and promote the culture of the dominant group or nation – as is the case in many western nation-states. Does a minority have the right to be equal at the state building level? Put differently and perhaps even more provokingly, does the majority nation have the right to claim as its nation state the state that it is sharing with other groups?

*602.* Many countries avoid the minority question from the very outset. They assume, based on concepts of individual equality, that they have no minorities. Does the minority have a right to be recognized as such? Does it have the right to be recognized as a group distinct from the majority?

## III. Minorities in Switzerland

*603.* As described above, Switzerland has a multicultural population. While the majority of the Swiss population is German-speaking, nonetheless, Switzerland is not regarded as the state of and for the German-speaking group. Switzerland accords an equal status to the different preexisting linguistic, religious and cultural groups on the state founding level as well as on the constitutional design level. Further, Switzerland does not rely on the 'melting pot' or 'colour blindness' idea like the United States, but expects and accepts that the 'Swiss People' is composed of different groups thus making the Swiss nation a composed nation.[1]

1. *See* e.g., Fleiner Thomas, 'Switzerland: Constitution of the Federal State and the Cantons', in: Basta Fleiner & Fleiner, 126–143; Rhinow, Verfassungsrecht, 43 *et seq.*; Schweizer Rainer J., 'Homogenität und Vielfalt im schweizerischen Staatsrecht', in: Thürer *et al.*, § 10, 161–177; Töpperwien Nicole, *Nation-State and Normative Diversity*, Helbing & Lichtenhahn, Basle 2001, 244–286.

*604.* Due to their equal status, it is more adequate to speak of different groups than to phrase the debate in minority/majority terms. At the federal level, among the traditional groups, only the Romansh-speaking community is, to some extent, in a minority position because their status is slightly different than that of the other linguistic groups, and because of their vulnerability due to their very small number (less than one percent of the population). In addition, new diversity is not accepted and expected in the same way as traditional diversity; therefore, it can be argued that the immigrants in Switzerland form a minority, or numerous minorities.

*605.* Historically, religious diversity was the main reason for tension in Switzerland. Today, however, linguistic diversity creates more tensions. Therefore the following discussion will be restricted mainly to linguistic issues.

§ 2. ACCOMMODATION OF LINGUISTIC GROUPS AT THE FEDERAL LEVEL

*606.* The *promotion of diversity* is a fundamental state principle (*see supra* Part II, Chapter I, § 1). The promotion of diversity is mainly realized through the mechanisms of self- and shared rule.

*607.* *Self-rule* is accorded to Cantons and by the Cantons to the municipalities. Most of all, when different groups are concentrated, territorially based self-rule can favour self-determination. Through self-rule, decisions on sensitive and dividing issues can be left to the decision-making process of the concerned community. Settled at the local level, these issues are less likely to lead to fragmentation at the higher level (for more specific information on self-rule, *see supra* Part II, Chapter I, § 2, II.). Based on self-rule each canton can designate the official language for its territory.

*608.* *Shared rule* leads to a political institutionalization of diversity. Through participation rights, different groups are accorded a special influence in the decision-making process of the federal level. Shared rule favours the generation of compromises and promises that the essential interests of the different communities will be respected (for more specific information on the shared rule arrangement, *see supra* Part II, Chapter 1, § 2, II.). The different linguistic groups are represented proportionally – with smaller groups sometimes represented in an over-proportional manner – in all federal institutions.[1]

1. *See* e.g., Fleiner Thomas & Misic Alexander, 'Föderalismus als Ordnungsprinzip der Verfassung', in: Thürer *et al.*, § 27, 429–439; Stauffer Thomas & Töpperwien Nicole, 'Balancing Self-Rule and Shared Rule', in: Basta Fleiner & Fleiner, 41–51.

*609.* In accordance with the value of diversity, Article 4 of the Swiss Federal Constitution of 1999 declared German, French, Italian, and Romansh as *national languages*, thus highlighting the equal value of all four languages.[1]

1. On the constitutional language policy, *see* Borghi Marco, 'Landessprachen und Amtssprachen', in Thürer *et al.*, § 37, 593–606; Borghi Marco, 'Sprachenfreiheit und ihre Schranken', in: Thürer *et al.*, § 38, 607–618; Hottinger Julian, 'La diversité culturelle', in: Fleiner *et al.*, 38–52; St. Galler Kommentar, Kägi-Diener Regula ad Article 4, 43–47; St. Galler Kommentar, Kägi-Diener Regula, 806–817; Fleiner Thomas, 'Switzerland: Constitution of the Federal State and the Cantons', in: Basta Fleiner & Fleiner, 126–143.

*610.* The four national languages are also considered *official languages* (Article 70(1) of the Constitution). All Swiss who are German-, French-, Italian-, or Romansh-speaking can address the federal authorities in their mother tongue and will receive answers in their language.

*611.* German, French, and Italian speakers have a slightly better status than the Romansh. While individual acts, orders, and decisions will be addressed in Romansh, general ones will in most cases only be published in German, French, and Italian. Thus, all federal legal texts are published in German, French and Italian, with all three versions having the same validity. When the three versions suggest different interpretation, the judge or civil servant who is interpreting or applying the law cannot just rely on the language version in which the legal text was drafted but also has to use the most convincing of the three versions.

*612.* While on the one hand the Romansh language is to some extent disfavoured, the Romansh and the Italian on the other hand are favoured by the Constitution. According to Article 70(5) of the Constitution, the Confederation must support the measures taken by the Cantons of Grisons and Ticino to maintain and to promote Romansh and Italian.

*613.* These two languages were accorded a *preferential status* because they are regarded as more vulnerable than the two dominant languages – German and French. Thus, the Confederation is supposed to support the two concerned Cantons, which have Switzerland's largest Italian- and Romansh-speaking populations.

*614.* Based on a similar logic, the Constitution mandates the Confederation to support the bilingual Cantons and the trilingual Canton. According to Article 70(4) of the Constitution, the Confederation shall support the plurilingual Cantons in the fulfilment of their particular tasks.

*615.* In addition, the Confederation shall take measures to encourage better understanding between the different language groups (Article 70(3) of the Constitution). Even though Switzerland as such is plurilingual, most Swiss citizens are monolingual. The Confederation and the Cantons shall therefore take measures so that a true exchange and understanding between different groups can develop. In this respect language instruction in schools is heatedly debated because some Cantons want to introduce English as the first foreign language taught to students, instead of a national language as previously done.

*616.* Finally the Constitution accommodates linguistic groups is by guaranteeing the freedom of language in Article 18.[1]

1. *See* St. Galler Kommentar, Kägi-Diener Regula, 270–276.

## § 3. Linguistic Accommodation on the Cantonal and Municipal Level

*617.* Of the twenty-six Swiss Cantons and half Cantons, seventeen are German-speaking,[1] four are French-speaking,[2] one is Italian-speaking,[3] three are bilingual (German/French),[4] and one Canton is trilingual (German, Italian, Romansh).[5]

1. (1) Zurich, (2) Lucerne, (3) Uri, (4) Schwyz, (5) Obwalden and (6) Nidwalden, (7) Glarus, (8) Zug, (9) Solothurn, (10) Basle-City and (11) Basle-Land, (12) Schaffhausen, (13) Appenzell Outer Rhodes and (14) Appenzell Inner Rhodes, (15) St. Gallen, (16) Aargau, and (17) Thurgau.
2. (1) Vaud, (2) Neuchâtel, (3) Geneva, and (4) Jura.
3. Ticino.
4. (1) Berne (French-speaking minority), (2) Fribourg (German-speaking minority), (3) Valais (German-speaking minority).
5. Grisons.

*618.* Problems arise most often in the bilingual and trilingual Cantons.[1] The Cantons have the right to regulate which languages shall be the official languages in their territory for communication with cantonal and municipal authorities. For the designation of official languages, the Cantons are requested to abide by the territoriality principle and to take indigenous linguistic minorities into account (Article 70(2) of the Constitution). Both requests are introduced in order to *preserve peaceful relations* among the different linguistic groups. Smaller linguistic groups shall not have to fear that they or their territory will be dominated by the majority language.

1. For minorities at the cantonal level, *see* e.g., Fleiner Thomas, 'Switzerland: Constitution of the Federal State and the Cantons', in: Basta Fleiner & Fleiner, 130–143.

*619.* In order to take *indigenous linguistic minorities* into account, bilingual and trilingual Cantons normally designate all languages that are indigenous to their territory as official languages for the purpose of communicating with cantonal authorities.

*620.* Article 70(5) implies that the Cantons of Ticino and Grisons can adopt *special measures* (positive discrimination) for the protection of the Italian and the Romansh (e.g., prohibition to advertise other than in the vulnerable language, Decision of the Federal Court 116 Ia 345).

*621.* For purposes of communication with municipal authorities, the *territoriality principle* is of prime importance. The territoriality principle maintains the territorial linguistic *status quo*, meaning the language that is traditionally spoken by the population of the territory is designated as official language. Only when there is a high and stable influx of persons from another language group will the language status of the territory be adjusted. In an *obiter dictum*, the Federal Court suggested that only when the newly immigrated language group forms about one half of the population will they have the right to have their language designated as an official language (Decision of the Federal Court 106 Ia 345).

*622.* For instance, German-speaking Swiss who take up residence in a French-speaking municipality will have to address the municipal authorities in French and will normally have to send their German-speaking children into French-speaking schools. As example, a municipality in the Canton of Grisons with a minority of Romansh speakers (20 per cent) did not offer school instruction in Romansh and was not willing to pay for the costs of sending the children to a Romansh-speaking school. The Federal Court upheld the municipality actions as constitutional (Decision of the Federal Court, 100 Ia 462) However, according to a newer decision concerning the Canton of Fribourg, when parents are willing to send their children to private schools in a different municipality or another municipality accepts the children and the parents cover the additional costs, the canton must not intervene (Decision of the Federal Court, 122 I 236). The canton can even restrict the use of another national language for instruction in private schools (Decision of the Federal Court, 91 I 480).

*623.* Therefore, the territoriality principle, like some measures of positive discrimination, is in conflict with the freedom of language. In most cases the Federal Court gave precedence to the aim of harmonious relationships between the different linguistic groups and therefore to the territoriality principle over the freedom of language.[1]

1. On the tensions between territoriality principle and the freedom of language, *see* e.g., Fleiner Thomas, 'Switzerland: Constitution of the Federal State and the Cantons', in: Basta Fleiner & Fleiner, 136–138; Hottinger Julian, 'La diversité culturelle', in: Fleiner *et al.*, 42–45.

*624.* International law restricts the territoriality principle to some extent. For example, according to the European Convention on Human Rights all arrested and accused persons must be informed of the reasons for their arrest or accusation in a language that they understand (Articles 5(2) and 6(3) of the European Convention on Human Rights).

## § 4. New Minorities

*625.* One of the main purposes of the Swiss state is to maintain and promote diversity (*see supra* Part II Chapter 1, § 1). This promotion of diversity, however, is limited to traditional or indigenous diversity. The understanding what diversity merits promotion is therefore relatively static.[1]

1. *See* e.g., Basta Fleiner Lidija R., 'Minority and Legitimacy of a Federal State: An Outsider Perception of the Swiss Model', in Basta Fleiner & Fleiner, 99–102; Schindler Dietrich, 'Schweizerischer Föderalismus – Europäischer Föderalismus', in: Daniel Thürer & Elmar Ledergerber, Schulthess Polygraphischer Verlag, Zurich 1995, 53–54; Töpperwien Nicole, *Nation-State and Normative Diversity*, Helbing & Lichtenhahn, Basle 2001, 279–283.

*626.* As will be shown below, immigrants are supposed to assimilate in order to receive Swiss citizenship. A Portuguese-speaking Swiss does not enjoy the same institutionalization of diversity, as do the German-, French-, Italian-, or Romansh-speaking Swiss, even though Portuguese-speaking Swiss outnumber the Romansh-speaking Swiss.

*627.* Only in very few instances has a redefinition of the diversity to be promoted been reached.

- With the foundation of the Canton of Jura in 1978, the people of the Canton received a state composing status like the people of the other Cantons.
- The voting right for women that was accorded at the federal level only in 1971 led to the inclusion of women into the political body. The Swiss tradition of unofficial quota led to a comparably quick representation of women in political institutions.
- On the cantonal level, some Cantons recently granted Jewish religious communities public law status, like that of Christian communities. This is a particularly noteworthy example because although Switzerland granted Jewish people equal rights as individuals in 1874, it took another one hundred years for Jewish communities to be granted equality as a group.

*628.* The inequality in status which is not expressed in unequal rights but in a missing institutionalization of diversity could only be eradicated when either the new diversity would be equally institutionalized, or when the Swiss state would cease to maintain and promote diversity. Both approaches would at this moment question the legitimacy of the state and could jeopardize the balance between the different composing groups. This issue of new diversity is still unsolved.

# Chapter 4. Legal Position of Aliens

## § 1. Legal Sources

*629.* Today about one fifth of the Swiss population does not have Swiss citizenship ('Four-fifths democracy', Thomas Fleiner).

*630.* Until 1925, regulation concerning foreigners was a cantonal matter. However, in 1848 the federal level attained the power to order the expulsion of foreigners for political reasons, and between 1910 and 1925 the Federal Government restricted immigration by decrees without relying on a constitutional basis. In 1925, the Federal Constitution of 1874 was amended so as to establish a federal competence concerning immigration, emigration, residence, domicile of foreigners, and asylum. The main aim of federal laws concerning foreigners is to limit the number of foreigners as well as to protect the security and economic interests of the country.[1]

1. For an outline of the Swiss foreigners law, *see* e.g., Auer/Malinverni/Hottelier, Vol. I, 141–169 (with further references); Ehrenzeller Bernhard (ed.), *Das schweizerische Ausländerrecht*, St. Gallen 2003; Fleiner Thomas, 'Rechtsstaatsdefizite für Ausländerinnen und Ausländer im schweizerischen Verwaltungsrecht', in: Mélanges Morand, Basle 2001, 231 *et seq.*; Kälin Walter, 'Die Bedeutung des Freizügigkeitsabkommens für das Ausländerrecht', in: Cottier & Oesch (eds.), *Die sektoriellen Abkommen Schweiz-EG, Ausgewählte Fragen zur Rezeption und Umsetzung der Verträge vom 21. Juni 1999 im schweizerischen Recht*, Berne 2002, 11 *et seq.*; Malinverni Giorgio, 'Le droit des étrangers', in: Thürer *et al.*, § 63, 979–991; Nguyen Minh Son, *Droit public des étrangers*, Berne 2002; Rhinow, Verfassungsrecht, 62 *et seq.*; Uebersax Peter/Münch Peter/Arnold Martin (eds.), *Ausländerrecht, Ausländerinnen und Ausländer im öffentlichen Recht, Privatrecht, Strafrecht, Steuerrecht und Sozialrecht der Schweiz*, Helbing & Lichtenhahn, Basle 2002.

### I. Provisions in the Federal Constitution

*631.* The Federal Constitution outlines only the distribution of competencies concerning legislation on foreigners and limits the federal power to expel foreigners. According to Article 121 of the Constitution, legislation on immigration, emigration, residence and domicile of foreigners, and on granting asylum are federal matters. Foreigners who endanger Switzerland's security may be removed from Switzerland by force.[1]

1. *See* St. Galler Kommentar, Cavelti Urs ad Article 121, 1249–1259.

*632.* However, no person shall be removed by force to a state where he or she is threatened by torture, or other means of cruel and inhuman treatment or punishment (Article 25(3) of the Constitution). Refugees are additionally protected against extradition to states in which they are persecuted (Article 25(2) of the Constitution).[1]

1. *See* St. Galler Kommentar, Breitenmoser Stefan ad Article 25, 322–327.

## II. Further Federal Provisions

*633.* The *Residence and Domicile of Foreigners Act of 26 March 1931* (SR 142.20, cited as Federal Foreigners Act) is the main legal text concerning foreigners. This statute merely provides for general rules and principles, leaving further more detailed regulation to the executive branch. The Federal Council adopted a number of decrees and directives based on the above mentioned statutory delegation. Of special importance is the decree of 6 October 1986 introducing quantitative and qualitative limits on immigration (SR.823.21). The directives issued by the Federal Council, however, are not always published and therefore can be problematic in view of the *Rechtsstaat* principle.

## III. International Law

*634.* International law is becoming an increasingly important source for Swiss immigration law. Switzerland has concluded treaties with eleven countries granting a *right* to domicile after a certain time of residence, and it also has treaties with more than thirty countries to facilitate the obtaining of domicile. Further, international multilateral treaties – e.g., concerning the dispensation of visa obligations, or for the protection of human rights – are gaining importance. The European Convention on Human Rights is in this respect the most important international document. In addition, the bilateral treaties between Switzerland and the European Union concerning the right to free movement for citizens of the European Union will bring far reaching changes and improvements for EU citizens.[1]

1. *See*, *inter alia*, Rhinow, Verfassungsrecht, 63 *et seq.*

## § 2. Access to Swiss Territory

*635.* Unless exceptions are granted, every foreigner needs a valid passport and a visa to enter Switzerland (Decree concerning the Entry and Declaration of Arrival of Foreigners of January 14, 1998, SR 142.211). Additionally he or she must not present a safety hazard to Switzerland, must not have been subjected to a prohibition to enter Switzerland or a measure of expulsion from Switzerland.[1]

1. Malinverni Giorgio, 'Le droit des étrangers', in: Thürer *et al.*, § 63, 982.

## § 3. Residence and Domicile

*636.* Foreigners need an authorization in order to receive the right to reside or to establish domicile on Swiss territory.[1] Unless specially provided by law or international treaty, there is no right to receive such authorization. The authorizations are issued exclusively by the Cantons and are valid only on the territory of the issuing canton. The Federal Government can only grant permits to asylum seekers or can allow in some cases provisional admission. Federal law, however, binds the Cantons by establishing quantitative (contingents) and qualitative (mainly labour related) limits. Additionally, for most authorizations concerning foreigners who are not citizens of the European Union, the Cantons need the approbation of the Federal Government in order to render the authorization valid.

1. *See* Auer/Malinverni/Hottelier, Vol. I, 147–156; Malinverni Giorgio, 'Le droit des étrangers', in: Thürer *et al.*, § 63, 983–984.

*637.* Those who request a working permit are normally issued a single authorization combining the residency and working authorization. In this case, the cantonal labour department has to first give its approval based on the labour market situation. Following approval, the cantonal immigration bureau can then refuse the authorization on non-economic grounds, such as safety concerns.

*638.* Swiss law distinguishes between residency and domicile. The *residence permit* is always limited in time. The *domicile authorization* gives an unlimited and unconditioned right to establish domicile in the canton that issued the authorization. Some international treaties extend the right to domicile to the whole of Switzerland. A domicile authorization is normally granted after five to ten years of residency, and it includes a work permit. Persons married to a Swiss citizen have the right to receive a domicile permit after five years of uninterrupted residence in Switzerland. Minor children and the spouse of a person who was issued a domicile authorization are included under the permit as long as they live in the same household.

## § 4. Removal from Swiss Territory

*639.* As a rule, everyone who does not have a valid authorization to stay in Switzerland and who is not in danger of suffering persecution, cruel and inhumane treatment or punishment in the country to which they would be expelled, can be removed from the territory.[1] The authorization can either have ceased to be valid or the persons never obtained an authorization.

1. *See* Auer/Malinverni/Hottelier, Vol. I, 162–169; Malinverni Giorgio, 'Le droit des étrangers', in: Thürer *et al.*, § 63, 987–988.

*640.* Authorizations of residence are limited in time and therefore *expire* unless they are prolonged. Both authorizations of domicile and of residence can be *revoked* when the person, at the time of applying for the authorization made false declarations. Authorizations of residence can also be revoked when the person's conduct in Switzerland provokes strong complaints.

*641.* Authorizations of residence and domicile will *cease* when the person receives an authorization in a different canton. Authorizations of domicile also cease when the person leaves the country for more than six months (this period can be extended to two years upon demand).

*642.* *Expulsion* is a further reason for authorizations to lose validity. Expulsions can be ordered based on legal, administrative, or political reasoning. As a *legal measure*, expulsion is a supplementary sentence (Article 55 Criminal Code) for crimes punishable with imprisonment or reclusion and it will be declared for three to fifteen years or for life in case of repeat offenders. As an *administrative measure*, expulsion can be ordered by the canton against foreigners who, during their imprisonment or reclusion, demonstrate that they are not willing to adapt to the Swiss public order, who threaten the public order due to mental disease, or who burden Swiss social services on a long term basis. Finally, as a *political measure*, foreigners can be expelled from the country when they are a risk to the internal and external security of Switzerland.

*643.* When the foreigner does not have a valid authorization – either because it was never issued, has expired, was revoked, ceased to be valid, or because the person was ordered expelled – the authorities will set a deadline for the person to leave the canton and/or the country, depending on which authorities – cantonal and/or federal – are setting the deadline.

*644.* When the person does not leave the country voluntarily or is expected to plan to stay illegally, authorities can adopt coercive measures, including detention. When extradition is not possible, illicit, or not reasonable due to practicality considerations, the foreigner will receive a provisionary authorization.

*645.* Except in cases of expulsion, extradition does not include a prohibition or restriction for a future return to Switzerland.

## § 5. Status of Foreigners

*646.* International law fixes minimal standards upon Switzerland, such as a prohibition on imposing military service on foreigners, or arbitrarily expelling foreigners. International law also calls for the recognition of certain fundamental rights.

*647.* According to Swiss law, foreigners have an equal or similar status as Swiss citizens in nearly all fields of law. Restrictions or difference in treatment are only admissible when they are justified by objective reasons.[1]

1. *See* Auer/Malinverni/Hottelier, Vol. I, 156–162; Häfelin & Haller, 371–372.

*648.* On the federal level, *political rights* are limited to Swiss citizens. However, the Cantons can grant political rights for elections and popular referenda in cantonal and communal matters. Until June 2001, only three Cantons accorded or provided the possibility to accord political rights to foreigners. The Canton of Neuchâtel, for example, accords foreigners who have a domicile permit the right to vote on the municipal level after thirteen months of domicile in the canton, but foreigners cannot be elected. The Canton of Jura accords the right to vote and to be elected on the cantonal and municipal levels to foreigners after ten years of domicile in the canton. The Canton of Vaud allows the voting rights of foreigners in its new constitution. The provision should be implemented by April 2003. The Canton of Appenzell Outer Rhodes has foreseen the possibility that the municipalities introduce voting rights to foreigners who demand them and have resided in Switzerland for ten years – five of which must have been in the Canton. Finally, in the Canton of Thurgau, foreigners have a consultative vote on the municipal level.

*649.* As mentioned above, foreigners normally do not have an unlimited right to choose a place of domicile. For persons with a residence permit, economic freedom is limited insofar as the working permit can be granted with conditions. Some professions that demand a special loyalty to and understanding of Switzerland are restricted to Swiss citizens, for instance, the profession of police, judges, and in some Cantons notary public. Today – although not historically – the freedom of expression, assembly, and association are guaranteed to foreigners to the same degree they are guaranteed to Swiss citizens. Until 1998, political speech received only limited freedom of expression protection. It was allowed only with prior authorization.[1]

1. Cf. Decision of the Federal Court, 96 I 266: Unauthorized political speech in which a foreigner criticized the police of the Canton of Zurich was regarded as reason for expulsion.

*650.* To give further examples of differences in treatment: a foreigner cannot hold bonds of the Swiss National Bank, and the majority of the Boards of Directors of a Swiss corporation must have Swiss citizenship and a domicile in Switzerland (Article 708 of the Code of Obligations). Additionally, there are some limits with respect to the acquisition of real estate (authorization requirement according to the Federal Act concerning the acquisition of real estate by foreigners (SR 211.412.4).

*651.* As a general rule, foreigners with a domicile permit and, in some cases, persons with a residence permit can invoke the right to reunion of the family. This right is anchored both in Article 17(2) of the Federal Foreigners Act (and in Article 8 of the European Convention on Human Rights (Article 8).

# Chapter 5. Judicial Control of Administrative Action

## § 1. Overview

*652.* The purpose of this chapter is to discuss the forms of administrative process that are subject to judicial control (*infra*, § 2), and the basic structure of the administrative process and its administrative control (*infra*, § 3). The last part of the chapter will deal with the most important instrument of judicial control of administrative action before the Federal Court: the Administrative Court Action (*infra*, § 4).

## § 2. Forms of the Administrative Process

### I. Overview of the Forms of the Administrative Process

#### *A. Overview*

*653.* *Action* is one of the main features of the administration and one of the legitimizing elements of its existence. The implementation of these multiple and complex administrative tasks, prescribed by law, must follow *standardized types* of procedures and forms. The most important forms of administrative action in Swiss administrative law are the *administrative order* and, to a much lesser extent, the *public contract.*

*654.* Other forms of administrative action, such as an *administrative plan* (especially in zoning law) or an *actus realis*, are not mentioned by the Administrative Procedure Act (although they are important in practice). The emergence of new forms of administrative action, such as *cooperative informal action as a particularly important form of the actus realis,* e.g., gentlemen's agreements or arrangements between the administration and the addressee(s), still is a dogmatically unexplored area in administrative law. *See* for such cooperative agreements, for example, Articles 9–11 of the Federal Price Control Act (SR 942.20), Articles 29–30 and 37 of the Federal Antitrust Act (SR 251) or Article 41a of the Federal Environmental Protection Act (SR 814.01).

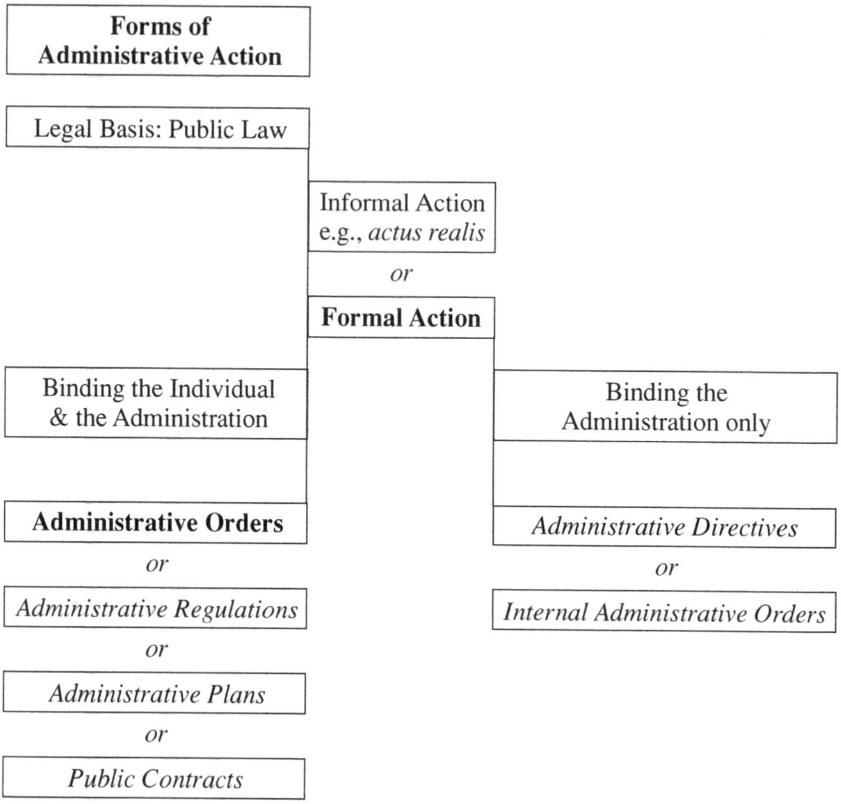


*655.* One main problem of practical importance connected with the emergence of new forms of administrative action is the insufficiency of the set of available judicial remedies. The Administrative Procedure Act focuses exclusively on *administrative orders as a prototype form of administrative action* (Article 5 of the Administrative Procedure Act). An Administrative Court Action is only available against administrative orders based upon Federal law (Article 97 of the Federal Judicial Act).

## *B. The Administrative Order*

### 1. The Centrality of the Administrative Order

*656.* The administrative order is the most important instrument of the administrative process.[1] Swiss administrative law is deeply influenced by French and German administrative law, especially by the theory of the *acte administratif.* According to the Swiss concept, agency action can only be brought before court in cases where the administrative procedure has been declared terminated in substance as in form, followed by the issuance of an administrative order.

1. *See, inter alia*, with further references: Fleiner-Gerster, 157 *et seq.*; Häfelin & Müller, 177 *et seq.*; Kölz & Häner, 71–79; Moor, 151 *et seq.*; Rhinow *et al.*, 186–189; Tschannen *et al.*, 156 *et seq.*; Zimmerli *et al.*, 37 *et seq.*

*657.* According to Article 97 of the Federal Judicial Act, the most important remedy against administrative action – the Administrative Court Action – is only available if there is an administrative order. Hence, the definition of an administrative order is crucial to Swiss administrative law – as it was in Germany in the late 1960s before the introduction of the theory of subjective public rights (*subjektive öffentliche Rechte*).

## 2. The Definition of the Administrative Order

*658.* Article 5 of the Federal Administrative Procedure Act provides a legal definition of the administrative order. According to this central provision, an administrative order is the *final and unilateral decision of an agency*, in a *concrete and individual case*, imposing upon the individual a set of *obligations* or granting a set of *rights*, based upon *federal public law*. According to Article 5(3) of the Administrative Procedure Act, an administrative order is not required if:

(1) it is *excluded* by statute; or
(2) the statute entitles the agency to *act in another form* of the administrative process, e.g., in the form of a public contract (Article 49(c) of the Federal Expropriation Act [SR 511] or Articles 16(2) and 19 of the Federal Subsidy Act [SR 616.1]).[1]

1. For more detail *see*: Fleiner-Gerster, 157 *et seq.*; Häfelin & Müller, 177 *et seq.*; Kölz & Häner, 71–79; Moor, 151 *et seq.*; Rhinow *et al.*, 188 *et seq.*; Tschannen *et al.*, 156 *et seq.*; Zimmerli *et al.*, 37 *et seq.*

## 3. Element of the Definition: An *Agency*

*659.* Article 1(2) of the Administrative Procedure Act determines which *agencies* must decide in the form of an administrative order, e.g., the Federal Council, the Federal Departments, the Federal Chancery, the Federal Administration, Federal Commissions, independent federal enterprises, or other organs outside the Federal Administration implementing delegated tasks of the Confederation, based upon public law.

## 4. Element of the Definition: *Unilateral* Decision

*660.* The administrative order as defined in Article 5 of the Administrative Procedure Act is a final and unilateral decision. The requirement that the agency give its order unilaterally does not imply that the agency can take its decision without the participation of the concerned individual(s). On the contrary, the parties concerned dispose of a set of multiple participatory rights (Articles 18, 26, 29, 31, and 33(1) of the Administrative Procedure Act). However, the power to make a unilateral decision means that the agency is authorized to issue an administrative order regardless of the parties' approval. Furthermore, the unilateral decision-making power is dogmatically necessary to distinguish the administrative order from contracts based upon public or private law.

5. Element of the Definition: Individual and Concrete Case

*661.* The administrative order is a unilateral decision in an individual and concrete case. From a dogmatic perspective, this element is necessary to distinguish the administrative order from *rules*. The administrative order determines the rights and duties of a single addressee or a determined and limited number of addressees, whereas rules are *general*, binding everyone. Furthermore, the administrative order deals with a *concrete* set of facts that have already occurred in a determined place and in a determined time, whereas rules are abstract, applying to an indeterminable, and yet virtual, plurality of facts.

6. Element of the Definition: *Binding* Decision of an Agency

*662.* The administrative order determines the *legal relationship* between the addressee(s) and the administration with binding (executory) force. The content of the legal relationship is the creation, modification or termination of rights and duties (Article 5(1)(a) of the Administrative Procedure Act), or the determination of the (non-) existence, or the extent of rights and duties (Article 5(1)(b) of the Administrative Procedure Act), or petitions of the addressee (to create, modify, terminate rights or duties or determine their (non-) existence) inadmissible in substance or in form (Article 5(1)(c) of the Administrative Procedure Act). The *element of the binding legal force* of the administrative order is dogmatically necessary to distinguish the administrative order from the *actus realis*, which is *merely factual*, lacking a legal relationship between the addressee(s) and the administration (e.g., recommendations, cautions, declarations of intent, reports and other administrative forms of communication and information).

7. Element of the Definition: Based Upon Federal Public Law

*663.* The administrative order must have its legal basis in federal public law. Determining whether the legal basis is federal or cantonal public law is sometimes difficult and complex and has an *important impact upon the available remedy before the Federal Court*. The judicial remedy against administrative orders based upon cantonal public law is the Public Law Action (Article 84 *et seq.* of the Federal Judicial Act, *see supra*, Part IV, Chapter 2, § 4, III.), whereas an Administrative

Court Action is available against administrative orders based upon federal public law (Article 97 *et seq.* of the Federal Judicial Act, *see infra*, § 4, II.).

*C. The Public Contract*

*664.* Although the administrative order is the most important instrument of administrative action, the administration can also act in the form of public contracts, which are bilateral agreements between at least two legal subjects in order to create a concrete administrative relationship based upon public law. Provisions concerning the creation of contracts of the Code of Obligations are applicable *per analogiam*; there are no special or formal requirements and the Administrative Procedure Act is not applicable.

*665.* Public contracts are only admissible in cases where the use of an administrative order is inadequate. Hence, public contracts are *subsidiary* to administrative orders and rather rare in practice.[1]

1. *See* Moor, 351–430; Häfelin & Müller, 217–237 (with further references).

## § 3. The Structure of the Administrative Process and its Administrative Control

### I. Overview

*666.* The administrative process and its judicial control is divided into three stages:

*First*, the administrative process of preparing, formulating and issuing the administrative order (adjudication) and, in the absence of an appeal, the enforcement of the order (*see infra*, II.).

*Second*, in case the order is contested in substance or in form, the relevant Administrative Procedure Act determines the procedure of appeal before an (internal and hierarchically superior) administrative body (*see infra*, III.).

*Third*, the judicial control of the regularity of the administrative action before a cantonal Administrative Court or the Federal Court (*infra*, § 4). It is one of the basic goals of judicial reform to prevent cases that cannot be brought before a judicial instance.

### II. The Process of Adjudication

*667.* The general process of adjudication is determined by Articles 1–43 of the Federal Administrative Procedure Act.[1] Special statutory provisions may provide for a different procedural framework, e.g., special procedural provisions concerning hearings in Asylum Law. However, such derogations may not be contrary to the general process of adjudication of the Federal Administrative Procedure Act.

1. *See, inter alia,* with further references: Fleiner-Gerster, 191 *et seq.*; Häfelin & Müller, 341 *et seq.*; Kölz & Häner, 83 *et seq.*; Moor, 181 *et seq.*; Rhinow *et al.*, 211 *et seq.*; Tschannen *et al.*, 183 *et seq.*

*668.* The basic principles of the process of adjudication are set out in Articles 7–43 of the Federal Administrative Procedure Act. Apart from the special statutory provisions of the Act, these provisions are equally applicable to the procedure of appeal before an administrative body.

*669.* The process of adjudication is divided into four stages:

(1) the preliminary stage;
(2) the investigation;
(3) the decision as a result of the fact-finding process; and
(4) the execution.

## *A. The Preliminary Stage of Adjudication*

*670.* During the preliminary stage of the process of adjudication the agency must examine its *competence* for the matter concerned.[1] An agreement of competency (prorogation) between the agency and the party is inadmissible (Article 7 of the Federal Administrative Procedure Act). Furthermore, the agency must examine possible personal conflicts ('Ausstandsregeln') (Article 10 of the Federal Administrative Procedure Act) and verify the capacity of the individual as a party as well as a participant in the process of adjudication (Articles 6 and 48 of the Federal Administrative Procedure Act).

1. *See* Kölz & Häner, 83–89; Rhinow *et al.*, 213–217.

## *B. The Investigation*

*671.* During the investigatory phase of the process of adjudication the agency must establish the relevant facts of the case (Articles 12–19 of the Federal Administrative Procedure Act).[1] It is a main feature of European continental administrative law that the process of adjudication be characterized by the *inquisitory principle*, which holds that the agency is not bound by the facts brought forward by the parties. In theory, the agency must find the relevant facts itself and prove their existence (so-called principle of substantive truth). Admissible evidence in Swiss administrative law includes public writings, statements made by the party, or by a non-party, inspections, and expert testimony (Article 12 of the Federal Administrative Procedure Act).[2]

1. *See, inter alia,* Fleiner-Gerster, 200–207; Häfelin & Müller, 344–345, 352–358; Kölz & Häner, 96–120 (with further references); Moor, 255 *et seq.*; Rhinow *et al.*, 217 *et seq.*; Tschannen *et al.*, 190–193.

2. *See* Kölz Alfred, *Prozessmaximen im schweizerischen Verwaltungsprozess*, 2nd ed., Schulthess, Zurich 1974, 93 *et seq.*, 128 *et seq.*

*672.* However, the inquisitory principle does not imply that the parties are completely dispensed from the *obligation to participate* in the fact-finding process. A party can even be statutorily obliged to participate in the process of investigation, as a violation of duty to participate, can result in the agency not deciding the matter (Article 13 of the Federal Administrative Procedure Act).

*673.* Furthermore, by granting the *right to a hearing* (Article 29 of the Federal Administrative Procedure Act), the agency has to determine the parties' legal position and establish the *applicable law*.

### *C. The Decision*

*674.* An administrative order resulting from the agencies' investigatory process must contain a description of relevant facts as well as an explanation of legal grounds for the decision. According to Article 34(1) of the Federal Administrative Procedure Act, an administrative order must be issued *in writing* as a prerequisite for its validity.

*675.* According to Article 70 of the Constitution, the *official languages* of the Confederation are German, French, and Italian. Romansh is one of the official languages of communication with Romansh-speaking people. Consequently, federal administrative orders have to be written in the official language of the party who has made the request (or who could possibly make a request). Administrative orders issued by the last cantonal instance must be written in the official language of the canton (Article 37 of the Federal Administrative Procedure Act). The non-observance of the language provisions affects the *validity* of the administrative order insofar as the material legal effect of the order and the running of the statute of limitations are suspended (Article 38 of the Federal Administrative Procedure Act).

*676.* Moreover, the order must inform the addressee of the existence of remedies, the competent administrative body or court, and the running of the statute of limitations (Article 35 of the Federal Administrative Procedure Act). According to the Federal Court, should the agency gives *inadequate or even wrong information of the available remedy*, the principle of good faith does not protect an addressee who might have found the error with due diligence (Decision of the Federal Court 124 I 255, 258; 112 Ib 417, 422). Good faith does protect the addressee of an administrative order against the *wrong indication of the statute of limitations*. Nonetheless, the protection of good faith is not available if the addressee is a lawyer and could have easily found the error by studying the relevant legal provisions (Decision of the Federal Court 117 Ia 421, 423).

*D. The Execution of an Administrative Order*

*677.* As a rule, if the individual does not act within thirty days after the issuance of the order and if the individual does not appeal to higher authorities against the order, it can then be enforced like a judgment after the thirty-day period has elapsed. Therefore, it is possible for an order to be enforced even though the order itself or its preparation procedure was unlawful.[1]

1. *See* Rhinow *et al.*, 227–228.

## III. Administrative Control of the Process of Adjudication

*A. Overview*

*678.* According to the still valid legal framework (*see supra*, Part II, Chapter 5, § 2, II., B., 4.), an administrative order issued by a federal agency can be subject to an appeal before a superior federal agency (the Department), or, in the case of an existing legal basis, before an Administrative Tribunal (e.g., in asylum law cases). Subsequently, on the federal level, the decisions of the Department or the Administrative Tribunal can be brought with an Administrative Court Action before the Federal Court. Most Cantons have followed this concept of a combined internal administrative and judicial administrative control.[1]

1. *See, inter alia*, with further references: Fleiner-Gerster, 216 *et seq.*; Häfelin & Müller, 364 *et seq.*; Kölz & Häner, 170 *et seq.*; Moor, 503 *et seq.*, 527 *et seq.*; Rhinow *et al.*, 233 *et seq.*; Zimmerli *et al.*, 90 *et seq.*

*679.* Articles 44 *et seq.* of the Federal Administrative Procedure Act contain relevant provisions for the internal administrative control of agency action. The cantonal process of internal administrative control of agency action is usually enacted in the cantonal Administrative Judiciary Acts.

*B. Impact of Judiciary Reform*

*680.* One of the basic innovations of judiciary reform is the creation of a new *Federal Administrative Court*, which is to be seated in the city of St. Gallen. This court shall have jurisdiction as a first instance over administrative orders issued by federal agencies – replacing *in general* the process of internal administrative control of administrative action unless a statutory provision first allows for an appeal before an internal administrative body. Unless a special statute rules otherwise, the decisions of the Federal Administrative Court can be reviewed by the Federal Court. The abolition of the internal administrative control of cantonal administrative orders is also a trend that can be observed in the Cantons (e.g., in the Canton of Zurich). However, there is considerable opposition against this pillar of judiciary reform.

*681.* Since the future of the internal administrative control of agency action is still uncertain, the following paragraphs will briefly present the available formal and informal remedies.

### *C. The Ambivalent Nature of Internal Administrative Control*

*682.* According to Article 49 of the Federal Administrative Procedure Act, in case of an administrative complaint, the supervising organ of the process of internal administrative control can subject an agency decision to an *extensive* factual and legal control and also review *discretionary elements* of the agencies' decision. Furthermore, an agency decision can be overruled on the grounds of *inappropriateness*.

*683.* The main advantage of internal control of administrative action is that the controlling administrative instance can immediately correct undue practices of agency action or misapplications of the applicable law. However, the fact that the controlling organ is itself a part of the agency – in most cases it will be the superior administrative level of the agency that issued the order – may also affect the *impartiality* of the controlling body. It could occur that the objectivity and neutrality of the superior instance may be overshadowed by a certain solidarity with the inferior decision-making instance. This is one of the main reasons why judiciary reform provides for the abolition of internal administrative control.

### *D. Formal and Informal Remedies*

*684.* The available remedies for the internal control of agency action are divided into two categories, formal and informal remedies, which differ completely from each other in form and substance.

#### 1. Formal Remedies

*685.* *Formal remedies* of internal administrative control oblige the controlling organ to issue a formal and binding decision, which is comparable to a judgment. Formal remedies are bound to certain formal requirements and to the statute of limitations. The available formal remedies are an administrative complaint (*Verwaltungsbeschwerde*), an administrative objection (*Einsprache*), and a request for revision (*Revisionsgesuch*). In case of an administrative complaint, the controlling organ is usually an administrative instance hierarchically superior to the agency that issued the administrative order. The agency that issued the administrative order has jurisdiction over administrative objections and requests for revision.

##### a. The Administrative Complaint

*686.* The *administrative complaint* is by far the most important remedy of internal administrative control of administrative orders (Article 5(1)(c) of the Federal Administrative Procedure Act).

The rules concerning standing correspond with the Administrative Court Action (*see infra*, § 4, II.).

*687.* According to Article 49 of the Federal Administrative Procedure Act, the administrative complaint is available in cases of violation of federal provisions, including the violation of federal constitutional law, misapplication of agency discretion, wrong or incomplete determination of relevant facts, and inappropriateness of the decision. The latter is especially unique, because it is only in very limited and rare cases that the Federal Court will squash an administrative order on the grounds of inappropriateness.

*688.* As a general rule, an administrative complaint suspends the execution of an administrative order (Article 55 of the Federal Administrative Procedure Act). However, the decision-making agency or the controlling body can deny suspension of the administrative order – e.g., in all cases where the administrative order does *not* deal with a pecuniary debt of the addressee of the order. According to the Federal Court, denying suspension of an order following an administrative complaint can result only after weighing public versus private interests (Decision of the Federal Court 127 II 132, 137).

b. The Administrative Objection and the Request for Revision

*689.* An *administrative objection* is a formal remedy that is only available if provided for by statute (e.g., in construction and taxation law). An administrative order will be re-examined by the agency that issued the order.

*690.* Citizens have a very limited right to ask for a *revision* of an administrative order. According to Article 66(2) of the Federal Administrative Procedure Act, it is up to the addressee of the administrative order to prove (1) the existence of new relevant evidence, (2) that the controlling organ did not take into account important facts relevant to its case, (3) that it violated the right to a hearing, or (4) that the authority issuing the order was composed of members having a direct personal interest in the matter.

2. Informal Remedies

*691.* Two informal remedies are available: (1) a request for reconsideration (*Wiedererwägungsgesuch*) or (2) a complaint before the supervisory authority (*Aufsichtsbeschwerde*). Contrary to formal remedies, the agency is not obliged to treat the case. Furthermore, there are no requirements regarding the form and no statute of limitations has to be observed. A request for reconsideration is treated by the decision-making agency, whereas a complaint is heard before the (hierarchically superior) supervisory authority. The main focus of the Federal Administrative Procedure Act is on formal remedies with the exception of Article 71, which allows for complaints before the supervisory authority.

## § 4. The Judicial Control of Administrative Action

### I. Overview

*692.* Administrative action can be reviewed either by ordinary administrative courts or by special administrative courts. *Ordinary administrative courts* have general jurisdiction over all administrative cases and controversies. From an organizational perspective, ordinary administrative courts either form an independent and autonomous part of the judiciary (e.g., in the Canton of Zurich), or are part of the superior cantonal ordinary courts, which also have jurisdiction over civil and criminal cases. The Federal Court belongs to the latter category because its public law department has jurisdiction over public law and administrative law cases.[1]

1. *See* Häfelin & Müller, 389.

*693.* *Special administrative courts* have limited jurisdiction in a certain area of administrative law defined by statute (e.g., in the field of zoning and construction law, social security law, takings, or immigration law). On the Federal level, social security cases are heard by an autonomous section of the Federal Court, the Federal Assurance Court in Lucerne (Article 122 *et seq.* of the Judicial Act). Furthermore, different Administrative Tribunals are granted judicial independence and have special jurisdiction over cases in various areas of administrative law, such as asylum, customs, and certain areas of administrative economic law. Under the new judiciary reform, the Federal Administrative Court will replace the numerous Administrative Tribunals.

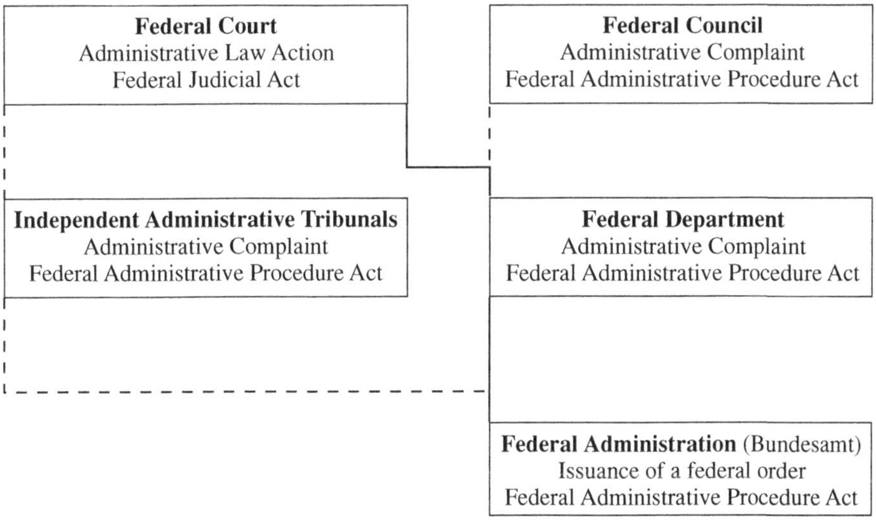


*694.* The reform will abolish internal administrative control of agency action. According to Article 74(a) of the Federal Administrative Procedure Act, the Federal Council can hear cases if the Administrative Law Action before the Federal Court is inadmissible.

*695.* Generally, under the judiciary reform, the existing quasi-judicial competence of the Federal Council shall be abolished. The Federal Council is primarily a political body and its jurisdiction can be considered in conflict with Article 29(a) of the Constitution and Article 6 of the European Convention on Human Rights. However, a proposal of the Federal Senate provides for the Federal Council to continue hearing cases against administrative orders in the field of national and international security, neutrality, diplomatic protection and other matters of foreign affairs. The statute may create a new competency for the Federal Council.

*696.* Considering the currently available judicial remedies against administrative action on the federal level, the most important remedy is an *Administrative Court Action* before the Federal Court. The reform provides for a merger of the Administrative Court Action and the Public Law Action into one single remedy in order to facilitate the complicated current system of remedies before the Federal Court.

## II. The Administrative Court Action before the Federal Court

### *A. Generally*

*697.* According to Article 97 of the Judicial Act, the Federal Court has jurisdiction as last instance for *administrative orders based upon federal law* (Article 5 of the Federal Administrative Procedure Act). In the event of the existence of a Federal administrative order, the Court will first examine which lower authority, e.g., one of the Administrative Tribunals, the Departments, or the Federal agencies, has issued or reviewed the order. The Court will then examine whether the administrative order deals in substance and in form with a matter falling within the *negative list* of Articles 99–101 of the Judicial Act. The extensive and very detailed negative list excludes the review of an administrative order for various reasons, which also includes the highly or purely technical nature of the issue, or political reasons. If the administrative order falls within the negative list, the Administrative Court Action is excluded (although an administrative complaint before the Federal Council is eventually available, Articles 72–74 of the Federal Administrative Procedure Act).[1]

1. *See*, *inter alia*, with further references: Häfelin & Müller, 396 *et seq.*; Kölz & Häner, 298 *et seq.*; Moor, 588 *et seq.*; Rhinow *et al.*, 278 *et seq.*; Zimmerli *et al.*, 62 *et seq.*

### *B. The Distinction between Administrative Court Action and Public Law Action*

*698.* The distinction between an Administrative Court Action and a Public Law Action is complex in practice.[1] *See* generally for the Public Law Action, *supra*, Part IV, Chapter 2, § 4, III. As a general rule, a Public Law Action against *cantonal* orders or decisions regarding the violation of constitutional freedom and liberties is only *subsidiarily* available (Article 84(2) of the Judicial Act). If an administrative order *based upon federal law* violates the citizens' constitutional freedoms and liberties, the available remedy is an Administrative Court Action – not a Public Law Action. Moreover, only federal administrative orders can be the litigated object of an Administrative Court Action, whereas a Public Law Action is available for litigated administrative orders as well as for *cantonal statutes and rules.*

1. *See* Zimmerli *et al.*, 287–292; Kälin Walter & Müller Markus, 'Vom ungeklärten Verhätnis zwischen Verwaltungsgerichtsbeschwerde und staatsrechtlicher Beschwerde', in *Schweizerisches Zentralblatt für Staats- und Verwaltungsrecht* (ZBl) 1993, 433 *et seq.*, Moor, 576 *et seq.*

### *C. Administrative Orders as Main Object of Litigation*

*699.* As a general rule, the litigated administrative order must be based upon federal administrative law (Article 97 of the Judicial Act). In practice, as the Administrative Court Action is less rigid than the Public Law Action and therefore preferred by lawyers, the term 'based upon Federal administrative law' has led to a complex case law. An Administrative Law Action is also available against:

(1) cantonal administrative orders *that should have been based upon federal administrative law* (e.g., Decision of the Federal Court, 127 II 1, 3);
(2) cantonal administrative orders based upon dependent cantonal executory laws *purely in implementation of exhaustive federal laws* (e.g., Decision of the Federal Court, 126 II 171, 173); or
(3) administrative orders based upon cantonal law which have a *narrow substantive nexus* with federal administrative law (e.g., Decision of the Federal Court, 123 II 359, 361).[1]

1. *See* Moor, 581–588.

*700.* Furthermore, the distinction between independent and dependent cantonal executory laws is particularly complex in the areas of zoning and taxation, where the Confederation can only establish principles on zoning and the harmonization of taxes (Articles 75(1) and 129(1) of the Constitution).

### *D. Grounds for the Action*

*701.* According to Article 104 of the Judicial Act, the main grounds for the Administrative Court Action are:

(1) the violation of federal (constitutional) law, including the excess or abuse of discretionary powers;
(2) wrong or incomplete factual findings, if a previous reviewing court has determined the relevant facts either in a manifestly wrong or incomplete manner, or in violation of essential procedural provisions (Article 105(2) of the Judicial Act); or
(3) in very rare cases, the Court can review administrative orders for inappropriateness.[1]

1. *See, inter alia*, with further references: Häfelin & Müller, 400–402; Kölz & Häner, 335–341; Moor, 660 *et seq.*; Rhinow *et al.*, 289–291; Zimmerli *et al.*, 90 *et seq.*

*E. Standing*

*702.* The standing requirements for internal administrative control of agency action and an Administrative Court Action are basically identical. Whereas cantonal administrative procedures can be taken before Federal Court with the remedy of the Administrative Court Action, cantonal administrative provisions concerning standing may not be narrower than the standing provisions for the Administrative Court Action (Article 98(a)(3) of the Judicial Act). The judiciary reform will not change the provisions concerning standing.

1. Standing of the Addressee of the Administrative Order and Third-party Standing

*703.* According to Article 103(a) of the Judicial Act, an addressee of an administrative order has standing for an Administrative Court Action if one: (a) is *affected* by the administrative order in question; and (b) has a *legitimate interest to be protected by the Court* to remove or modify the administrative order. The legitimate interest to be protected by the Court can be based upon *legal* grounds or – contrary to the standing requirement for the Public Law Action (*supra*, Part IV, Chapter 2, § 4, III, B, 2.) – can be merely *factual* (e.g., economical or ideal grounds). Since the presence of a factual legitimate interest to be protected by the Court is sufficient, third parties may take action against an administrative order as well, if their relationship to the administrative order at stake is *special, remarkable, and sufficiently close* (e.g., Decision of the Federal Court, 123 II 376, 378).[1]

1. *See, inter alia,* with further references: Häfelin & Müller, 402–404; Kölz & Häner, 324 *et seq.*; Moor, 626 *et seq.*; Zimmerli *et al.*, 115–125.

2. Agency Standing

*704.* According to Article 103(b) of the Judicial Act, the federal departments and agencies competent to issue an order (and to review it in the process of internal administrative control) have standing for an Administrative Court Action. In addition, the standing of federal agencies must be provides for by federal law, as the standing of cantonal or municipal agencies must be allowed for by a special statute (e.g., Article 34(2) of the Federal Zoning Law, granting Administrative Court Action standing to the Cantons and their municipalities). Authorities listed in Article 103(b) of the Judicial Act have standing only in cases or controversies against agencies *outside the federal administration*, such as the Federal Administrative Tribunals, or the supreme cantonal instances.[1]

1. *See, inter alia,* with further references: Häfelin & Müller, 404; Kölz & Häner, 325–328; Moor, 650–653; Zimmerli *et al.*, 125–127.

3. Standing of Associations

*705.* Associations have standing either as:

(1) a party affected by an administrative order;
(2) a third party; or
(3) in the interest of their members.

Furthermore, standing for the preservation of public interests – so-called *ideal standing* – is granted to certain associations (Article 103(c) of the Judicial Act). Ideal standing is only granted to associations expressly authorized by federal law, such as national environmental organizations, which:

(1) have been founded at least ten years before the Administrative Court Action is heard before the Federal Court;
(2) are challenging federal or cantonal administrative orders;
(3) involve an administrative order concerning the planning, erection or modification of non-removable constructions; and
(4) satisfy an environmental compatibility test, based upon Article 55(1) of the Federal Environmental Protection Act. National associations for the protection of nature or monuments must fulfil similar requirements to get ideal standing for an Administrative Court Action.[1,2]

1. *See*, *inter alia*, with further references: Häfelin & Müller, 404–406; Kölz & Häner, 328–329; Moor, 653–659; Zimmerli *et al.*, 128–134.
2. *Rechtsstaat principle* v. *economic freedom and democratic principle*? The ideal standing of associations is a highly and emotionally debated issue in Swiss politics. On September 7, 2003, the people of the Canton of Zurich voted with a clear majority for the construction of a new stadium for the European Soccer Championship 2008. They approved a private special zoning plan allowing derogations from the general zoning regime ('privater Gestaltungsplan' in the sense of §§ 83–87 of the Zurich Zoning and Construction Law) and the transfer of land to a private investor. Owing to the investor's plans to use the premises of the stadium also for leisure facilities, such as a shopping center and a cinema complex, the Traffic Club of Switzerland, an association with ideal standing in the meaning of Article 55 of the Federal Environmental Protection Act, and other affected residents and interest groups protested against the project on the basis of not unfounded concern about expected increased traffic flows to and around the new stadium. The administrative appeal before the Zurich Administrative Court was insofar successful for the petitioners as the court essentially held that the projected traffic flows to the stadium are above the legally permitted maximum and must therefore be reduced to a lower level in conformity with the law. The private investors claiming, *inter alia*, that a reduction of the traffic flow to the stadium would put the profitability of the project into question, appealed before the Federal Court. Tragically, Zurich might not be able to co-host the European Soccer Championship 2008. – The neuralgic points concerning the institution of ideal standing of associations could be summarized as follows: (1) *Economic liberty* v. *Rechtsstaat principle*: Private investors claim that associations with ideal standing are trying to block *per se* investments and the realization of major construction project, especially shopping centers. Associations with ideal standing argue that litigation could be avoided if the private sector presented projects in conformity with the law. Note the cases decided in favor of associations with ideal standing (e.g., Decisions of the Federal Court 124 II 272; 124 II 75; 122 II 81; 118 Ib 599). (2) *Democratic principle* v. *Rechtsstaat principle*: If a project is not in conformity with the law, a minority of affected petitioners can reverse the outcome of a popular vote (in the Zurich stadium case, a clear majority of 60 per cent voted for the project.) Proposals to withdraw ideal standing to challenge

democratic decisions are being discussed in Federal Parliament. *See* for the antagonistic relationship between the democratic principle and the *Rechtsstaat* principle, *supra*, General Introduction, Chapter II, § 1 and 3. (3) The concept of ideal standing of associations is a logical consequence of the Swiss concept of judicial review of administrative action which is predominantly based upon the question whether the legal order and the public interest as such have been violated by the administrative action (objective control), rather than the rights of individuals (subjective control, Individualrechtsschutzkontrolle.).

### *F. Statute of Limitation*

*706.* An Administrative Court Action must be filed before the Federal Court within thirty days after the issuance of an administrative order (Article 106(1) of the Judicial Act).

### *G. Effects of the Action*

*707.* Contrary to internal administrative control of administrative action (Article 55 of the Federal Administrative Procedure Act), an Administrative Court Action before the Federal Court normally does not suspend an administrative order (Article 111 of the Judicial Act). A suspension of an order is only provided for in cases of administrative orders obliging the addressee to pay a sum of money. Furthermore, suspension of an administrative order may be granted either upon the initiative of the President of the competent Chamber of the Federal Court, or upon the request of a party.

# Part V. Specific Problems

## Chapter 1. War, Treaty, and Foreign Affairs Powers

### § 1. War Powers

#### I. The Swiss Army as Militia

*708.* Switzerland has no professional army. Rather, its army is organized as a militia, whose main functions, due to the principle of neutrality (*supra* General Introduction, Chapter 2, § 3), are the prevention of war, maintenance of peace, defence of the country and the protection of the population. It also supports civil authorities in efforts to repel serious threats to internal security or other exceptional circumstances (Article 58(2) of the Constitution).[1]

1. *See* St. Galler Kommentar, Meyer Hansjörg ad Article 58, 726–733.

*709.* According to Article 59 of the Constitution, every Swiss man must render military service. In the case of non-observation of this fundamental obligation (*Grundpflicht*), Article 81 of the Federal Military Penal Act allows for imprisonment of up to eighteen months. While alternative service is possible, it lasts longer than the military service. Military service is voluntary for Swiss women. Regarding the participation of members of the Army in international peace-keeping operations *see*, *supra*, General Introduction, Chapter 2, § 3.

#### II. Threats to National Security

*710.* The deployment of the Army is a federal matter. The Federal Council is entitled to take measures to secure the external security, independence, and neutrality of Switzerland (Article 185(1) of the Constitution).[1]

1. *See* Ruch Alexander, 'Äussere und innere Sicherheit', in: Thürer *et al.*, § 56.

*711.* According to Article 168(1) of the Constitution, in cases of external threats to national security, if a larger contingent of troops is assigned or ordered to combat, *Federal Parliament must elect the General of the Swiss Army* (Article 85(1) of the Federal Military Act, SR 510.10), who is then the Commander-in-Chief of the Army. Until his election, however, the control of the military remains in the hands of the Federal Council, to be used on a provisionary basis (Article

85(2) of the Federal Military Act). After the General's election, the Federal Council remains the supreme organ of the executive branch giving the General his commission (Article 86 of the Federal Military Act). The General is elected only in the event of, and only during the time of a major external threats to national security. The last General was General Henri Guisan, elected in 30 August 1939.

*712.* For reactions to internal threats to cantonal or national security, *see supra* Part III, Chapter 2, § 1, III.

## § 2. Treaty Powers

### I. Overview

*713.* According to Article 54 of the Constitution, treaty powers are a *federal matter*. Due to this extensive competency, the Confederation is entitled to conclude treaties – based upon international public law – concerning matters that would normally fall within the competencies of the Cantons, such as taxation, police, or education. However, the Cantons may participate in the decisions of foreign policy that concern their powers or their essential interests. This implies that the Confederation must inform the concerned Cantons in a full and timely manner, as well as consult them. The position of the Cantons has particular weight when the treaty concerns their powers. Whenever appropriate, the Cantons are entitled to participate in international negotiations.[1]

1. *See* St. Galler Kommentar, Ehrenzeller *et al.* ad Article 54, 659 *et seq.*; Häfelin & Haller, 554 *et seq.*; Müller Georg, 'Rechtssetzung und Staatsverträge', in: Thürer *et al.*, § 70; Rhinow, 355 *et seq.*; Rhinow, Verfassungsrecht, 584 *et seq.*

### II. Procedure for the Conclusion of Treaties

#### *A. Negotiation and Approval*

*714.* According to Article 184 of the Constitution, the Federal Council represents Switzerland abroad. With respect to the participatory rights of Federal Parliament (Article 166(1) of the Constitution), the Federal Council conducts foreign relations, nominates and instructs the Swiss delegation, and grants authorization to the members of the delegation to sign the negotiated treaty.

*715.* Treaties based upon international public law are subject to approval by Federal Parliament, which has the authority to only accept or reject the treaty (Articles 166(2) and 184(2) of the Constitution). Although the approval by Federal Parliament is a necessary prerequisite for the ratification of the treaty, it does not constitute a binding commission for the Federal Council to ratify it. The Federal Council may refrain from ratifying the treaty, even after approval by Federal Parliament.[1]

1. *See* Häfelin & Haller, 556–558; St. Galler Kommentar, Thürer Daniel ad Article 184, 1838–1839.

*B. Optional and Mandatory Referendum for International Treaties*

*716.* International treaties are subject to an *optional referendum* if they are:

(1) of unlimited duration and may not be terminated;
(2) provide for entry into an international organization; or
(3) involve a multilateral unification of law, such as the bilateral treaties between the Swiss Confederation and the European Union or the European Convention on Human Rights (Article 141(1)(d)(1)–(3) of the Constitution).[1]

1. *See* St. Galler Kommentar, Thürer Daniel ad Article 141, 1499–1502.

*717.* These categories of international treaties are submitted to the vote of the People, at the request of either 50,000 Swiss citizens entitled to vote or of eight Cantons (Article 141(1) of the Constitution).

*718.* Furthermore, Federal Parliament may submit further international treaties outside the scope of Article 141(1)(d) of the Constitution to an optional referendum.

*719.* The main difference between an optional and a *mandatory referendum* is that the latter is *decided by the majority of the People and the Cantons.* According to Article 140(1)(b) of the Constitution, the People and the Cantons must decide on the entry of the Swiss Confederation into organizations for collective security, such as the United Nations, or into supranational communities, such as the European Union.

*720.* In 16 March 1986, the Swiss People and the Cantons rejected the entry of the Swiss Confederation into the United Nations. But in a second mandatory referendum, in 3 March 2002, Switzerland became the 190th member of the United Nations.

*721.* On 6 December 1992, the Swiss People and the Cantons rejected the entry of Switzerland into the European Economic Community. Although this agreement did not constitute a supranational organization within the meaning of Article 140(1)(b) of the Constitution, the question was submitted to the People and the Cantons as a mandatory referendum due to its important impact upon the Swiss economy and political system.[1]

1. *See* Häfelin & Haller, 559.

*C. Ratification and Publication*

*722.* Upon ratification, the international treaty gains binding force under international public law. Ratification is within the powers of the Federal Council (Article 184(2) of the Constitution).

*723.* Because Switzerland has adopted the monistic system, further transformation is not required. As a rule, international treaties must be published in the

Official Register of Federal Law (Article 2 of the Federal Publication Act). Upon publication, the self-executing provisions of the international treaty gain binding force for the individual (Article 10 of the Federal Publication Act).

| | | |
|---|---|---|
| Negotiations | Federal Council | Article 184(2) of the Constitution |
| Signature | Federal Assembly | Article 184(1) of the Constitution<br>Article 166(1) of the Constitution |
| Authorization | Federal Assembly | Article 166(2) of the Constitution |
| [Referendum] | People | Article 141(1)(d) the Constitution<br>Article 141(2) of the Constitution |
| | People and Cantons | Article 140(1)(b) of the Constitution |
| Ratification | Federal Council | Article 184(2) of the Constitution |
| Publication | Federal Chancery | |

## III. The Relationship between Treaties and National Law

*See* discussion *supra*, Part I, § 1, III.

§ 3. Foreign Affairs Powers

## I. Foreign Policy in the New Constitution: A Change of Paradigm

*724.* The provisions of the Constitution of Switzerland concerning foreign policy reflect a fundamental change of paradigm from Switzerland's 19th century position as an 'introverted' (Rhinow) nation-state to a modern and open constitutional state. In the Preamble of the Constitution, the Swiss People and the Cantons renew their alliance to strengthen liberty and democracy, independence and peace in solidarity, and openness towards the world. National and foreign policy have become highly interdependent. Thus, the basic purpose of the Confederation is not only the protection of the liberty and the rights of the People, as well as the independence and security of the country (Article 2(1) of the Constitution), but also the promotion of a just and peaceful international order (Article 2(4) of the Constitution).[1]

1. Rhinow, Verfassungsrecht, 583 *et seq.*

## II. The Pillars of Swiss Foreign Policy

*725.* The importance of foreign policy is also systematically highlighted in Title 3, Chapter 2 of the Constitution, which immediately follows the chapter regarding the relationship between the Confederation and the Cantons. The foreign policy of Switzerland aim is to contribute to the alleviation of the needs and poverty of the world, and promoting respect for human rights, democracy, the peaceful coexistence of nations, and the preservation of natural resources (Article 54(2) of the Constitution).

*726.* The provision outlines the various pillars of Swiss foreign policy, which are:

(1) the policy concerning the relationship between Switzerland and Europe;
(2) the peace and security policy; and
(3) the development policy.

Surprisingly, considering the importance of trade with foreign nations for Switzerland, the Constitution does not expressly mention foreign trade policy, except for Article 101(1) of the Constitution, which grants the Confederation the power to safeguard the interests of the Swiss economy abroad.[1]

1. *See* Epiney Astrid, 'Beziehungen zum Ausland', in: Thürer *et al.*, § 55; Goetschel *et al.*, Schweizerische Aussenpolitik, Zurich 2002; St. Galler Kommentar, Kley Roland Vorbemerkungen Article 54–56, 649 *et seq.*; Rhinow, 355 *et seq.*

## III. The Cantons and Foreign Affairs

*727.* The concept of Swiss federalism as an equilibrium between self-rule and a constitutionally guaranteed shared rule has already been set out (*supra*, Part III, Chapter 1, § 2). The same concept is evident in the *traditional instruments* of the Cantons to influence foreign policy, such as consultation procedure, initiatives by the Cantons, representation in the Senate, the double majority requirement for important treaties, and the cantonal referendum.

*728.* In the Constitution of 1999, the element of *cooperation*, also included in the shared rule principle, has gained importance as a compensation for diminished cantonal autonomy (*supra*, Part III, Chapter 1, § 3, III.).[1] In the context of foreign affairs, the Constitution underlines the role of the Cantons in the decision-making process of foreign policy, and the relations between the Cantons and foreign nations. Furthermore, although foreign relationships are a federal matter

(Article 54(1) of the Constitution), the Confederation has to take into consideration the powers of the Cantons as well as the protection of their interests (Article 54(3) of the Constitution).[2]

1. *See* Fleiner Thomas & Misic Alexander, 'Föderalismus als Ordnungsprinzip der Verfassung', in: Thürer *et al.*, § 27, 438.
2. *See* St. Galler Kommentar, Pfisterer Thomas ad Article 54, 674–679 (with further references).

*729.* According to the concept of cooperative federalism, Article 55(1) of the Constitution integrates the Cantons into the *decision-making process of the preparation of foreign policy*, which concern the powers and the essential interests of the Cantons. In order to avoid centralization through foreign policy, the Federal Participation Act also reconfirms the role of the Cantons in the foreign policy process of the Confederation, but without adding new substance to Article 55 of the Constitution. In addition to the right of the canton to be *timely and fully informed*, and the possibility of the Confederation to *consult* the Cantons (Article 55(2) of the Constitution), the Constitution grants to the Cantons *further appropriate participatory rights in international negotiations* (Article 55(3) of the Constitution). Furthermore, the position of the Cantons shall have particular weight when their powers are concerned.[1]

1. *See* St. Galler Kommentar, Pfisterer Thomas ad Article 55, 680 *et seq.* (with further references).

*730.* From an institutional perspective, as a result of the inadequate flow of information during the negotiations for entry into the European Economic Community in the 1990s, the *Conference of the Cantonal Governments* (*Konferenz der Kantonsregierungen*) was created in 1993. The Conference is not focused exclusively on Foreign or European Union policy, but rather, it aims at coordinating the decision-making process among Cantons in order to exercise joint influence on the federal level. All twenty-six Cantons are members of the Conference, of which the vote of eighteen Cantons is sufficient to make a decision. Additionally, the Conference sends a delegate to the European Union in Brussels, who serves for informational purposes for the Conference and also to augment the Conference's influence on the European Union.

*731.* Furthermore, the Constitution regulates the *relationship between the Cantons and foreign nations*. According to Article 56(1) of the Constitution, the Cantons are entitled to conclude treaties with foreign nations. The Constitution requires that:

(1) the matter is within the scope of cantonal powers Cantons (Article 56(1) of the Constitution);
(2) the treaty between one or more Cantons and the foreign nation is not contrary to the law or the interests of the Confederation or to the laws of other Cantons (Article 56(2) of the Constitution); and
(3) the Cantons inform the Confederation before concluding a treaty (Article 56(2) *in fine* of the Constitution).

*732.* The Cantons are allowed to deal *directly* with lower ranking foreign authorities (Article 56(3) of the Constitution), while in all other cases, the Confederation will act on their behalf.[1]

1. *See* St. Galler Kommentar, Pfisterer Thomas ad Article 56, 694 *et seq.* (with further references).

# Chapter 2. Taxing Power, Financial Equalization and Spending Power

## § 1. Taxing Power

*733.* All three levels of government may raise taxes. Citizens pay about one third of their taxes to each governmental level. According to Article 127(1) of the Constitution, the general principles of taxation – particularly the circle of taxpayers, the object of the tax and its calculation – shall be established by statute.[1]

1. *See* St. Galler Kommentar, Vallender Klaus A. & René Wiederkehr ad Article 127, 1297–1299; Auer/Malinverni/Hottelier, Vol. I, 382–383; Stauffer Thomas, 'The Case of Switzerland', in: Richard Bird & Thomas Stauffer (eds.), *Intergovernmental Fiscal Relations in Fragmented Societies*, Helbing & Lichtenhahn, Basle 2001, 54–57.

### I. Exclusive and Concurrent Powers

*734.* The federal level may only levy taxes that are explicitly provided for in the Constitution. Federal taxing power is exclusive in the fields of value added tax (VAT), special consumption tax, as well as stamp and withholding tax (Article 134 of the Constitution). In the areas of personal and corporate income tax, as well as corporate capital tax, the federation and the Cantons have concurrent powers. These taxes can be levied at all three governmental levels. Further, the Cantons can introduce additional taxes.[1]

1. *See* Auer/Malinverni/Hottelier, Vol. I, 390–394; Stauffer Thomas, 'The Case of Switzerland', in: Richard Bird & Thomas Stauffer (eds.), *Intergovernmental Fiscal Relations in Fragmented Societies*, Helbing & Lichtenhahn, Basle 2001, 54–57; St. Galler Kommentar, Vallender Klaus A. ad Article 134, 1395–1403.

### II. Federal Taxes

*735.* The most important *federal taxes* are the direct taxes (income of natural persons, profit, capital and reserves of legal entities) and the Value Added Tax (VAT). As the constitutional federal power to levy direct taxes and the VAT expires in 2006 (Articles 13 and 14 Transitory Provisions), the Federal level is only accorded with a provisional power and its federal taxing power is additionally limited insofar as the constitution sets maximum tax rates (Articles 128(1) and 130(1)–(2) of the Constitution). For example, the Federal level may not set the tax rate above 11.5 per cent on the income of natural persons, and it cannot set the

VAT higher than 7.6 per cent on the supply of goods and services, including own use, and on imports. An increase of the tax rate needs a constitutional amendment. Tax scales shall be established by taking the burden of direct cantonal and municipal taxes into account (Article 128 of the Constitution). Mainly due to these constitutional limitations the level of fiscal centralization in Switzerland is comparatively low.[1]

1. *See* Locher Peter, 'Finanzordnung des Bundes', in: Thürer *et al.*, § 77, 1211–1224; St. Galler Kommentar, Vallender Klaus A. ad Article 128, 1323–1343.

## III. Cantonal and Municipal Taxes

*736.* Direct taxes form the most important part of *cantonal and municipal tax revenue*. According to Article 127(3) of the Constitution, intercantonal double taxation is prohibited and the Confederation shall take the necessary measures to prevent it. Cantonal income tax is levied at the place of residence. For corporate taxes, the tax base is allocated to the branches where it has been generated in order to prevent intercantonal double taxation. This tax splitting favours fiscal competition. Within the limits of the Federal Constitution, the Cantons can decide on the type of taxes it wants to levy, on the tax base, the tax scale, the tax rate, and the exempt amounts.

*737.* Direct taxes, including the federal taxes are assessed and collected by the Cantons (Article 128(4) of the Constitution). In some cases (*see infra* Part V, Chapter III), religious communities also have the right to levy taxes, which are then equally assessed and collected by the Cantons.[1]

1. *See* e.g., Oberson Xavier & Guillaume Pierre-Alain, 'Le régime financier dans le droit constitutionnel des cantons', in: Thürer *et al.*, § 78, 1225–1243; Stauffer Thomas, 'The Case of Switzerland', in: Richard Bird & Thomas Stauffer (eds.), *Intergovernmental Fiscal Relations in Fragmented Societies*, Helbing & Lichtenhahn, Basle 2001, 54–57.

## IV. Harmonization of Taxes

*738.* The Swiss taxing system has, *inter alia,* consequences with regard to inequalities of taxes among Cantons and municipalities. The global tax burden of a representative tax payer differs decisively from one canton to the other (57 to 131 index points by a mean of 100). Depending on their domicile, citizens must pay up to 2.5 times more taxes than citizens of another canton. The Constitution provides only a limited federal competence to harmonize the cantonal taxation system (Article 129(2) of the Constitution). Tax scales, tax rates and tax-exempt amounts are decided either by a cantonal parliament or by popular cantonal referendum without intervention of the federal level. Federal harmonization only concerns tax liability, tax object, taxation period as well as procedural and criminal law on taxation.[1]

1. *See* e.g., Dafflon Bernard, *Péréquation fédérale-cantonale en Suisse: Evolutions possibles et souhaitables*, Fribourg August 2001, 4.

§ 2. Financial Equalization

*739.* Not only the tax burden but also the canton's financial capacity differs decisively among Cantons (*see supra* § 1). The authoritative financial capacity of the Cantons is established by Federal Regulations[1] and it is based on a balancing of different indices, such as the GDP per inhabitant, fiscal burden, fiscal revenue, and cantonal financial need. The financially weakest canton has a 7.27 times lower financial capacity than the financially strongest canton.

1. *See* e.g., the Federal Ordinance on the Financial Capacity of the Cantons for the years 2000 and 2001 of November 17, 1999 (SR. 613.11).

*740.* Due to these differences, financial equalization, which aims to give the Cantons enough finances to assure that they can provide a minimal – not an equal – level of services has gained importance.[1] In Article 46(3) of the Constitution, the Confederation is mandated to ensure an equitable financial equalization, the basis of which certain financial equalization is provided in Article 135 of the Constitution, stating that the Confederation shall promote financial equalization among Cantons. When granting subsidies, the Confederation shall take the financial capacities of the Cantons and the special situation of the mountainous regions into account.[2] Article 128(4) of the Constitution ensures that at least one sixth of the amount raised with federal direct taxes shall be used for financial equalization among Cantons.

1. *See* Stauffer Thomas, 'The Case of Switzerland', in: Richard Bird & Thomas Stauffer (eds.), *Intergovernmental Fiscal Relations in Fragmented Societies*, Helbing & Lichtenhahn, Basle 2001, 60–64; Dafflon Bernard, *Péréquation fédérale-cantonale en Suisse: Evolutions possibles et souhaitables*, Fribourg August 2001, 7–19.
2. *See* St. Galler Kommentar, Vallender Klaus A. & Wiederkehr René ad Article 135, 1404–135.

*741.* Today, some Cantons are, to a significant extent, dependent on federal subsidies. For instance, the Canton of Jura depends on federal subsidies for 43.3 per cent of its expenditures, in comparison to the Canton of Geneva with 7 per cent. As a cantonal average, there is a dependency of 17.1 per cent (all figures from 1998). In addition, to federal subsidies and revenue sharing that take the financial capacity of the Cantons into account, the amount of financial cantonal contributions to the funding of federal tasks also depends on the financial capacity.[1]

1. Data provided in Dafflon Bernard, *Péréquation fédérale-cantonale en Suisse: Evolutions possibles et souhaitables*, Fribourg August 2001, 24.

*742.* The system of financial equalization applied today is complicated and not exactly satisfactory because it has developed into a system of uncoordinated and hardly controllable measures and is based, to an extent, on conditioned grants thus applying different formulas for the distribution of payments to the Cantons. Therefore, it has been under general discussion and will be fundamentally modified.[1] The main goal is to allow cantonal policy more autonomy by giving global grants to support intercantonal cooperation, giving economically weak Cantons more federal resources, and financing cantonal tasks, which are particularly costly because of their specific circumstances. Additionally, the reform aims to introduce a system of mandatory compensation payments for spillovers while at the same time, it would readjust and standardize formulas for the distribution of payments. The financially stronger Cantons are mainly opposed to the new system, although non-governmental organizations (NGOs) have voiced their concern as well. NGOs primary fear that with the introduction of more unconditioned grants, the financially stronger Cantons will be more reluctant to continue over-proportionally financing common social programs. Many of the new systems opponents regard it as a de-solidarization among the Cantons.

1. *See Der Neue Finanzausgleich zwischen Bund und Kantonen, Bericht über die Vernehmlassung, Eidgenössisches Finanzdepartment und Konferenz der Kantonsregierungen*, Berne March 2000; Reich Markus, 'Grundzüge der föderalistischen Finanzverfassung', in: Thürer *et al.*, § 76, 1207–1209.

## § 3. Spending Power

*743.* In 1997, the federal budget accounted for 32 per cent, the cantonal budgets for 41 percent, and the municipal budgets for 28 per cent of the total public expenditures. In the following, only the federal spending power shall be dealt with.

*744.* According to Article 183 of the Federal Constitution, the Federal Council shall prepare the financing plan, draft the budget and establish the federal accounts.[1] Federal Parliament decides on federal spending, adopts the budget and approves the federal accounts (Article 167 of the Constitution).[2] These decisions can be taken by simple federal decree and so are not submitted to a referendum. There is no financial referendum at the federal level. For decisions granting subsidies, authorizing credit lines, and establishing spending ceilings, which cause new one-time expenditures exceeding 20 million Swiss Francs, or new recurrent expenditures exceeding 2 million Swiss Francs, a special quorum is required. In these cases, not only a majority of those voting but a majority of the members of both Chambers of Parliaments must approve (Article 159(3)(b) of the Constitution).

1. *See* St. Galler Kommentar, Stauffer Thomas ad Article 183, 1825–1832.
2. *See* St. Galler Kommentar, Stauffer Thomas ad Article 167, 1647–1655.

*745.* On 2 December 2001, in order to counteract the mounting deficit, the People and the Cantons accepted an amendment of the Constitution that aims at establishing a balanced budget. According to Article 126(1) of the Constitution, the Confederation shall in the long term keep its expenditures and receipts in balance. This mandate is further solidified in Article 126(2). Taking into account the economic situation, the maximum of the total expenditures which may be budgeted shall be determined by the expected receipts; for extraordinary expenses the maximum amount may be increased based on receipts and the economic situation (Article 126(3) of the Constitution). The increase can only be decided by a majority of the members of both Chambers of Federal Parliament (Articles 126(3) and 159(3)(c) of the Constitution). An excess of expenditures must be compensated in the following years (Article 126(4) of the Constitution).[1]

1. *See* St. Galler Kommentar, Stauffer Thomas ad Article 126, 1283–1294.

# Chapter 3. The Constitutional Relationship between Religion and State

## § 1. Historical Background

*746.* Switzerland is mainly divided into two religious groups: Protestant (Zwingli and Calvin) and Roman Catholic. While Switzerland had managed to stay out of European religious conflicts, the short civil war of 1847 was partly attributed to religious tensions (*supra* General Introduction, Chapter 1) because religious divisions overlapped with political ones. Essentially, the Protestant parts of Switzerland opted for a stronger centralization and democratization, while, in violation of the Confederal Treaty, the conservative Catholic Cantons formed a secret union (*Sonderbund*) in order to protect their interests. When the union was revealed, the diet, the only confederal institution, demanded the dissolution of the union to which the conservative Catholic Cantons resisted and left the diet so the progressive Protestant Cantons decided to dissolve the union by force, the short civil war that followed led to the defeat of the Catholic Cantons.

*747.* One of the main challenges for and achievements of constitution making in 1848 was to assure the loyalty of both religious communities. Any regulation of the relationship between religion and the state on the federal level threatened to lead to an unbridgeable cleavage between the Catholic and Protestant parts of Switzerland. The Federal Constitution of 1848 as well as the other federal Constitutions that followed tried to find mechanisms so as not to alienate any of the two religious groups, as well as to protect the individual although, slightly disfavouring to the Catholic Church.[1]

1. *See* Kreis Georg, 'Totalrevisionen als soziale Bewegunge – Zu den fünf Verfassungsphasen der neueren Schweizergeschichte', in: Sitter-Liver, 176; Steinberg, 222–223.

## § 2. Provisions in the Federal Constitution

### I. Rule

*748.* According the Swiss Federal Constitution of 1999, as had been the case under the 1848 and 1874 Constitutions, it is within the powers of the Cantons to regulate the relationship between religion and the state (Article 72(1) of the Constitution).[1]

1. *See* Häfelin & Haller, 129–130; Kiener Regina, 'Bildung, Forschung und Kultur', in: Thürer *et al.*, 912–913.

## II. Limits and Related Provisions

*749.* The Cantons are not completely free in their power, however. The federal level maintains a peacekeeping or mediating function in order to promote peace between the different communities and to protect the individual from intrusions by the state.

*750.* a. The federal level can adopt measures to maintain or achieve peace between different religious groups (Article 72(2) of the Constitution).[1]

1. *See* St. Galler Kommentar, Cavelti Urs Josef ad Article 72, 830–832.

*751.* b. The Federal Constitution guarantees the freedom of religion and philosophy, including the right to enter and leave a religious community free from state coercion and to practice the religion alone and in communities (Article 15 of the Constitution).[1]

1. *See* Hafner Felix, 'Glaubens- und Gewissensfreiheit', in: Thürer *et al.*, § 44, 707–719; Häfelin & Haller, 121–130.

*752.* c. The Federal Constitution prohibits mandatory religious instruction at schools and guarantees the religious neutrality of public schools.

*753.* d. Further provisions that can have an impact on the rights and duties of the State and of religious communities are, for instance, the right to a decent burial as well as provisions of criminal law (e.g., prohibition of drugs), safety regulations (e.g., duty to wear a helmet when driving a motorcycle), and the law for animal protection (e.g., prohibition of slaughtering by bleeding without previous narcotization). A constitutional provision that provided for the need for a federal approval for the institution of new bishoprics was repealed in 2001.

## § 3. Cantonal Solutions

*754.* There are four different models of relationships between the state and church, or more appropriately stated, between the state and religion. (1) A state can be a theocracy, where the authority of the state is supposed to derive directly from a divine source. (2) There can be a state religion, although state religions and their influence can vary decisively. In all cases, however, the state religion must have an exclusive, official status in the state. (3) The third model is characterized by the recognition of a special status for more than one religion, i.e., it is possible within this system that one religion has a preferential status. And (4), there can be a separation between the state and religion, or state neutrality regarding religion based on the concept of privatizing religion.[1]

1. *See* Fleiner, 2nd ed., Staatslehre, 386–396.

*755.* None of the Cantons are organized as a theocracy. All Cantons have chosen either a relative separation form, the recognition of a special status for more than one religious community, or a form of state religion.

## I. Separation between State and Religion

*756.* The Canton of Geneva (since 1907) and the Canton of Neuchâtel (since 1941) have opted for a separation between religion and state. Religious communities must rely on the forms of private law for their organization. The separation is relative insofar as the religious communities can raise voluntary taxes and the state collects the taxes either free of charge (Neuchâtel) or against an emolument (Geneva).

## II. Public Law Status for certain Religious Communities

*757.* The majority of the Cantons opt for this solution. Today most Cantons allow for a public law status for the Protestant and Roman Catholic Church, although some Cantons also grant public law status to other religious communities, such as the Jewish community (Berne, Basle-City, Fribourg) and the Christ-Catholic Church (Berne). Even though the Muslim population greatly outnumbers the Jewish and Christ Catholic communities, the Muslim community has not yet achieved a public law status in any of the Cantons. According to the provisions of the Canton of Fribourg, a religious community can achieve public law status when it:

(a) is a traditional religious movement in Switzerland or of universal importance;
(b) is a member of the ecumenical council of churches or has been represented in the canton for thirty years; and
(c) when it respects the fundamental principles of the Swiss legal order.

*758.* Some Cantons accord equal rights to the religious communities with public law status (Glarus, Aargau, Grisons, Saint Gallen, Thurgau), while others privilege one of the communities, which are sometimes called a state church.

*759.* Religious communities with a public law status normally have the right to raise taxes that are then collected by the state. These taxes are only mandatory for the adherents of the religious communities. In Cantons that denominate a so-called state church, adherence to this religious belief is normally expected, based on the territoriality principle. Any person who does not want to belong to the community must revoke his or her membership. Enterprises are mandated to pay church taxes in most of the Cantons. According to the Federal Court, they cannot claim the right to religious freedom in order to leave a religious community, and therefore cannot be exempted from taxes.

*760.* In addition, religious communities with a public law status can receive state subsidies. In exchange, they are supposed to offer some social services.

## III. State Church

*761.* The Canton of Vaud is in a process of revising its Constitution. Its Constitution of 1885, as well as the proposals for a new constitution, declare the

Protestant Church as the state church, thus making it the only religious community with a special status. Substantive changes on this part of the Constitution are planned for a later time. Membership in the Church is presumed, in accordance with the freedom of religion, but can be revoked. The clergy are civil servants of the Cantons.

# Index

# Annex

## Text of the Constitution of Switzerland

of 18 April 1999

**Contents**

# The Constitution of the Swiss Confederation

of 18 April 1999

Agreed by Federal Parliament on 18 December 1998.
Adopted by public vote on 18 April 1999.
Application Decree of Federal Parliament: 28 September 1999.
In force since 1 January 2000.

## Preamble

In the name of God Almighty!
The Swiss People and the Cantons,
Conscious of their responsibility towards creation,
Resolved to renew their alliance, so as to strengthen liberty, democracy, independence and peace in a spirit of solidarity and openness towards the world
Determined to live together and respecting each other with their diversities in unity,
Conscious of their common achievements and of their duty to take responsibility for future generations,
Knowing that only those remain free who use their freedom, and that the strength of the People is measured by the well being of its weakest members,
*Agree upon the Constitution which follows*:

## Part One. General Provisions

*Article 1. The Swiss Confederation*
The People and the Cantons of Zurich, Berne, Lucerne, Uri, Schwyz, Obwalden, Nidwalden, Glarus, Zug, Fribourg, Solothurn, Basle-City, Basle-Land, Schaffhausen, Appenzell Outer Rhodes, Appenzell Inner Rhodes, St. Gallen, Grisons, Aargau, Thurgau, Ticino, Vaud, Valais, Neuchâtel, Geneva, and Jura form the Swiss Confederation.

*Article 2. Aims*
(1) The Swiss Confederation shall protect the liberty and rights of the People and safeguard the independence and security of the country.
(2) It shall promote common welfare, sustainable development, internal cohesion and cultural diversity of the country.
(3) It shall seek to guarantee its citizens the greatest possible equality of chances.
(4) It shall commit itself to supporting the long-term preservation of natural resources and in favor of a peaceful and just international order.

*Article 3. Cantons*
The Cantons are sovereign insofar as the Federal Constitution does not limit their sovereignty; they exercise all rights which are not delegated to the Confederation.

*Article 4. National Languages*
The National Languages are German, French, Italian, and Romansh.

*Article 5. The Rule of Law*
(1) The law is the foundation and limitation of all state activity.
(2) State activity must be in the public interest and proportionate to the goals pursued.
(3) Public authorities and private persons must act in good faith.
(4) The Confederation and the Cantons shall respect international law.

*Article 6. Individual and Social Responsibility*
Every person shall take responsibility for herself and himself; as far as they can, they shall contribute to achieving the tasks of state and society.

## Part Two. Fundamental Rights and Liberties, Citizenship and Social Goals

### Chapter One. Fundamental Rights and Liberties

*Article 7. Human Dignity*
Human dignity ought to be respected and protected.

*Article 8. Equality*
(1) All persons are equal before the law.
(2) No one should be discriminated against simply because of their origin, race, sex, age, language, social position, way of life, religious, philosophical, or political convictions, or because of a physical, mental or psychological disability.
(3) Men and women have equal rights in law. The law shall provide for equality in law and in fact, particularly in the family, during education, and in the workplace. Men and women have the right to equal pay for work of equal value.
(4) The law shall provide for measures to eliminate discrimination against persons with disabilities.

*Article 9. Protection Against Arbitrariness and Principle of Good Faith*
Every person has the right to be treated by state authorities in a non arbitrary way and according to the rules of good faith.

*Article 10. The Right to Life and to Personal Freedom*
(1) Everyone has the right to life. The death penalty is abolished.
(2) Everyone has the right to personal liberty, particularly to physical and mental integrity, and to freedom of movement.
(3) Torture and all other forms of cruel, inhuman, or degrading treatment or punishment are prohibited.

*Article 11. The Protection of Children and Young People*

(1) Children and young people have the right to special protection of their personal integrity and also to encouragement of their development.

(2) They exercise their rights by themselves to the extent of their intellectual capacities to discern.

*Article 12. The Right to Aid in Distress*

Whoever is in a situation of distress, and is not in a position to care for herself or himself, has the right to help and assistance and also the right to benefit from the indispensable means for living in dignity.

*Article 13. Rights to Privacy*

(1) Everyone has the right for respect of their private and family life, their domicile, their correspondence and their telecommunications.

(2) Everyone has the right to be protected against any abuse of personal data relating to them.

*Article 14. Rights to Marriage and Family*

The freedom to marry and the right to family are guaranteed.

*Article 15. Freedom of Religion and Conscience*

(1) Freedom of religion and conscience is guaranteed.

(2) Everyone has the right to freely choose their religion and their philosophical convictions and to expound them individually or in community with others.

(3) Everyone has the right to join or belong to a religious community and to receive a religious instruction.

(4) No one may be forced to join or belong to a religious community, to perform religious acts or to undergo a religious instruction.

*Article 16. Freedom of Opinion and Information*

(1) The freedom of opinion and of information is guaranteed.

(2) Everyone has the right to form, express, and disseminate their opinions freely.

(3) Everyone has the right to receive information, to gather it from generally accessible sources and to disseminate it freely.

*Article 17. Freedom of the Media*

(1) The freedom of the press, radio and television, along with other forms of distributing productions and information deriving from public telecommunications is guaranteed.

(2) Censorship is prohibited.

(3) Journalistic confidentiality is guaranteed.

*Article 18. Freedom of Language*

The freedom of language is guaranteed.

*Article 19. The Right to Primary School Education*

The right to a sufficient and free primary school education is guaranteed.

**Switzerland – Text of the Constitution**

*Article 20. The Freedom of Science*
The freedom of teaching and of scientific research is guaranteed.

*Article 21. The Freedom of Art*
The freedom of art is guaranteed.

*Article 22. Freedom of Assembly*
(1) The freedom of assembly is guaranteed.
(2) Everyone has the right to organize meetings and to choose whether to participate in them or not.

*Article 23. Freedom of Association*
(1) The freedom of association is guaranteed.
(2) Everyone has the right to form associations, to join them or to belong to them and to participate in their collective activities.
(3) Nobody shall be forced to join or to belong to an association.

*Article 24. Freedom of Residence*
(1) Swiss citizens have the right to establish their residence anywhere within the country.
(2) They have the right to leave or to return to Switzerland.

*Article 25. Protection against expulsion, extradition, and removal by force*
(1) No Swiss may be expelled from the country; they may only be extradited to a foreign authority with their consent.
(2) Refugees may not be returned by force to nor handed back to the control of the authorities of a country where they have been persecuted.
(3) Nobody may be removed by force to a state where they are threatened by torture or any other form of cruel and inhuman treatment or punishment.

*Article 26. The Right to Property*
(1) The right to property is guaranteed.
(2) Expropriation and restrictions of ownership equivalent to expropriation requires compensation in full.

*Article 27. Economic Freedom*
(1) Economic freedom is guaranteed.
(2) This involves above all the freedom to choose one's profession, and to enjoy both free access to, and free exercise of, a remunerative private activity.

*Article 28. Freedom of Coalition*
(1) Workers, employers, and their organizations have the right to coalesce in organizations to protect their interests, to form unions and to decide whether to join them or not.
(2) As far as possible, conflicts shall be resolved through negotiation and mediation.

(3) Strikes and lockouts are permissible when they relate to labor relations, and when they conform with obligations to keep the 'labor peace' or to resort to conciliation.
(4) Legislation may prohibit certain categories of persons from striking.

*Article 29. General Procedural Guarantees*
(1) In legal or administrative proceedings, everyone person has the right to have their case treated equitably and decided within a reasonable time.
(2) The parties to a case have the right to be heard.
(3) Every person lacking the necessary funds has the right to free legal assistance, unless their case appears to be without any chance of success. They have, moreover, the right to free legal representation to the extent that this is necessary to protect their rights.

*[Article 29a. Guarantee of Access to a Judge]*
[Note: This provision was approved by popular vote on 12 March 2000. The provision will come into force with the overall reform of the judiciary.]

[Everyone has the right to have legal disputes judged by a judicial authority. The Confederation and the Cantons may, in exceptional cases, exclude the access to a judge.]

*Article 30. Guarantees in Judicial Proceedings*
(1) Everyone whose case must be decided by judicial proceedings has the right to have this done in a court established by law, has jurisdiction and is both independent and impartial. Special courts are prohibited.
(2) Every person against whom a civil action is brought has the right to have the case heard before a court at his or her domicile. Legislation may prescribe another jurisdiction.
(3) Court hearings and verdicts shall be public. Legislation may provide for exceptions.

*Article 31. Habeas Corpus*
(1) No one may be deprived of their liberty except in the cases and in the forms provided by law.
(2) Everyone deprived of their liberty has the right to be informed immediately, and in a language that they understand, of the reasons for their detention and of the rights they enjoy. They must have the opportunity to assert their rights. In particular, they have the right to have their close friends and relations informed.
(3) Everyone taken into preventive detention has the right to be brought before a judge without delay; the judge shall decide whether they should remain in detention or should be released. Everyone held in preventive detention has the right to be judged within a reasonable time.
(4) All those who are deprived of their liberty without trial have the right to bring their case before a court at any time. The court shall decide as soon as possible whether their detention is legal.

*Article 32. Criminal Procedure*
(1) Everyone is presumed innocent until proved guilty and sentenced by a court.
(2) All accused persons have the right to be informed fully and as soon as possible of the accusations. They must be able to exercise their rights of legal defense.
(3) Every sentenced person has the right to judicial review by a higher court. This does not apply to cases where the Federal Court sits as a court of first instance.

*Article 33. Right of Petition*
(1) Everyone has the right to address petitions to the authorities without incurring any adverse consequences.
(2) The authorities must take notice of the petition.

*Article 34. Political Rights*
(1) Political rights are guaranteed.
(2) Guarantees of political rights protect the free formation of opinion and the unaltered expression of their will.

*Article 35. Implementation of Fundamental Rights and Liberties*
(1) Fundamental rights and liberties must be implemented throughout the entire legal system.
(2) Whoever exercises a state function must respect fundamental rights and liberties and contribute to their implementation.
(3) The authorities shall ensure, where applicable, that fundamental rights and liberties are also respected in relations amongst private parties.

*Article 36. Limitations of Fundamental Liberties*
(1) Any limitation of a fundamental liberty requires a legal basis. Grave limitations must be expressly prescribed by law. Exempt are cases of clear and present danger.
(2) Any limitation of a fundamental liberty must be justified by public interest or by the need to protect the fundamental liberties of others.
(3) Limitations of fundamental liberties must be proportionate to the goal pursued.
(4) The core of fundamental liberties is inviolable.

## Chapter Two. Nationality, Citizenship and Political Rights

*Article 37. Nationality and Citizenship*
(1) Everyone who holds citizenship of a Municipality, and of the Canton has Swiss citizenship.
(2) No one should enjoy privileges or be discriminated against because of their citizenship. Exceptions are possible to regulate political rights in bourgeoisies and corporations, and to provide for participation in their assets, unless cantonal legislation provides otherwise.

*Article 38. Acquisition and Loss of Citizenship*
(1) The Confederation shall regulate the acquisition and the loss of citizenship through descent, marriage and adoption. Moreover, it shall also regulate the

loss of Swiss citizenship on other grounds, along with the reinstatement of citizenship.

(2) It shall set minimum requirements for the naturalization of foreigners by the Cantons, and shall grant naturalization permits.

(3) It shall facilitate the naturalization of stateless children.

*Article 39. Exercise of Political Rights*

(1) The Confederation shall regulate the exercise of political rights at the federal level; the Cantons shall regulate the exercise of these rights at the cantonal and municipal levels.

(2) Political rights shall be exercised in the citizen's domicile. The Confederation and the Cantons may prescribe exceptions.

(3) No one may simultaneously exercise political rights in more than one Canton.

(4) The Cantons may require that newly established residents undergo a waiting period, of no more than three months, before exercising political rights in cantonal and communal affairs.

*Article 40. Swiss Citizens Living Abroad*

(1) The Confederation shall encourage links both amongst Swiss citizens with a domicile abroad, and between them and Switzerland. It may support organizations which pursue this goal.

(2) It shall legislate on the rights and obligations of Swiss citizens with a domicile abroad, in particular on the exercise of the political rights at the federal level, on the duty to render military or alternative service, on the assistance to those in need and on social security.

## Chapter Three. Social Goals

*Article 41.*

(1) In addition to personal responsibility and private initiatives, the Confederation and the Cantons shall ensure that:

a. everyone benefits from social security;
b. everyone benefits from the necessary health care which they need;
c. families, as communities of adults and children, are protected and encouraged;
d. everyone capable of working should be able to support themselves by work carried on under equitable conditions;
e. everyone looking for housing should be able to find appropriate housing for themselves and their family at affordable conditions;
f. children and young people, together with people of working age, should be able to benefit from initial and continuing education according to their aptitudes;
g. children and young people are encouraged to develop into independent and socially responsible persons, and are supported in their social, cultural, and political integration.

(2) The Confederation and the Cantons shall ensure that everyone is insured against the economic consequences of old age, disability, illness, accidents, unemployment, maternity and against being orphaned or widowed.
(3) They shall undertake to achieve these social goals within the framework of their constitutional powers and with the means available to them.
(4) These social goals shall not be interpreted as conferring any justiciable right to state services.

# Part Three. Confederation, Cantons, and Municipalities

## Chapter One. Relations between the Confederation and the Cantons

### Section 1. Competences of the Confederation and the Cantons

*Article 42. The Tasks of the Confederation*
(1) The Confederation shall accomplish the tasks which are attributed to it by the Constitution.
(2) It shall take on those tasks which require uniform regulation.

*Article 43. The Tasks of the Cantons*
The Cantons shall define the tasks which they undertake to accomplish within the framework of their powers

### Section 2. Cooperation between the Confederation and the Cantons

*Article 44. Principles*
(1) The Confederation and the Cantons support each other in the fulfillment of their tasks and collaborate with each other.
(2) They owe each other respect and support. They shall mutually grant each other administrative and judicial assistance.
(3) Disputes between the Cantons, or between Cantons and the Confederation, shall, as far as is possible, be resolved through negotiation or mediation.

*Article 45. Participation in the Federal Decision-Making Process*
(1) In the cases specified by the Federal Constitution, the Cantons shall participate in the decision-making process at the federal level, in particular in formulating federal legislation.
(2) The Confederation shall fully and timely inform the Cantons of its plans; it shall consult them if their interests are likely to be affected.

*Article 46. Implementation of Federal Law*
(1) The Cantons shall implement federal law in conformity with the Constitution and with statute law.
(2) The Confederation shall leave the Cantons appropriate discretionary powers, and shall take their specificities into account.

(3) The Confederation shall take into account the financial burden associated with the implementation of federal laws by leaving sufficient sources of financing to the Cantons, and by ensuring equitable financial harmonization.

*Article 47. Cantonal Autonomy*
The Confederation shall respect the autonomy of the Cantons.

*Article 48. Intercantonal Treaties*
(1) The Cantons may conclude intercantonal treaties, and may create common organizations and institutions. In particular, they may join forces collectively to fulfill tasks of regional significance.
(2) The Confederation may participate in such organizations or institutions within the limits of its powers.
(3) Intercantonal treaties may not be contrary ether to the law or the interests of the Confederation, nor yet to the rights of other Cantons. The Confederation must be notified of such treaties.

*Article 49. Supremacy of and Respect for Federal Law*
(1) Federal law takes precedence over contrary cantonal law.
(2) The Confederation ensures that the Cantons respect federal law.

## Section 3. Municipalities

*Article 50.*
(1) Communal autonomy is guaranteed within the limits fixed by cantonal law.
(2) In its activities, the Confederation shall as well take into account the possible consequences for the Municipalities.
(3) In so doing, it shall also consider the special situations of the cities, the suburban areas and of the highlands and alpine regions.

## Section 4. Federal Guarantees

*Article 51. Cantonal Constitutions*
(1) Every Canton shall adopt a democratic constitution. The cantonal constitution must be approved by the People, and must be subject to revision if a majority of the electorate so requires.
(2) The cantonal constitutions must be guaranteed by the Confederation. The Confederation will grant this guarantee provided the constitutions are not contrary to federal law.

*Article 52. Constitutional Order*
(1) The Confederation shall protect the constitutional order of the Cantons.
(2) It shall intervene if the public order of a Canton is disturbed or threatened and cannot be restored by the Canton whether alone or with the help of other Cantons.

*Article 53. Cantonal Existence, Status and Territory*
(1) The Confederation shall protect the existence and the territory of the Cantons.
(2) All alterations to the number of the Cantons, or to their status, are subject to the assent of the relevant electorate and of the Cantons concerned, and also of a double vote of the People and the Cantons.
(3) All changes to the territory of a Canton are subject to the approval of the electorate of the Cantons concerned, and to the assent of the Federal Assembly in the form of a federal decree.
(4) Intercantonal boundary settlements may be made by treaty between the Cantons concerned.

## Chapter Two. Powers

### Section 1. Relations with Foreign Countries

*Article 54. Foreign Affairs*
(1) The Confederation is competent for foreign affairs.
(2) The Confederation shall seek to preserve the independence and prosperity of Switzerland and its welfare; in particular it shall contribute to alleviating need and poverty in the world, and to promoting respect for human rights, democracy, the peaceful coexistence of peoples and the conservation of natural resources.
(3) It shall take the powers of the Cantons into consideration, and shall safeguard their interests.

*Article 55. Cantonal Participation in External Policy Decisions*
(1) The Cantons shall work together with the Confederation on the preparation of decisions on foreign policy which affect their powers or their essential interests.
(2) The Confederation shall fully and timely inform the Cantons, and shall consult them.
(3) The recommendations of the Cantons shall be given particular weight when their responsibilities are involved. In such cases, and in an appropriate manner, the Cantons will participate in international negotiations.

*Article 56. Cantonal Relations with Foreign Countries*
(1) The Cantons may conclude treaties with foreign countries in those fields within their powers.
(2) These treaties may not be contrary to the law, nor to the interests of the Confederation, nor to the laws of other Cantons. Before concluding a treaty, the Cantons must inform the Confederation.
(3) The Cantons may deal directly with lower ranking foreign authorities; in other cases, cantonal relations with foreign countries shall be conducted by the Confederation, acting on their behalf.

## Section 2. Security, National and Civil Defense

*Article 57. Security*

(1) The Confederation and the Cantons shall provide, within the framework of their powers, for the security of the country and the protection of its population.
(2) They shall coordinate their efforts in the field of internal security.

*Article 58. The Army*

(1) Switzerland has an army. This shall be organized predominantly on the militia principle.
(2) The army shall contribute to preventing war and to maintaining peace; it shall ensure that the country is defended and its population is protected. It shall lend support to the civil authorities when they have to repel serious threats to internal security or to cope with other exceptional circumstances. The law may prescribe further tasks.
(3) The use of the army is a Confederal competence. The Cantons may mobilize their troops to maintain public order on their territory, if the means available to their civil authorities no longer enable them to master serious threats to internal security.

*Article 59. Military and Alternative Service*

(1) Every Swiss male must render military service. The law shall provide for an alternative form of service.
(2) Swiss women may serve in the army on a voluntary basis.
(3) Swiss males who perform neither military nor alternative service must pay a tax. The tax is levied by the Confederation but is assessed and collected by the Cantons.
(4) The Confederation shall legislate on fair compensation for loss of income.
(5) Those whose health is affected as a result of their military or alternative service have the right to appropriate compensation from the Confederation. If they loose their lives while on service their next of kin also have a right to equal support.

*Article 60. The Organization, Instruction, and Equipment of the Army*

(1) Legislation on military matters and on the organization, training and equipment of the army, is a Confederal competence.
(2) Within the limits of federal law, the Cantons shall have the power to raise cantonal troops, to appoint and to promote the officers of such troops, and to furnish a part of their clothing and equipment.
(3) The Confederation may take over cantonal military installations provided fair compensation is paid.

*Article 61. Civil Defense*

(1) Legislation on civil defense is a Confederal competence. Civil defense is designed to protect people and property in the case of armed conflicts.
(2) The Confederation shall legislate on the involvement of civil defense in catastrophes and emergencies.

(3) The Confederation may make the civil defense service compulsory for men. For women, it shall be voluntary.
(4) The Confederation shall legislate on fair compensation for loss of income.
(5) Those whose health is affected as a result of their civil defense service have the right to appropriate compensation from the Confederation. If they loose their lives while on service their next of kin also have a right to equal support.

## Section 3. Education, Research and Culture

*Article 62. Education*
(1) Education is a cantonal competence.
(2) The Cantons shall ensure that there is a sufficient basic education, open to all children. This education shall be compulsory, and subject to state management or supervision. It shall be free in state schools. The school year shall begin between mid-August and mid-September.

*Article 63. Professional Education and Universities*
(1) The Confederation shall legislate on professional education.
(2) It shall manage technical universities. It may create, operate, or support other universities and institutions of higher education. It may make its support conditional upon measures of co-ordination being taken.

*Article 64. Research*
(1) The Confederation shall encourage scientific research.
(2) It may make its support conditional, in particular, upon coordination measures being taken.
(3) It may create, take over, or operate research institutions.

*Article 65. Statistics*
(1) The Confederation shall collect the necessary statistical data on the condition status and evolution of the population, the economy, the society, the territory, and the environment in Switzerland.
(2) To rationalize facilitate the collection of data, it may legislate on harmonizing and maintaining official records.

*Article 66. Support of Education*
(1) The Confederation may grant subsidies to the Cantons to cover the expenses they may incur in awarding scholarships and other educational grants.
(2) It may, moreover, while respecting cantonal autonomy in educational matters, complement cantonal measures and take its own measures to encourage education.

*Article 67. The Educational Needs of Adults and Young People*
(1) The Confederation and the Cantons shall, when fulfilling their tasks, take into account children's and young people's special needs for development and protection.

(2) The Confederation may complement cantonal measures and support both extra-curricular activities for children and young people and the training of adults.

*Article 68. Sport*
(1) The Confederation shall promote sport, particularly sporting education.
(2) It shall operate a sports school.
(3) It may legislate on the practice of sport by the young, and may make sports education in schools compulsory.

*Article 69. Culture*
(1) The field of culture is a cantonal competence.
(2) The Confederation may support cultural activities of national interest, and encourage artistic and musical expression, particularly by promoting education in these fields.
(3) In accomplishing its tasks, it shall take into account the cultural and linguistic diversity of the country.

*Article 70. Languages*
(1) The official languages of the Confederation are German, French, and Italian. Romansh shall be an official language for Confederal relations with Romansh speakers.
(2) The Cantons shall decide on their official languages. In order to preserve harmony between linguistic communities, the cantons shall respect the traditional territorial distribution of languages, and shall take indigenous linguistic minorities into account.
(3) The Confederation and the Cantons shall encourage understanding and exchange between the linguistic communities.
(4) The Confederation shall support the pluri-lingual Cantons in the fulfillment of their particular tasks.
(5) The Confederation shall support the measures taken by the Cantons of Grisons and Ticino to safeguard and promote Romansh and Italian.

*Article 71. Cinema*
(1) The Confederation may encourage Swiss film production and cinematic culture.
(2) It may legislate to encourage the variety and the quality of cinematographic works produced.

*Article 72. Church and State*
(1) Regulation of the relationship between church and state is a cantonal competence.
(2) The Confederation and the Cantons may, within the limits of their powers, take measures to maintain public peace between the members of the various religious communities.
(3) [The 'Diocesan' article, making the creation of Catholic bishoprics dependent on governmental approval was abrogated by popular vote on 10 June 2001.]

## Section 4. Environment and Zoning

*Article 73. Sustainable Development*
The Confederation and the Cantons shall work to establish a durable equilibrium with nature, in particular enhancing both its capacity to renew itself and the way it is used by man.

*Article 74. Protection of the Environment*
(1) The Confederation shall legislate to protect mankind and its natural environment against harmful and offensive damage.
(2) It shall ensure that such damage is avoided. Polluters shall pay for the costs of protection and making good.
(3) Implementation of federal regulations shall fall to the Cantons, insofar as the law does not reserve this for the Confederation.

*Article 75. Zoning*
(1) The Confederation shall lay down principles for zoning. Their implementation shall fall to the Cantons, and shall serve to achieve a considered and moderate use of the soil and a rational occupation of the land.
(2) The Confederation shall encourage and coordinate the efforts of the Cantons, and shall collaborate with them.
(3) In fulfilling their tasks, the Confederation and the Cantons shall take the needs of land use planning into account.

*Article 76. Water*
(1) Within the limits of its powers, the Confederation shall ensure the rational use and the protection of water resources, and shall combat the harmful effects of water.
(2) It shall establish principles on the conservation and development of water reserves, on the use of water both for the production of energy and for cooling purposes and also on other interventions in the water cycle.
(3) It shall legislate on water protection, on securing sufficient residual water, on hydraulic engineering, on the safety of dams and on actions to influence rainfall.
(4) The Cantons shall have control over their own water resources. Within the limits of federal law, they may levy dues for water use. The Confederation shall have the right to use water for its transport operations; and where it does it shall pays dues and compensation.
(5) In consultation with the cantons concerned, the Confederation shall decide on the rights to water resources of interest to other states and shall set the rates for their use. If the Cantons concerned cannot agree on rights to inter-cantonal water reserves, the Confederation will decide the matter.
(6) In fulfilling its tasks, the Confederation shall take into account the interests of those Cantons from which the water originates.

*Article 77. Forests*
(1) The Confederation shall ensure that forests may fulfill their protective, economic and social functions.

(2) It shall establish principles for the protection of forests.
(3) It shall encourage measures for the conservation of forests.

*Article 78. Nature and Cultural Heritage*
(1) The protection of nature and of cultural heritage is a cantonal competence.
(2) In fulfilling its tasks, the Confederation shall take into account the objectives of the protection of the natural and cultural heritage. It shall protect landscape, the physiognomy of localities, historical sites and natural and cultural monuments; it shall preserve them in their entirety if the public interest so requires.
(3) It may support efforts towards the protection of nature and the cultural patrimony and may, by contract or by expropriation, acquire or preserve things of national importance.
(4) It shall legislate on the protection of animal and plant life and on the preservation of their diverse natural environments. It shall protect endangered species from extinction.
(5) Marshes and wetlands of special beauty and national significance shall be protected. No installations may be built on them, and no alterations of any kind may be made to the land. Exception is made for installations serving to ensure their protection or their continuing use for agricultural purposes.

*Article 79. Hunting and Fishing*
The Confederation shall establish principles for hunting and fishing, notably principles that preserve the diversity of fish, wild animals and birds.

*Article 80. The Protection of Animals*
(1) The Confederation shall legislate on the protection of animals.
(2) In particular it shall regulate:

a. the keeping and care of animals;
b. experiments on and abuse of living animals;
c. the use of animals;
d. the import of animals and products of animal origin;
e. trade in and transport of animals;
f. the slaughter of animals.

(3) The implementation of such Confederal regulations is the task of the Cantons, insofar as the law does not reserve this for the Confederation.

## Section 5. Public Works and Transport

*Article 81. Public Works*
The Confederation may, in the interest of the country, or of a large part of it, carry out and build and operate public works, or encourage their development.

*Article 82. Road Traffic*
(1) The Confederation shall legislate on road traffic.
(2) It exercises ultimate supervision over roads of national importance; it may determine which transit roads must remain open to traffic.

(3) The use of public roads shall be free. The Federal Assembly may authorize exceptions.

*Article 83. National Highways*

(1) The Confederation shall ensure the construction of a network of national highways and shall see that such highways are usable.
(2) The Cantons shall build and maintain their national highways in conformity with federal policies, subject to ultimate Confederal supervision.
(3) The Confederation and the Cantons shall jointly bear the costs of the national highways jointly. The cost to be borne by each Canton shall be calculated taking into account the burdens which national highways impose on them, their interest in these highways and their financial resources.

*Article 84. Alpine Transit*

[Note: *See also* Transitional Provisions of the Federal Constitution.]

(1) The Confederation shall protect the alpine regions from the negative effects of transit traffic. It shall limit the nuisances caused by such traffic to a level which is harmful neither to people, animals and plants, nor to their environment.
(2) Transalpine freight in border-to-border transit hall be carried by rail. The Federal Council shall take the necessary measures. Exceptions are only permitted if they are inevitable. They shall be specified by statute.
(3) The capacity of transit roads in the alpine regions may not be increased. By-passes to relieve the pressure of through transit traffic in towns and villages are excluded from this provision.

*Article 85. Financial Dues for Heavy Goods Lorries*

[Note: *See also* Transitional Provisions of the Federal Constitution.]

(1) The Confederation may levy dues on heavy goods lorries proportional to the benefits provided or the consumption involved where heavy goods traffic creates public costs which are not already covered by other fees or charges.
(2) The net revenue from the dues shall be used to cover costs arising from road traffic.
(3) The Cantons shall receive shares of the net revenue from the dues. These shall be calculated by taking into account the particular repercussions of the levy in mountainous and remote regions.

*Article 86. Motor Fuels Consumption Tax and other Traffic Charges*

(1) The Confederation may raise a consumption tax on motor fuels.
(2) It shall raise a tax on the use of national highways by those motor vehicles and trailers which are not subject to heavy lorry dues.
(3) Half of the net revenue both from the motor fuels consumption tax and from the national highway tax shall be used for the following purposes and costs linked to road traffic:

a. Construction, maintenance and operation of national highways;
b. Measures to promote combined traffic and the transit of accompanied goods road vehicles, or to separate railway traffic from road traffic;

c. Contributions towards the construction of main roads;
d. Contributions towards the construction of protective works against natural disasters and towards measures of protection of the environment and landscape made necessary by road traffic;
e. General participation in the financing by the Cantons of highways open to motor vehicles and to the equalization of financial charges in matters relating to roads;
f. Contributions to the Cantons without national highways, and to Cantons with alpine roads carrying international traffic.

(4) If the revenues are insufficient to meet these needs, the Confederation can raise a surcharge on the motor fuels consumption tax.

*Article 87. Transport*
[Note: *See also* Transitional Provisions of the Federal Constitution.]

Legislation on rail traffic, cable cars, navigation, aviation, and space travel is a Confederal competence.

*Article 88. Footpaths and Hiking Trails*
(1) The Confederation shall establish principles applicable to networks of footpaths and hiking trails.
(2) It may support and coordinate measures taken by of the Cantons for the management and upkeep of such networks.
(3) In fulfilling its tasks, it shall take into account networks of footpaths and hiking trails, and shall replace those paths and trails which it has to close.

## Section 6. Energy and Communications

*Article 89. Energy Policy*
(1) Within their respective powers, the Confederation and the Cantons shall work to develop a sufficient, diversified, reliable and economic energy supply, compatible both with the protection of the environment and with the economical and efficient use of energy.
(2) The Confederation shall establish principles on the use of domestic and renewable energy, and for the economical and efficient use of energy.
(3) The Confederation shall legislate on the consumption of energy by fixed installations, vehicles and appliances. It shall promote the development of energy techniques, particularly in the fields of energy saving and renewable energy.
(4) Measures concerning the use of energy in buildings are primarily a cantonal competence.
(5) In its energy policy, the Confederation shall take into account the efforts of the Cantons, of the Municipalities and of economic interests; it shall take into consideration conditions in the various regions and the limitations of what is economically feasible.

*Article 90. Nuclear Energy*
[Note: *See also* Transitional Provisions of the Federal Constitution.]

Legislation on nuclear energy is a Confederal competence.

*Article 91. Energy Transport*
(1) The Confederation shall legislate on the transport and supply of electricity.
(2) Legislation on pipelines for the transport of liquid or gaseous fuels is a Confederal competence.

*Article 92. Postal and Telecommunication Services*
(1) Postal and telecommunication services are a Confederal competence.
(2) The Confederation shall ensure adequate and universally available basic postal and telecommunication services, at reasonable rates, across all regions. Rates shall be fixed according to uniform principles.

*Article 93. Radio and Television*
(1) Legislation on radio and television and other forms of public broadcasting of features and information is a Confederal competence.
(2) Radio and Television shall contribute to education and cultural development, to the free formation of opinion and to entertainment. They shall take into account the particularities of the country and the needs of the Cantons. They shall present events factually and shall reflect diverse opinions fairly and adequately.
(3) The independence of radio and television and the autonomy of their programs are guaranteed.
(4) The situation and the role of other media, in particular the press, should be taken into account.
(5) Complaints about programs may be submitted to an independent authority.

## Section 7. Economy

*Article 94. The Principles of Economic Order*
(1) The Confederation and the Cantons shall respect the principle of economic freedom.
(2) They shall seek to safeguard the interests of the national economy and, together with the private sector of the economy, to contribute to the welfare and economic security of the population.
(3) Within the limits of their respective powers, they shall seek to create favorable conditions for the private sector of the economy.
(4) Derogations from the principle of economic freedom, in particular measures threatening competition, are shall be allowed only if prescribed by the Federal Constitution or if based on cantonal monopolies.

*Article 95. Remunerative Private Economic Activity*
[Note: *See also* Transitional Provisions of the Federal Constitution.]

(1) The Confederation may legislate on the exercise of remunerative private economic activities.
(2) It shall seek to create a unified Swiss economic area. It shall guarantee that individuals having a university degree, or a federal or cantonal education certificate, or an education certificate recognized by a Canton, may exercise their profession throughout Switzerland.

*Article 96. Competition Policy*
(1) The Confederation shall legislate so as to curtail economically or socially damaging effects of cartels and other restrictions on competition.
(2) It shall take measures

a. to prevent abusive price fixing by firms or by private and public law entities also enjoying a dominant position on the market;
b. against unfair competition.

*Article 97. Consumer Protection*
(1) The Confederation shall take measures to protect consumers.
(2) It shall legislate to make remedies available to consumer organizations. In the field of federal legislation against unfair competition, these organizations shall have the same rights as professional and economic associations.
(3) The Cantons shall provide a conciliation procedure or a simple and speedy judicial procedure for litigants in cases involving sums below a specified amount. The Federal Council shall specify the amount in question.

*Article 98. Banking and Insurance*
(1) The Confederation shall legislate on banking and stock exchanges, taking account of the special role and status of cantonal banks.
(2) It may legislate on other types of financial services.
(3) It shall legislate on private insurance.

*Article 99. Monetary Policy*
(1) Money and currency are a Confederal competence. The Confederation shall have the sole and exclusive right to strike coins and to issue bank notes.
(2) As an independent central bank, the Swiss National Bank shall follow a monetary policy, which serves the general interest of the country. The policy shall be administered with the cooperation, and under the supervision of, the Confederation.
(3) The Swiss National Bank shall create sufficient monetary reserves from its profits; a part of these reserves shall be held in gold.
(4) At least two thirds of the net profits of the Swiss National Bank shall be credited to the Cantons.

*Article 100. Economic Development Policy*

(1) The Confederation shall take measures to ensure consistent economic development and, in particular, to prevent and fight inflation and unemployment.
(2) It shall take note of the economic development of the various regions. It shall cooperate with the Cantons and economic actors.
(3) In the fields of credit and currency, in foreign trade and in public finance, it may, if necessary, depart from the principle of economic freedom.
(4) In their budgetary policy, Confederation, Cantons and Municipalities shall take the economic cycle into account.
(5) In order to stabilize the economy, the Confederation may temporarily levy surcharges, or grant rebates on federal taxes and dues. The accumulated funds thus raised are shall be frozen; when they are released, direct surcharges shall be individually reimbursed, and indirect surcharges be shall be used to grant rebates or to create employment.
(6) The Confederation may oblige firms businesses to accumulate anti-crisis reserves. To facilitate this it may grant tax privileges, and may also oblige the Cantons to grant such privileges. After the release of the reserves, firms shall be free to decide how to use them within the guidelines provided by law.

*Article 101. Foreign Trade*

(1) The Confederation shall safeguard the external interests of the Swiss economy.
(2) In special cases, it may take measures to protect the domestic economy. It may, if necessary, depart from the principle of economic freedom.

*Article 102. Maintaining Stocks of Essential Goods and Services*

[Note: *See also* Transitional Provisions of the Federal Constitution.]

(1) The Confederation shall ensure the country's stocks of essential goods and services in order to meet any threats of war, other manifestations of force or severe shortages which the economy cannot counteract by itself. It shall take preventative measures.
(2) It may, if necessary, depart from the principle of economic freedom.

*Article 103. Structural Policy*

[Note: *See also* Transitional Provisions of the Federal Constitution.]

The Confederation may support economically threatened regions, and promote branches of the economy and professions, if the measures of self-help that can reasonably be expected of them are insufficient to ensure their existence. It may, if necessary, depart from the principle of economic freedom.

*Article 104. Agriculture*

(1) The Confederation shall ensure that agriculture, by way of an output which responds to the demands both of sustainable development and of the market, contributes substantially

a. to securing the provisioning of the population;
b. to the conservation of national resources and the upkeep of the rural landscape.
c. to a decentralized pattern of settlement on the land.

(2) In addition to the measures of self-help that may reasonably be expected from agriculture and, if need arise, departing from the principle of economic freedom, the Confederation shall promote cultivation of the land by peasant farms.
(3) It shall conceive the measures in such a way that agriculture may fulfill its multiple functions. Its powers and tasks shall, above all, be the following:

a. It shall complement peasant agricultural revenues by direct payments, so as to secure a fair and adequate remuneration for the services rendered, provided that the farmer can prove compliance with ecological requirements;
b. It shall promote, by way of economically advantageous incentives, forms of farming production which are particularly close to nature and respectful of both the environment and animals;
c. It shall legislate on the declarations of origin and on quality, production methods and processing processes for foodstuffs;
d. It shall protect the environment against pollution due to excessive use of fertilizers, chemicals and other auxiliary substances;
e. It may encourage agricultural research, counseling, and education in agriculture and also subsidize investments;
f. It may legislate on the consolidation of rural property.

(4) To these ends it shall invest specially targeted agricultural credits and the Confederation's general funds.

*Article 105. Alcohol*
Legislation on the production, the importing, the refining , and the sale of distilled spirits is a Confederal competence. The Confederation shall, in particular, take into account the harmful effects of the consumption of alcohol.

*Article 106. Gambling*
[Note: *See also* Transitional Provisions of the Federal Constitution.]

(1) Legislation on gambling and lotteries is a Confederal competence.
(2) A federal license from the Confederation shall be required to establish and run a gambling casino. When issuing a federal license, the Confederation shall take regional circumstances and the dangers of gambling into account.
(3) The Confederation shall levy a tax on the revenues from casinos a tax on their revenues; this tax shall not exceed 80 per cent of the gross revenues from games of chance. The yield shall be used to cover the Confederal subsidy to old age, survivors', and disability insurance.
(4) Approval of gambling machines involving an element of skill and where money can be won is a cantonal competence.

*Article 107. Weapons and Military Material*
(1) The Confederation shall legislate against the misuse of weapons, associated equipment, and munitions.
(2) It shall legislate on the production, acquisition, distribution, import, export and transit of military materiel.

## Section 8. Housing, Work, Social Security and Health

*Article 108. Promotion of the Construction and of the Acquisition of Dwellings*

(1) The Confederation shall encourage the construction and the purchase of flats and family houses for individuals' own use and the activity both of developers and of organizations working to build social housing.
(2) It shall promote, in particular, the acquisition and development of land for housing purposes, the rationalization of building techniques and the reduction of construction and housing costs.
(3) It may legislate on the development of land for the erection of housing and on the rationalization of construction techniques.
(4) In fulfilling this task, it shall, in particular, takes special note of the interests of families and of the elderly, the needy and the disabled.

*Article 109. Leasehold*

(1) The Confederation shall legislate against abuses in tenancy arrangements, particularly against unfair rents, on the quashing of abusive notices of termination, and on the extension of tenancies only for short periods.
(2) It may legislate to confer generally binding effect on general contracts between landlords and tenants. Contracts may become generally binding only if they take fairly into account justified minority interests and regional differences, and respect the principle of equality before the law.

*Article 110. Labor*

(1) The Confederation may legislate on:

a. the protection of workers;
b. the relationship between employers and workers, in particular the common regulation of matters concerning business or professional activity;
c. recruitment services;
d. extending the application of collective labor contracts.

(2) Collective labor contracts may have their scope extended only if they fairly take into account justified minority interests and regional differences, and also respect both the principle of equality before the law and the freedom to unionize.
(3) August 1 is the National Day of the Confederation. In labor law, it is treated as if it were assimilated to a Sunday, and is paid.

*Article 111. Social Security*

(1) The Confederation shall take measures so as to ensure an adequate social security for the elderly, survivors, and the disabled. This social security shall be based on three pillars, namely on the Federal old age, survivors' and disability insurance; company pension plans; and on arrangements made by individuals for their own future.
(2) The Confederation shall ensure that the Federal old age, survivors', and disability insurance, and company pension plans can durably fulfill their purpose.

(3) It may require the Cantons to exempt from taxation both the institutions of the federal old age, survivors', and disability insurance, and company pension plans, while also granting tax relief to persons insured and their employers both on contributions paid and on monies set aside for future benefits.
(4) In cooperation with the Cantons, the Confederation shall encourage individuals to provide for their own future, particularly through by fiscal measures and by policies encouraging the acquisition of property.

*Article 112. Old Age, Survivors' and Disability Insurance*
[Note: *See also* Transitional Provisions of the Federal Constitution.]

(1) The Confederation shall legislate on the old age, survivors', and disability insurance scheme.
(2) In doing so, it shall respect the following principles:

a. Insurance is compulsory;
b. Pensions must be sufficient to cover basic living expenses;
c. The maximum pension must not be more than twice the minimum;
d. Pensions must at least keep up with price inflation.

(3) Insurance shall be financed:

a. by contributions from the insured; in the case of employees half their contributions are to be met by their employers;
b. by subsidies from of the Confederation and, if the law so provides, from the Cantons.

(4) Together, the subsidies of the Confederation and the Cantons shall not exceed half the total disbursements made under the scheme.
(5) Confederal subsidies shall be primarily financed by the net proceeds of the tax on tobacco, the tax on distilled spirits, and the tax on the revenue from the operation of gaming houses.
(6) The Confederation shall encourage the integration of persons with disabilities, and also support efforts to assist the elderly, survivors, and the disabled. To this end, it may use the funds of the old age, survivors' and disability insurance.

*Article 113. Company Pension Plans*
[Note: *See also* Transitional Provisions of the Federal Constitution.]

(1) The Confederation shall legislate on pension plans provided by companies.
(2) In doing so, it shall respect the following principles:

a. Company pension plans, together with the old age, survivors', and disability insurance, should permit the insured to maintain their previous standard of living in an appropriate way;
b. Company pension plans shall be mandatory for employees; The law may prescribe exceptions;

c. Employers shall insure their employees with a pension institution. If necessary, the Confederation shall give them the possibility of insuring their employees with a federal pension institution;
d. The self-employed may voluntarily insure themselves with a pension institution;
e. The Confederation declare company pension schemes obligatory for particular groups of the self-employed, whether in general or just for specific particular risks.

(3) Company pension plans shall be financed through contributions by the insured themselves; at least half the contribution of employees shall be paid by their employers.
(4) Pension institutions must satisfy minimum federal requirements; the Confederation may prescribe nationwide measures to resolve particular problems.

*Article 114. Unemployment Insurance*
(1) The Confederation shall legislate on unemployment insurance.
(2) In doing so, it shall respect the following principles:

a. The insurance shall guarantee an appropriate compensation for loss of earnings, and shall support measures to prevent and fight unemployment;
b. Insurance shall be mandatory for employees; the law may provide for exceptions;
c. The self-employed may voluntarily insure themselves.

(3) Unemployment insurance shall be financed by the contributions of the insured themselves. The employers shall pay half the contribution of their employees.
(4) In exceptional circumstances, the Confederation and the Cantons shall provide subsidies.
(5) The Confederation may legislate on social assistance to the unemployed.

*Article 115. Assistance to Persons in Need*
Persons in need shall be assisted by the Cantons of their domicile. The Confederation may provide for exceptions, and shall determine the competent authorities.

*Article 116. Family Allowances and Maternity Insurance*
(1) In fulfilling its tasks, the Confederation shall take into account the needs of the family. It may support measures to protect the family.
(2) It may legislate on family allowances and operate a federal family compensation fund.
(3) It shall institute a maternity insurance scheme. It may also oblige people who cannot benefit from the insurance to contribute.
(4) The Confederation may declare mandatory both the joining of a family compensation fund and maternity insurance, whether generally or for certain categories of persons, and may make its subsidies dependent upon equitable contributions by the Cantons.

*Article 117. Health and Accident Insurance*

(1) The Confederation shall legislate on health and accident insurance.

(2) It may declare mandatory health and accident insurance generally or for certain categories of persons.

*Article 118. Health Protection*

(1) Within the limits of its powers, the Confederation shall take measures for the protection of health.

(2) It shall legislate on:

a. the use of foodstuffs and of therapeutics, drugs, organic materials, chemicals and things which may be dangerous to health;
b. the fight against contagious, widespread or other diseases which are particularly dangerous to humans and animals;
c. the protection against ionizing radiation.

*Article 119. Medically Assisted Procreation and Genetic Engineering involving humans*

(1) Human beings should be protected against the abuse of medically assisted procreation and genetic engineering.

(2) The Confederation shall legislate on the use of human reproductive and genetic material. In doing so it shall ensure the protection of human dignity, of the personality, and of the family, and, in particular, it shall respect the following principles:

a. All forms of cloning and interference with genetic material of human reproductive cells and embryos are prohibited;
b. Non-human reproductive and genetic material may neither be introduced into nor combined with human reproductive material;
c. Methods of medically assisted procreation are only authorized when sterility or the danger of transmission of a serious illness cannot be otherwise avoided; but neither in order to induce certain characteristics in the child nor to conduct research. The fertilization of human ova outside a woman's body ova shall be permitted only under conditions determined by the law. No more human ova may be developed into embryos outside a woman's body than are capable of being immediately implanted into her;
d. The donation of embryos and all forms of surrogate maternity are prohibited;
e. No trade may be conducted in human reproductive material or in any product obtained from embryos;
f. An individual's person's genetic material may only be analyzed, registered or disclosed with their consent, or if a statute so provides;
g. Every person shall have access to the data concerning their ancestry.

*Article 119a. Medical Transplantation*
[Note: Added 7 February 1999 by popular vote, certified as accurate by decision of the Federal Government of 23 March 1999 and based on the Federal Decree of 26 June 1998.]

(1) The Confederation shall establish rules in the field of transplantation of organs, tissues and cells. In doing this it shall seek to safeguard human dignity, personality and health.
(2) It shall in particular establish principles for a fair distribution of organs.
(3) The donations of human organs, tissues and cells shall be free of charge. Trade in human organs is prohibited.

*Article 120. Genetic Engineering in the Non-Human Field*
(1) Individuals and their environment should be protected against the abuse of genetic engineering.
(2) The Confederation shall legislate on the use of the reproductive and genetic material of animals, plants, and other organisms. In doing so, it shall respect the integrity of living organisms and the security of man, animal and environment, and shall protect the genetic diversity of animal and vegetal species.

## Section 9. The Establishment and Residence of Foreigners

*Article 121.*
(1) Legislation on immigration, emigration, establishment and residence and domicile of foreigners and on granting asylum is a Confederal competence.
(2) Foreigners who endanger Switzerland's security may be removed from Switzerland by force.

## Section 10. Civil and Criminal Law, Weights and Measures

*Article 122. Civil Law*
[Note: Amendment of 12 March 2000.]

(1) Legislation in the field of civil law and civil procedure is a Confederal competence.
(2) Judicial organization and the administration of civil law are cantonal responsibilities except where the law provides otherwise.
(3) Civil judgments having the force of law are executable throughout Switzerland

*Article 123. Criminal Law*
[Note: The amendment of 12 March 2000 eliminated the old paragraph 3 which read 'Judicial organization, procedure and administration in penal matters are a cantonal competence'.]

(1) Legislation in the field of criminal law and criminal procedure is a Confederal competence.

(2) Judicial organization and the administration of criminal justice along with the execution of sentences and other criminal law measures are cantonal responsibilities except where the law provides otherwise.
(3) The Confederation can make financial contributions to the cantons

a. for the building of penal institutions;
b. for improving the carrying out of sentences and penalties;
c. for the support of institutions providing educational services designed for children, adolescents and young adults.

*Article 123a.*
[Note: Adopted by popular vote 8 February 2004.]

(1) Sexual or violent offenders who are considered highly dangerous and untreatable by experts at the time of conviction, shall be sentenced to life imprisonment due to the serious risk of recidivism. Early release on parole and leave shall not be permitted.
(2) Only on the basis of new scientific evidence proving that the offender is treatable and is thus no longer a threat to the community, can a new forensic-psychiatric assessment be conducted. If a detainee is granted parole based on this new assessment, the authority that ordered the release is liable in case of the offender's recidivism.
(3) All assessments evaluating violent and sexual offenders are to be carried out by two unconnected experts, taking into account all essential grounds for the assessment.

*Article 124. Aid to Victims of Criminal Acts*
The Confederation and the Cantons shall ensure that the victims of criminal acts against bodily, corporal, mental, or sexual integrity receive assistance and also appropriate compensation if, as a consequence of such criminal acts, they suffer financial difficulties.

*Article 125. Weights and Measures*
Legislation on weights and measures is a Confederal competence.

## Chapter Three. Financial System

*Article 126. Financial Management*
[Note: Adopted by popular vote 2 December 2001.]

(1) The Confederation shall keep its expenditure and receipts in balance over the medium term.
(2) The ceiling for total expenditure, which must be agreed in the budget is set by the expected receipts, taking into account the economic situation.
(3) Exceptional financial needs may justify an appropriate increase in the ceiling as defined in para 2. Any such increase must be agreed by the Federal Assembly in conformity with Article 159(3) lit. c of the Federal Constitution.

(4) If the total expenditures recorded in the annual accounts exceed the maximum amount according to subsections 2 or 4, the overspend shall be rectified in the following years.
(5) The law shall regulate the detailed arrangements.

*Article 127. Principles of Taxation*
(1) The general principles regulating of taxation, particularly on liability to tax, on decisions on what should be taxed and on its calculation, shall be established by law.
(2) To the extent that the nature of the tax allows it, the principles of universality, of equality of tax treatment and of taxation in proportion according to economic capacity shall be followed.
(3) Intercantonal double taxation is prohibited. The Confederation shall take any the necessary measures.

*Article 128. Direct Taxes*
[Note: *See also* Transitional Provisions of the Federal Constitution.]

(1) The Confederation may raise direct taxes:

(a) of at most 11.5 per cent on the income of individuals;
(b) of at most 9.8 per cent on the net profit of corporate bodies;
(c) of at most 0.0825 per cent on the capital and the reserves of corporate bodies.

(2) In establishing tax scales, the Confederation shall take into account the burden of direct taxes on the Cantons and Municipalities.
(3) Periodic adjustment to individuals' tax position will be made to avoid inflation inadvertently lifting them into higher tax brackets.
(4) The Cantons shall assess and collect the taxes. Three tenths of the gross tax yield shall be due to the Cantons; at least one sixth of this amount shall be used for financial equalization among the Cantons.

*Article 129. Harmonization of Taxes*
(1) The Confederation shall establish principles for the harmonization of direct taxes of the Confederation, Cantons, and Municipalities; it shall take into account the efforts of the Cantons to harmonize their taxes.
(2) Harmonization shall extend to the duty to pay taxes, to what is to be taxed, to the time scale of calculation and to procedural and criminal law on taxation. It does not cover tax scales, tax rates, and levels of exemption.
(3) The Confederation may legislate against arrangements granting unjustified tax advantages.

*Article 130. Value Added Tax*
[Note: *See also* Transitional Provisions of the Federal Constitution.]

[Note *ad* para. 3: Federal Parliament has made use of this authority. *See* Article 36 (1)–(3) of the Federal Value Added Tax Act of 2 September 1999 (SR 641.20), according to which the value added tax rates are, with effect from 1 January 2001, 7,6 per cent (normal rate), 2,4 per cent (reduced rate) und 3,6 per cent (special rate for services of accommodation).]

(1) The Confederation may levy a value added tax with a maximum tax rate of 6.5 per cent on the supply of goods and services, including own use, and on imports.
(2) 5 per cent of the tax yield shall be used for measures in favour of low income groups.
(3) If, because of the development of the age structure, the financing of the old age, survivors' and disability insurance is no longer secured, the value added tax rate may be raised in a Federal statute, by at most 1 per cent point.[10]

*Article 131. Special Consumption Taxes*
[Note: *See also* Transitional Provisions of the Federal Constitution.]

(1) The Confederation may levy special consumption taxes on the following:

a. tobacco and tobacco products;
b. distilled spirits;
c. beer;
d. automobiles and their components;
e. petrol, other mineral oils, natural gas and products obtained by refining them, and also on motor fuels.

(2) It may levy a surcharge on motor fuels.
(3) One tenth of the net yield of the tax on distilled spirits is to be allocated to the Cantons. The Cantons will use such funds to fight the causes and effects of substance addiction.

*Article 132. Stamp and Withholding Taxes*
[Note: *See also* Transitional Provisions of the Federal Constitution.]

(1) The Confederation may levy a stamp tax on securities, on insurance premium receipts and other documents relating to trading operations Documents concerning operations in immovable property and mortgages shall be exempt from stamp tax.
(2) The Confederation may levy a withholding tax on the revenue from movable capital assets, on lottery winnings and on insurance benefits.

*Article 133. Customs Duties*
Legislation on customs duties and other levies on trans-border goods traffic is a Confederal competence.

*Article 134. Exclusion of Cantonal and Communal Taxation*
What federal legislation subjects to value added tax, to a special consumption tax, to stamp tax, or to withholding tax, or declares to be exempt from these taxes, may not then be taxed by the Cantons and the Municipalities with levies of the same kind.

*Article 135. Financial Equalization*
(1) The Confederation shall promote financial equalization among the Cantons.
(2) When granting subsidies, it shall take into account the financial capacity of the Cantons and the special situation of the mountainous regions.

# Part Four. People and Cantons

## Chapter One. General Provisions

*Article 136. Political Rights*
(1) All Swiss citizens who are 18 years or older, and are not under guardianship because of mental illness or incapacity, shall have political rights in federal matters. All Swiss shall have the same political rights and duties.
(2) They may participate in elections to the House of Representatives and in federal votations, and may launch and sign popular initiatives and demands for referenda in federal matters.

*Article 137. Political Parties*
Political parties shall contribute to the forming the People's opinion and will.

## Chapter 2. Initiative and Referendum

*Article 138. Popular Initiative for Total Revision of the Federal Constitution*
(1) Within 18 months since the official publication, any 100,000 citizens entitled to vote may propose a total revision of the Federal Constitution.
(2) This proposal must be submitted to the People by referendum.

*Article 139 (new). Popular Initiatives for Partial Revisions of the Federal Constitution in the form of a fully formulated proposal for an amendment*
[Note: Adopted by popular vote 9 February 2003, in force since 1 August 2003]

(1) Within 18 months since the official publication, any 100,000 citizens entitled to vote may propose a partial revision of the Federal Constitution in the form of a fully formulated proposal for an amendment.
(2) Where an initiative does not respect either the principles of unity of form and unity of matter, or the mandatory rules of international law, the Federal Assembly shall declare it invalid, whether in whole or in part.
(3) The People and the Cantons shall vote simultaneously on the initiative. The Federal Assembly may formulate a recommendation regarding approval or rejection of the initiative. It may submit its own counter-draft to the initiative.

*Article 139 (old). Popular Initiatives for Partial Revisions of the Federal Constitution*
[Note: This provision remains in force. The generally framed initiative is still possible, *see* Federal decree of 19 June 2003 (AS 2003 1953).]

(1) Any 100,000 citizens entitled to vote may propose a partial revision of the Federal Constitution.
(2) A popular initiative for a partial revision of the Federal Constitution may be conceived in general terms or as a fully formulated proposal for an amendment.
(3) Where an initiative does not respect either the principles of unity of form and unity of matter, or the mandatory rules of international law, the Federal Assembly shall declare it invalid, whether in whole or in part.
(4) If the Federal Assembly approves a generally framed initiative, it must prepare a partial revision in the sense of the initiative, and submit it to the vote of the People and the Cantons. If it rejects the initiative, it shall submit it to the vote of the People; the People shall decide whether the initiative should be followed up. Where the People approves such an initiative, the Federal Assembly shall formulate a corresponding draft.
(5) [...]
(6) The People and the Cantons shall vote simultaneously on the initiative and the counter-project. [...].

*Article 139a.*
[Note: Adopted by popular vote 9 February 2003. The provision is not in force yet.]

*Article 139b. Procedure on the Initiative and the Counter-Proposal*
[Note: Adopted by popular vote 9 February 2003. Paras. 2 and 3 entered into force 1 August 2003. Para. 1 will enter into force at a later stage.]

(1) [...]
(2) The voters may approve both drafts. They may indicate in the decisive question which draft they prefer, should both be approved.
(3) Should one of the drafts obtain the majority of the People's votes and the other the majority of the votes of the Cantons, the draft will enter into force that obtained the higher sum relative to the percentage of the People's votes and to the percentage of the votes of the Cantons regarding the decisive question.

*Article 140. Mandatory Referendum*
(1) The following shall be submitted to the vote of the People and the Cantons:

a. Revisions of the Federal Constitution;
b. Entry into organizations for collective security or into supranational communities;
c. Federal Statutes declared urgent but which lack a constitutional basis and whose validity exceeds one year; such Federal Statutes must be submitted to a vote within one year of their adoption by the Federal Assembly.

(2) The following are shall be submitted to the vote of the People alone:

a. Popular initiatives for total revision of the Federal Constitution;
b. Popular initiatives for partial revision of the Federal Constitution, conceived in general terms, which were rejected by the Federal Assembly;

c. The question whether a total revision of the Constitution should be carried out if both Chambers disagree.

*Article 141. Optional Referendum*
[Note: Adopted by popular vote 9 February 2003. Para. 1 entered into force 1 August 2003. Para. 2 is ineffective since 1 August 2003.]

(1) 100 days since its official publication, the following laws are submitted to the vote of the People at the request of any 50,000 citizens entitled to vote, or of eight Cantons:

a. Federal Laws;
b. Federal laws declared urgent with a validity exceeding one year;
c. Federal decrees to the extent the Constitution or statute law prescribes this;
d. International treaties which:

1. are of unlimited duration and may not be terminated;
2. provide for the entry into an international organization;
3. contain important legislative provisions or that require for their further implementation additional Federal laws.

(2) […]

*Article 141a. Implementation of International Treaties*
[Note: Adopted by popular vote 9 February 2003, in force since 1 August 2003.]

(1) Should the approving decree of an international treaty be submitted to a mandatory referendum, the Federal Assembly may include the amendments of the Federal Constitution that are necessary for the implementation of the treaty into the approving decree.
(2) Should the approving decree of an international treaty be submitted to an optional referendum, the Federal Assembly may include the amendments to Federal legislation that is necessary for the implementation of the treaty into the approving decree.

*Article 142. Required Majorities*
(1) Proposals submitted to the vote of the People shall be accepted if the majority of those voting approves them.
(2) Proposals submitted to the vote of the People and the Cantons shall be accepted if both the majority of those voting and the majority of the Cantons approve them.
(3) The result of a popular vote in a Canton determines the vote of that Canton.
(4) The Cantons of Obwalden, Nidwalden, Basle-City, Basle-Land, Appenzell Outer Rhodes and Appenzell Inner Rhodes each count for one half of a cantonal vote.

# Part Five. Federal Authorities

## Chapter One. General Provisions

*Article 143. Eligibility*
Every Swiss citizen entitled to vote is eligible for membership of the House of Representatives, the Federal Council and the Federal Court.

*Article 144. Incompatibilities*
(1) Members of the House of Representatives, of the Senate, of the Federal Council, and Judges on the Federal Court may not at the same time be members of another of these bodies.
(2) The members of the Federal Council and the full-time judges of the Federal Court may not carry out another function for the Confederation or for a Canton, nor may they exercise any other remunerative activity.
(3) The law may provide for other incompatibilities.

*Article 145. Length of Tenure*
The members of the House of Representatives, the Federal Council, and the Chancellor of the Confederation shall be elected for a term of four years. The judges of the Federal Court shall be elected for a term of six years.

*Article 146. Confederal Liability*
The Confederation shall be answerable for damage illegally caused by its servants in the exercise of their official activities.

*Article 147. Consultation Procedure*
Cantons, political parties and interested circles shall be invited to comment, during preparatory phases, on important legislative bills, on other projects with major implications and also on important international treaties.

## Chapter Two. The Federal Assembly

### Section 1. Organization

*Article 148. Status*
(1) Subject to the rights of the People and the Cantons, the Federal Assembly is the highest authority of the Confederation.
(2) It has two Chambers, the House of Representatives and the Senate, each endowed with equal powers.

*Article 149. Composition and Election of the House of Representatives*
(1) The House of Representatives shall be composed of 200 deputies of the People.
(2) The Members of Parliament are elected directly by the People according to the system of proportional representation. The House of Representatives shall be renewed in full every four years.

(3) Each Canton shall form an electoral constituency.
(4) Seats shall be distributed among the Cantons in proportion to their population. Each Canton has a right to have at least one seat.

*Article 150. Composition and Election of the Senate*
(1) The Senate shall consist of 46 deputies of the Cantons.
(2) The Cantons of Obwalden, Nidwalden, Basle-City, Basle-Land, Appenzell Outer Rhodes and Appenzell Inner Rhodes shall elect one deputy each, the other Cantons shall elect two.
(3) The Cantons shall decide on the rules for the election of their representatives to the Senate.

*Article 151.* Sessions
(1) The Chambers shall meet regularly for plenary sessions. The law regulates the summoning of meetings.
(2) One fourth of the members of a Chamber or the Federal Council may request that the two Chambers be called to an extraordinary session.

*Article 152. Presidency*
Each Council shall elect from amongst its members, for a one year term, a President, a first Vice-President and a second Vice-resident. These mandates are not renewable for the following year.

*Article 153. Parliamentary Committees*
(1) Each Council shall appoint committees from within its own ranks.
(2) The law may prescribe joint committees.
(3) The law may delegate certain powers, not of a legislative nature, to committees.
(4) To help them fulfill their tasks, the committees shall have the right to obtain information, to consult documents and to conduct inquiries. The law shall define the limits to these rights.

*Article 154. Groups*
The members of the Federal Assembly may form political groups.

*Article 155. Parliamentary Services*
The Federal Assembly shall benefit from parliamentary services. It may also call upon the services of the Federal Administration. The law shall regulate the precise details.

## Section 2. Procedures

*Article 156. Separate Deliberation*
[Note: Approved by popular vote 9 February 2003. Para. 3(a) and (d) entered into force 1 August 2003. Para. 3(b) and (c) will enter into force at a later stage.]

(1) The House of Representatives and the Senate shall deliberate separately.
(2) Decisions of the Federal Assembly shall require the approval of both Chambers.

(3) In case of disagreement between the Chambers, the law shall guarantee that Federal decrees can pass:

(a) regarding the question whether a popular initiative is valid or partly invalid;
(b) [...]
(c) [...]
(d) regarding the budget and its supplements.

*Article 157. Joint Deliberation*

(1) The House of Representatives and the Senate shall deliberate in common as the Federal Assembly in Joint Session, under the chairmanship of the President of the House of Representatives, in order to:

a. hold elections;
b. rule on jurisdictional disputes between the highest federal authorities;
c. to rule on petitions for pardon.

(2) The Federal Assembly in Joint Session shall assemble for special occasions, and to hear declarations by the Federal Council.

*Article 158. Public Nature of Sessions*

Meetings of the Chambers shall be public. The law may provide for exceptions.

*Article 159. Quorum and Majority*

(1) The Chambers may deliberate validly only if the majority of their members are present.
(2) Decisions are taken in both Chambers and in the Federal Assembly in Joint Session by the majority of those voting.
(3) However, the majority of the members of each Chamber shall be required for the following:

a. Declarations that Federal laws are 'urgent';
b. Provisions granting subsidies, authorizing credit lines, and establishing spending ceilings which cause new one-off time expenditures exceeding 20 Million Swiss Francs, or new recurrent expenditures exceeding 2 Million Swiss Francs;
c. Increases of total expenditure in case of extraordinary payment requirements as provided by Article 126(3) of the Federal Constitutions.

(4) The Federal Assembly may, by an ordinance, adjust to inflation the amounts set out under the terms of subsection 3(b) of the Federal Constitution.

*Article 160. Rights of Initiative and Proposition*

(1) All members of the Federal Assembly, all parliamentary groups, all parliamentary committees and all Cantons have the right to submit initiatives to the Federal Assembly.
(2) Members of the Federal Assembly and of the Federal Council may present propositions concerning a proposal under discussion.

*Article 161. Ban on Accepting Direction from Outside*
(1) The members of the Federal Assembly shall vote without instructions.
(2) They shall make public their links with interest groups.

*Article 162. Immunity*
(1) The members of the Federal Assembly and the Federal Council , together with the Federal Chancellor may not be held responsible for their statements in the Chambers and before parliamentary organs.
(2) The law may provide for further forms of immunity, and extend them to other individuals.

## Section 3. Powers

*Article 163. The Form of Acts Passed by the Federal Assembly*
(1) The Federal Assembly shall enact legally binding rules in the form of Federal Statutes or ordinances.
(2) Other acts shall be issued as federal decrees. Where a federal decree is not liable to challenge by referendum it shall be known as a 'simple' federal decree.

*Article 164. Legislation*
(1) All important provisions establishing binding legal rules of law must be enacted in the form of a Federal law. This is particularly so with fundamental provisions on:

a. the exercise of political rights;
b. the restriction of constitutional rights;
c. the rights and obligations of individuals;
d. the definition of a tax payer, decisions on what should be taxable and the calculation of taxes;
e. the tasks and services of the Confederation;
f. cantonal obligations when implementing and executing federal law;
g. the organization and procedures of federal authorities.

(2) A Federal Statute may delegate the power to legislate in binding form unless this is excluded by the Federal Constitution.

*Article 165. Urgent Legislation*
(1) A Federal Statute whose coming into force brooks no delay, may be declared 'urgent' by the majority of each Council and put into force immediately. There must be a time limit on its applicability.
(2) If a referendum is demanded against an urgent Federal Statute, the latter shall lapse one year after its adoption by the Federal Assembly, unless it is approved by the People within that time.

(3) An urgent Federal Statute that has no constitutional basis shall lapse one year after its adoption by the Federal Assembly unless, within that time, it is adopted by the People and the Cantons. There must be a time limit on its applicability.
(4) An urgent Federal Statute, which was not adopted by popular vote, may not be renewed.

*Article 166. Foreign Relations and International Treaties*
(1) The Federal Assembly shall participate in shaping foreign policy and shall supervise foreign relations.
(2) It shall approve international treaties with the exception of those which, by statute or international treaty, are within the powers of the Federal Council.

*Article 167. Finances*
The Federal Assembly shall consent to federal spending, agree the budget and approve federal accounts.

*Article 168. Elections*
(1) The Federal Assembly shall elect the members of the Federal Council, the Federal Chancellor, the judges of the Federal Court, and the General.
(2) The law may empower the Federal Assembly to carry out other elections or to confirm other nominations.

*Article 169. High Supervision*
(1) The Federal Assembly shall exercise ultimate supervision of the Federal Council, the Federal Administration, the Federal Courts and the other organs entrusted with tasks of the Confederation.
(2) Official secrecy shall not be used as a reason for preventing special delegations of responsibility to supervisory commissions where these are duly prescribed by statute.

*Article 170. The Evaluation of Efficacy*
The Federal Assembly shall ensure that the efficacy of measures taken by the Confederation is evaluated.

*Article 171. Mandates to the Federal Council*
The Federal Assembly may confer mandates on to the Federal Council. Statute shall regulate the precise details and, in particular, the instruments which the Federal Assembly may use to influence matters within the remit of the Federal Council.

*Article 172. Relations between the Confederation and the Cantons*
(1) The Federal Assembly shall oversee relations between the Confederation and the Cantons.
(2) It shall guarantee cantonal constitutions.
(3) Should the Federal Council or a Canton raise objections, it shall decide whether to approve intercantonal treaties and treaties between Cantons and foreign countries,

*Article 173. Other Tasks and Powers*

(1) Beside this the Federal Assembly shall have following further tasks and powers:

a. It shall take measures to safeguard the external security, independence, and neutrality of Switzerland;
b. It shall take measures to secure the internal security;
c. If extraordinary circumstances so require, it may issue ordinances or simple federal decrees to fulfill the tasks listed at letters a and b;
d. It shall orders active military service, and to this end, shall mobilize all or part of the army;
e. It shall take measures to enforce federal law;
f. It shall decide on the validity of those popular initiatives which that meet the formal requirements;
g. It shall cooperate in planning major state activities;
h. It shall decide on individual acts if a Federal Statute expressly so provides;
i. It shall rule on conflicts of jurisdiction between the highest federal authorities;
k. It shall decide on petitions for pardon and grant amnesties.

(2) The Federal Assembly shall, moreover, deal with all subjects that are within the remit of the Confederation but which are not attributed to another federal authority.
(3) The law may assign other tasks and powers to the Federal Assembly.

## Chapter Three. The Federal Council and the Federal Administration

### Section 1. Organization and Procedure

*Article 174. The Role of the Federal Council*

The Federal Council is the highest governing authority and the supreme executive authority of the Confederation.

*Article 175. Composition and Election*

[Note: Paras. (3) and (4) were adopted 7 February 1999, by popular vote; certified as accurate by decision of the Federal Government of 2 March 1999 and based on the Federal Decree of 9 October 1998.]

(1) The Federal Council shall consist of seven members.
(2) The members of the Federal Council shall be elected by the Federal Assembly after each full renewal of the House of Representatives.
(3) They are elected for four years from amongst Swiss citizens eligible for membership in the House of Representatives.
(4) The various regions and language communities must be equitably represented in the Federal Council.

*Article 176. Presidency*
(1) The President of the Confederation shall chair the Federal Council.
(2) The Federal Assembly shall elects, for a one-year term, one of the members of the Federal Council as President of the Confederation and another as Vice-President of the Federal Council.
(3) These mandates may not be renewed for the following year. The outgoing President of the Confederation may not be elected as Vice-President for the following year.

*Article 177. The Principle of Collective Authority and the Division into Departments*
(1) The Federal Council shall take its decisions as a collegial body.
(2) For the preparation and implementation of decisions, the business of the Federal Council shall be distributed amongst its members according to Departments.
(3) Decisions on business can be entrusted to Departments or to administrative units subordinated to them; in such cases the right of appeal shall be guaranteed.

*Article 178. The Federal Administration*
(1) The Federal Council shall direct the Federal Administration. It shall ensure that the tasks, which are entrusted to it, are effectively carried out.
(2) The Federal Administration shall be divided into Departments; each Department is directed by one member of the Federal Council.
(3) Statute may attribute administrative tasks to outside organizations and individuals provided that these are duly constituted under public or private law.

*Article 179. Federal Chancery*
The Federal Chancery is the general staff of the Federal Council. It shall be directed by the Chancellor of the Confederation.

## Section 2. Powers

*Article 180. Government Policy*
(1) The Federal Council shall determine the aims and means of its governmental policy. It shall plan and coordinate the activities of the state.
(2) It shall inform the public of its activity fully and in good time, unless overriding public or private concerns prevent this.

*Article 181. The Right of Initiative*
The Federal Council shall submit drafts of its legislative proposals to the Federal Assembly.

*Article 182. Legislation and Implementation*
(1) The Federal Council shall issue legally binding acts in the form of ordinances, insofar as the Constitution or the laws empower it to do so.
(2) It shall ensure the implementation of legislation, decrees of the Federal Assembly and judgments of the federal judiciary.

*Article 183. Finances*

(1) The Federal Council shall prepare estimates along with a draft budget, and keep the accounts of the Confederation.
(2) It shall ensure proper financial management.

*Article 184. Foreign Relations*

(1) The Federal Council is responsible for foreign affairs subject to the Federal Assembly's rights of participation; it shall represents Switzerland abroad.
(2) It shall sign and ratify treaties. It shall submit them to the Federal Assembly for approval.
(3) When the defense of the country's interests of the country so requires, the Federal Council may issue ordinances and take all necessary decisions. Such ordinances must have a definite expiry date.

*Article 185. External and Internal Security*

(1) The Federal Council shall take measures to preserve the external security, the independence and the neutrality of Switzerland.
(2) It shall take measures to safeguard internal security.
(3) It may use the present article to issue ordinances and orders to obviate existing, or imminent, major disturbances in public order which gravely threaten the external or internal. Such ordinances must have a definite expiry date.
(4) In urgent cases, it may mobilize troops. If it mobilizes more than 4,000 members of the armed forces for active duty, or if the mobilization is expected to last more than three weeks, the Federal Assembly must be convened without delay.

*Article 186. Relations between the Confederation and the Cantons*

(1) The Federal Council is responsible for relations between the Confederation and the Cantons, and shall collaborate with the latter.
(2) It shall approve cantonal legislation where the implementation of federal law so requires.
(3) It may raise objections against to treaties between the Cantons, or between Cantons and foreign countries.
(4) It shall ensure respect for the implementation of federal law, for cantonal constitutions and for intercantonal treaties, and shall take any measures necessary to this end.

*Article 187. Other Tasks and Powers*

(1) The Federal Council shall also have the following further tasks and powers:

a. Supervising the Federal Administration and the other organizations or persons entrusted with tasks of the Confederation;
b. Regularly informing the Federal Assembly of its stewardship and of the state of the country;
c. Making appointments that are not in the remit of other authorities;
d. Deciding on appeals where the law so provides.

(2) The law may attribute further tasks and powers to the Federal Council.

## Chapter Four. The Federal Court and other Judicial Authorities

*Article 188. The Role of the Federal Court*

(1) The Federal Court is the highest federal judicial authority of the Confederation.
(2) Its organization and its procedure shall be regulated by the law.
(3) The Federal Court shall decide on the organization of its administration.
(4) When judges of the Federal Court are elected, Federal Parliament shall ensure that the official languages will be represented.

*Article 189 (old). Jurisdiction of the Federal Court*
[Note: Abrogated by popular vote 12 March 2000, but still in force.]

(1) The Federal Court has jurisdiction over:

a. complaints regarding the violation of constitutional rights;
b. complaints regarding the violation of communal autonomy and other cantonal guarantees on the behalf associations of public law;
c. complaints regarding the violation of international or intercantonal contracts;
d. public law disputes between the Confederation and the Cantons or between Cantons.

(2) The law may provide for further grounds for jurisdiction of the Federal Court.

*Article 189 (new). Jurisdiction of the Federal Court*
[Note: Accepted by popular vote 12 March 2000, but not in force yet.]

(1) The Federal Court shall have jurisdiction over violations of:

a. federal law;
b. public international law;
c. intercantonal law;
d. cantonal constitutional rights;
e. communal autonomy and other guarantees granted by the Cantons to corporate public bodies;
f. federal and cantonal provisions on political rights.

(2) It shall adjudicate in public law disputes between the Confederation and the Cantons or amongst the Cantons.
(3) The law may confer other powers on the Federal Court.
(4) Enactments of the Federal Assembly and the Federal Council cannot be challenged before the Federal Court. The law may provide for exceptions.

*Article 190 (old). Jurisdiction in Civil, Criminal and Public Law*
[Note: Abrogated by popular vote 12 March 2000, but still in force.]

(1) The law provides for the jurisdiction of the Federal Court regarding civil, criminal and public law and in all other areas of the law.
(2) The Cantons may, with the consent of the Federal Assembly, assign to the Federal Court for its determination disputes of cantonal administrative law.

*Article 190 (new). Applicable Law*
[Note: Accepted by popular vote 12 March 2000, but not in force yet.]

Neither the Federal Court nor any other authority can refuse to apply a federal statute or international law.

*Article 191 (old). Applicable Law*
[Note: Abrogated by popular vote 12 March 2000, but still in force. *See* Article 190 (new).]

Federal statutes and public international law are the relevant laws for the Federal Tribunal and other law-applying public agencies.

*Article 191 (new). Access to the Federal Court*
[Note: Accepted by popular vote 12 March 2000, but not in force yet.]

(1) The law shall guarantee access to the Federal Court.
(2) For disputes that do not concern a legal question of fundamental importance, the law may provide for a threshold sum.
(3) The law may, for certain specified matters, exclude access to the Federal Court.
(4) For manifestly unjustified complaints the law may provide for a simplified procedure.

*Article 191a. Other Confederal Judicial Authorities*
[Note: Accepted by popular vote 12 March 2000. Para. (1) entered into force 1 April 2003. Paras. (2) and (3) will enter into force at a later stage.]

(1) The Confederation shall establish a federal criminal court. This will hear, as a court of first instance, those cases, which the law attributes to the jurisdiction of the Confederation. The law may confer other powers on the Federal Criminal Court.
(2) The Confederation shall establish federal judicial authorities to hear public law disputes arising from within the administrative jurisdiction of the Federal Administration.
(3) Other judicial authorities may be established by the law.

*Article 191b. Cantonal Judicial Authorities*
[Note: Accepted by popular vote 12 March 2000, but not in force yet.]

(1) The Cantons shall establish cantonal judicial authorities to judge civil and public law cases and criminal offences.
(2) They may establish common judicial authorities.

*Article 191c. Independence of the Judiciary*
[Note: Accepted by popular vote 12 March 2000, but not in force yet.]

All judicial authorities shall be independent in their judicial activity and are bound only by the law.

# Part Six. Revision of the Constitution and Transitional Provisions

## Chapter One. Revision

*Article 192. Principle*
(1) The Federal Constitution may be revised in whole or in part at any time.
(2) Where the Federal Constitution and legislation deriving from it do not provide otherwise the revision shall follow the legislative process.

*Article 193. Total Revision*
(1) A total revision of the Federal Constitution may be proposed by the People or by one of the two Chambers, or decreed by the Federal Assembly as a whole.
(2) If the initiative emanates from the People, or if the Chambers disagree, the People shall decide whether a total revision should be undertaken.
(3) Should the People accept a total revision, new elections to both Chambers shall be held.
(4) The mandatory provisions of international law may not be violated.

*Article 194. Partial Revision*
(1) A partial revision of the Federal Constitution may be requested by the People, or be decreed by the Federal Assembly.
(2) A partial revision must respect the principle of the unity of subject matter. Nor it may it violate the mandatory provisions of international law.
(3) A popular initiative for partial revision must, moreover, respect the principle of the unity of form.

*Article 195. Entry into Force*
The Constitution revised in whole total or in part shall enter into force as soon as the People and the Cantons accept it.

## Chapter Two. Transitional Provisions

*Article 196. Transitional Provisions pursuant to the Federal decree of 18 December 1998 on a new Federal Constitution*
[Note: Adopted by popular vote 3 March 2002.]

*1. Transitional Provision to Article 84 (Transalpine Traffic)*

The transfer of freight transit traffic from road to rail shall be completed within ten years of the date of the adoption of the popular initiative for the protection of the alpine regions from transit traffic.

*2. Transitional Provision to Article 85 (Flat Heavy Goods Vehicle Charge)*

(1) The Confederation shall levy an annual charge for the use of roads open to general traffic on each domestic and foreign motor vehicle and trailer having a total weight of over 3.5 tons.

(2) The charge shall be:

a. for lorries and articulated motor vehicles of

- over 3,5 up to 12t: CHF 650
- over 12 up to 18t: CHF 2,000
- over 18 up to 26t: CHF 3,000
- over 26t: CHF 4,000

b. for trailers of

- over 8 up to 10t: CHF 1,500
- over 10t: CHF 2,000

c. for coaches: CHF 650

(3) The rates may be adjusted by means of a Federal law, insofar as this is justified by the cost of road traffic.
(4) The Federal Council may, moreover, by means of an ordinance, bring the tariff categories that apply above 12 tons, as listed in paragraph 2, into line with possible amendments of the weight categories defined in the road traffic law.
(5) For vehicles which are not on the road in Switzerland during the whole year, the Federal Council shall lay down graduated rates related to time on the road, while taking into account the costs of collecting the charge.
(6) The Federal Council shall regulate the implementation of the charge. It may establish the rates for special categories of vehicles implied in subsection 2; exempt certain vehicles from the charge; and establish special regulations, particularly for journeys in border areas. Such regulations shall not result in vehicles registered abroad being treated more favorably than Swiss vehicles. The Federal Council may prescribe fines in case of infractions. The Cantons shall collect the charges on vehicles registered in Switzerland.
(7) The charge may be wholly or partly abolished by the law.
(8) The present article shall apply until the coming into force of the Federal law of 19 December 1997 on the levy on heavy goods vehicles.

*3. Transitional Provision to Article 87 (Railroad and other Traffic)*

(1) The Major Railroad Projects concerned are the New Alpine Crossing, Rail 2000, the linking of Eastern and Western Switzerland to the European high-speed railroad network, and the improvement of protection against noise along railway lines whether by active or by passive measures.
(2) In order to finance the Major Railroad Projects, the Federal Council may:

a. until the charge on heavy goods vehicles related to benefits or consumption envisaged by Article 85 comes into force, use the full yield of the flat rate heavy goods vehicle charge, set out in Article 196, subsection 2, and may, for this purpose, at most double the rates;

b. use no more than two thirds of the yield of the heavy goods vehicle charge related to benefits or consumption envisaged in Article 85;
c. use funds accruing from the tax on mineral fuels set out in Article 86, subsection 3, letter b to cover at most 25 per cent of the total costs of the base tunnels of the New Alpine Crossing;
d. raise funds on the capital markets up to a maximum of 25 per cent of the general costs of the new alpine crossing, Rail 2000, and the link of Eastern and Western Switzerland to the European high-speed railroad network;
e. raise by .1 per cent points all value added tax rates (including surcharges) set out in Article 196, subsection 14 and Article 130;
f. look for additional financing from private sources or international organizations.

(3) The financing of the Major Railroad Projects as defined in paragraph 1 shall be assured by a fund legally dependent on the Confederation, but with its own separate accounts. The proceeds from the tolls and taxes set out in paragraph 2 shall be credited to the financial accounts of the Confederation, and transferred into the fund that same year. The Confederation may advance monies to the fund. The Federal Assembly shall issue regulations for the fund by means of an ordinance.
(4) The four Major Railroad Projects listed in paragraph 1 shall be regulated by means of Federal laws. The overall necessity of each major project must be established, along with the stage reached in its planning. For the New Alpine Crossing project, the various construction phases shall be defined in the relevant Federal law. The Federal Assembly shall allocate the necessary funds through authorized credit lines. The Federal Council shall approve the relevant construction phases and determine the timetable.
(5) This provision shall apply until the construction of the Major Railroad Projects mentioned in paragraph 1 is completed, and their financing has ended and advances can be repaid.

*4. Transitional Provision to Article 90 (Nuclear Energy)*

No general, building, start-up or operating permits for new installations designed for the production of nuclear energy shall be granted before 23 September 2000.

*5. Transitional Provision to Article 95 (Gainful Private Economic Activity)*

Until federal legislation is adopted, the Cantons shall mutually recognize their education or training certificates.

*6. Transitional Provision to Article 102 (Supplying the Country)*

(1) The Confederation shall ensure the country is stocked with millable cereals and baking flour.
(2) This transitional provision shall remain in effect, at the latest, until 31 December 2003.

*7. Transitional Provision to Article 103 (Structural Policy)*

For up to ten years from the entry into force of the Constitution, the Cantons may continue to apply existing regulations which make the opening of new businesses in specific sectors of the hotel and restaurant industry conditional upon establishing a need for such.

*8. Transitional Provision to Article 106 (Games of Chance)*

(1) Article 106 shall become operative on the coming into effect of a new Federal law on gambling and casinos.
(2) Until that date, the following provisions shall apply:

a. It is forbidden to open and operate casinos.
b. Cantonal governments may, under specific conditions dictated by the public interest, authorize recreational gambling as was customary in Kursaals until the spring of 1925 if they are of the opinion that such gambling is necessary to maintain or develop tourism, and if it is organized by a Kursaal operator serving this purpose. The Cantons may also prohibit this type of gambling.
c. The Federal Council shall issue an ordinance on the conditions dictated by public interest. The stake shall be no more than 5 Swiss Francs.
d. Each cantonal gambling license must be approved by the Federal Council.
e. One fourth of the gross receipts of gambling operations shall be credited to the Confederation which will apply it, irrespective of its own needs, to the benefit of victims of natural disasters, and for generally useful public institutions.
f. The Confederation may also take necessary measures concerning lotteries.

*9. Transitional Provision to Article 110 Subsection 3 (National Day)*

(1) Until the entry into force of new federal legislation, the Federal Council shall decide on detailed implementation.
(2) Swiss National Day shall not be included in the number of holidays as laid down in Article 18, paragraph 2 of the Federal Labor Act.

*10. Transitional Provision to Article 112 (Federal Old Age, Survivors', and Disability Insurance)*

As long as the federal old age, survivors', and disability insurance do not cover basic living expenses, the Confederation shall grant the Cantons subsidies to cover the costs of supplementary benefits.

*11. Transitional Provision to Article 113 (Company Pension Plans)*

Insured persons who belong to the generation employed before the introduction of mandatory Company pension plans, and therefore did not contribute for the full period, shall receive the minimum statutory benefits, adjusted according to their income, for up to 10 to 20 years after the entry into force of the new law.

*12. Transitional Provision to Article 126 (Financial Management)*

(1) The deficit in the financial accounts of the Confederation shall be reduced by making savings until the accounts are largely in balance.
(2) The deficit in the 1999 accounts may not exceed 5 billion Swiss Francs nor that in 2000 more not exceed 2.5 billion francs. In 2001 accounts, it shall be reduced to a sum less than 2 per cent of receipts.
(3) If the economic situation so requires, the majority of the members of both Chambers may, by way of a decree, extend the deadlines set out in paragraph 2 by, at most, two years.
(4) The Federal Assembly and the Federal Council shall take into account the objectives of paragraph 2 when establishing the budget and the multi-annual financing plan, as it shall when considering any proposals with financial implications.
(5) When implementing the budget, the Federal Council shall use all opportunities for savings. To this end, it may freeze credits and credit lines already authorized. Allowances duly based on legal provisions and, formally guaranteed cash payments, shall not be affected.
(6) If the objectives laid out in paragraph 2 are not achieved, the Federal Council shall determine the additional amount to be saved. To this end,

    a. it shall decide on supplementary savings within its remit;
    b. it shall propose necessary amendments of the law to the Federal Assembly.

(7) The Federal Council shall establish the total sum of the additional savings needed in such a way that the objectives shall be achieved no more than two years after the expiry of the deadlines laid down in paragraph 2. Savings shall be made both in subsidies to third parties and in Confederation's own field of activity.
(8) The two Chambers shall decide on proposals from the Federal Council in the same session, and shall put their decree into force by following the procedure laid down in Article 165 of the Constitution; they shall be bound by the amount of savings fixed by the Federal Council under the terms of paragraph 6.
(9) Should the deficit later again exceed 2 per cent of receipts, the overspend must be brought back to the 2 per cent level in the course of the next financial year. If the economy so requires, the Federal Assembly may, by way of an ordinance, extend the period by no more than two years. In all other respects, the procedure in paragraphs 4 to 8 shall be applicable.
(10) This provision shall remain in effect until it replaced by constitutional law measures to limit the federal deficit and debt.

*13. Transitional Provision to Article 128 (Term of Tax Levy)*

The Federal direct tax may be levied until the end of 2006.

*14. Transitional Provision to Article 130 (Value Added Tax)*

(1) Until a statute on value added tax enters into force, the implementing provisions shall be established by the Federal Council. The following principles shall therefore apply:

a. The following shall be taxable:

1. The supply of goods and services that a business provides against payment within Switzerland (including own use);
2. The import of goods.

b. The following are shall be exempt from the tax, and there shall be no right to deduct withholding tax:

1. Postal services within the framework of its monopoly but excluding passenger transport;
2. Health services;
3. Social welfare and social security services;
4. Services related to education, teaching and the care of children and young people;
5. Cultural services;
6. Insurance transactions;
7. Money market and capital market transactions, with the exception of asset management and the recovery of debts;
8. Transfer, long term leasing, and letting of immovable property;
9. Betting, lotteries, and other games of chance;
10. Services rendered by non-profit organizations to their members against the payment of a fee fixed by their articles of incorporation;
11. Supply of official Swiss postage stamps used as such. To avoid interference with fair competition or to simplify the collection of the tax, both voluntary taxation of the transactions listed above and the right to deduct tax in advance may be permitted.

c. The following shall be free of tax but shall be liable to the deduction of withholding taxes:

1. The export of goods, and services rendered abroad;
2. Services in connection with the export or transit of goods.

d. The following shall not be subjected to the tax on transactions made within Switzerland:

1. Businesses with a total annual taxable turnover of no more than 75,000 francs;
2. Businesses with a total annual taxable turnover of no more than 250,000 francs, provided that the amount of tax, after deduction of withholding tax, does not consistently exceed 4,000 francs per year;

3. Farmers, foresters, and horticulturists who supply produce exclusively from their own businesses, and livestock dealers;
4. Painters and sculptors with respect to works of art created by them personally.

To avoid interference with fair competition or to simplify tax collection, the businesses and persons listed above may be permitted to pay tax on a voluntary basis, and their right to deduct withholding tax shall be accorded.

e. The tax rate shall be:

1. 2.0 per cent on the delivery transactions and importation of the following goods, which the Federal Council may define in greater detail:

   - piped water,
   - foodstuffs and beverages, with the exception of alcoholic drinks,
   - livestock, poultry, fish,
   - cereals,
   - seeds, tuberous vegetables, plant bulbs, growing plants, cuttings, grafts, and cut flowers and branches, including in the form of bouquets, wreaths and similar arrangements,
   - fodder, silage acids, straw, fertilizers, and pesticides,
   - medicines,
   - newspapers, magazines, books and other printed materials within the parameters to the extent defined by the Federal Council;

2. Up to 2.0 per cent on radio and television activities where these are not of a commercial character;
3. Up to 6.5 per cent on the supply and the importation of other goods and on all other taxable services.

f. The tax shall be calculated on the payment obtained, or, if there is no such payment, and in the case of imports, on the value of the goods or services received.

g. The following shall be liable to pay tax:

1. Taxpayers who generate taxable turnover;
2. The recipients of services originating abroad, provided that their annual value is above 10,000 francs per year;
3. Individuals who import goods, and who are liable to pay customs duty or to make a customs declaration.

h. Taxpayers must pay tax on their taxable turnover; if they use the goods supplied and the services received to generate taxable turnover within Switzerland or abroad, the following may be deducted from their liabilities as withholding tax:

1. the tax passed on to the taxpayer by other taxpayers; and
2. the tax paid on the importation of goods or on the receipt of services from abroad;

3. 2.0 per cent of the price of natural products purchased from businesses which, under the terms of letter d, point 3 above, are not subject to the tax.

The right to deduct withholding tax does not extend to non-commercial expenditures.

i. As a general rule, the accounting period for the tax and the deduction of withholding tax shall be quarterly.
k. Special provisions may be established for turnover taxation in the case of gold coins and refined gold, and of goods, which are already subject to special fiscal charges.
l. Simplifications may be made if they neither greatly alter tax revenues nor significantly affect competition, and always providing they do not create excessive tax accounting difficulties for other tax payers.
m. Tax evasion and the undermining of taxation are shall be punishable in ways analogous to those in other federal criminal provisions in the field of tax law.
n. The special provisions on the criminal liability of businesses prescribed by Article 7 of the Federal Administrative Criminal Law Act of 22 March 1974 may also be applied in cases where a fine of more than 5,000 francs is possible.

(2) During the first five years following the introduction of the value added tax, 5 per cent of the its yield shall be used to reduce health insurance premiums so as to benefit those individuals in lower income strata. The Federal Assembly shall decide how this part of the value added tax, dedicated to a specific purpose, shall be used after the expiry of this period.
(3) The Confederation may, by law, set a lower rate for the value added tax on tourist services in Switzerland, provided that such services are largely used by foreigners and that the competitive situation so requires.

[Note *ad* para. 3: Federal Parliament has made use of this authority. *See* Article 36(2) of the Federal Value Added Tax Act of 2 September 1999 (SR 641.20), according to which the value added tax rates is, with effect from 1 January 2001 until 31 December 2003, 3,6 per cent (special rate for services of accommodation).]

(4) The value added tax may be levied until the end of 2006.

*15. Transitional Provision to Article 131 (Beer Tax)*

Until the adoption of a new Federal Statute, the beer tax shall be levied according to the law presently in force.

*16. Transitional Provision to Article 132 (Cantonal Share of Withholding Tax)*

Until the new financial equalization among the Cantons, the cantonal share of the yield of the withholding tax shall be 12 per cent. If the tax rate for the withholding tax exceeds 30 per cent, the share of the Cantons shall be 10 per cent.

*Article 197. Transitional Dispositions after Acceptance of the Federal Constitution of 18 April 1999*
[Note: Adopted by popular vote 3 March 2002.]

I. Swiss Membership of the UN

(1) Switzerland shall be a member of the United Nations Organization.
(2) The Federal Council is authorized to send the Secretary General of the UN a request that Switzerland be admitted to the UN and a declaration of acceptance of the obligations contained in the UN Charter.

Date of Entry into Force: 1 January 2000

**Final Provisions of the Federal Decree of 18 December 1998**

II.

(1) The Federal Constitution of 29 May 1874 is hereby abrogated.
(2) The following provisions of the Federal Constitution of 29 May 1874, which must be converted into statutory law, shall remain applicable until such new statutory provisions come into force:

a. Article 32$^{quater}$ subs. 6
Hawking and other forms of itinerant sale of spirits are prohibited.
b. Article 36$^{quinquies}$ subs. 1, first sentence, 2, sentences 2 to 5, and 4, second sentence

(1) For the use of first and second-class national highways, the Confederation shall levy an annual charge of 40 francs on domestic and foreign motor vehicles and trailers up to a total weight of 3.5 tons each . . .
(2) [...] The Federal Council It may exempt specific vehicles from the charge and issue special regulations, particularly for journeys in frontier areas. Such regulations shall not result in vehicles registered abroad being treated more favorably than Swiss vehicles. The Federal Council may establish fines for infringements. The Cantons shall collect the charge for vehicles registered in Switzerland, and shall ensure that all vehicles comply with the relevant rules.
(4) [...] The law may also extend the charge to other categories of motor vehicles, which are not subject to the charge on heavy goods vehicles.

c. Article 121$^{bis}$, subs. 1, 2, and subs. 3, first and second sentence

(1) Should the Federal Assembly prepare a counter-project, three questions shall be submitted to the voters on the same ballot. Every voter may state:

1. whether they prefer the popular initiative to the existing law;
2. whether they prefer the counter-project to the existing law;

3. which of the two texts should be applied in the case that the People and the Cantons prefer both texts to the existing law.

(2) The absolute majority shall be calculated separately for each question. Where questions are not answered such ballots shall not be counted.
(3) Should both the popular initiative and the counter-project be accepted, the vote on the third question shall be decisive. The text, which enters into force, will be that which obtains most votes from the People and Cantons in response to this question. [...]

III.

The Federal Assembly shall adapt the form of amendments of the Federal Constitution of 29 May 1874, to the new Constitution. Decrees of this kind shall not be subject to referendum.

IV.

(1) This decree shall be submitted to the votation of the People and the Cantons.
(2) The Federal Assembly shall determine the date of entry into force of the Constitution.

# Index

The numbers refer to the articles of the Federal Constitution of the Swiss Confederation of 18 April 1999.

**Index**